Women Talk More than Mei

Do women talk more than men? Does text messaging make you stupid? Can chimpanzees really talk to us? This fascinating textbook addresses a wide range of language myths, focusing on important big-picture issues, such as the rule-governed nature of language and the influence of social factors on how we speak. Case studies and analysis of relevant experiments teach readers the skills to become informed consumers of social science research, while suggested open-ended exercises invite students to reflect further on what they've learned.

With coverage of a broad range of topics (cognitive, social, historical), this textbook is ideal for non-technical survey courses in linguistics. Important points are illustrated with specific, memorable examples: invariant *be* shows the rule-governed nature of African-American English; vulgar female speech in Papua New Guinea shows how beliefs about language and gender are culture-specific. Engaging and accessibly written, Kaplan's lively discussion challenges what we think we know about language.

ABBY KAPLAN is an assistant professor (lecturer) in the Department of Linguistics at the University of Utah.

Women Talk More than Men

. . . And Other Myths about Language Explained

Abby Kaplan
University of Utah

CAMBRIDGE
UNIVERSITY PRESS

University Printing House, Cambridge CB2 8BS, United Kingdom

One Liberty Plaza, 20th Floor, New York, NY 10006, USA

477 Williamstown Road, Port Melbourne, VIC 3207, Australia

4843/24, 2nd Floor, Ansari Road, Daryaganj, Delhi - 110002, India

79 Anson Road, #06-04/06, Singapore 079906

Cambridge University Press is part of the University of Cambridge.

It furthers the University's mission by disseminating knowledge in the pursuit of education, learning and research at the highest international levels of excellence.

www.cambridge.org
Information on this title: www.cambridge.org/9781107446908

First published 2016

A catalogue record for this publication is available from the British Library

Library of Congress Cataloging in Publication data
Names: Kaplan, Abby, author.
Title: Women talk more than men : –and other myths about language explained /Abby Kaplan.
Description: Cambridge ; New York : Cambridge University Press, [2016]
Identifiers: LCCN 2015042976 | ISBN 9781107446908 (paperback)
Subjects: LCSH: Language and languages–Sex differences. | Language and languages–Usage. | Language and languages–Miscellanea. | Discourse analysis. | Historical linguistics. | Sociolinguistics.
Classification: LCC P120.S48 K37 2016 | DDC 401/.9–dc23
LC record available at http://lccn.loc.gov/2015042976

ISBN 978-1-107-08492-6 Hardback
ISBN 978-1-107-44690-8 Paperback

Contents

Figures

Tables

Acknowledgments

This book has been long in the making, and it has benefited from the assistance of many people. Helen Barton at Cambridge University Press has been a helpful guide throughout. Derron Borders, Howard Giles, Jim McCloskey, Sean Redmond, and Fernando Rubio provided pointers to helpful literature. Special thanks to Ruth Kramer for help with Egyptian hieroglyphs, and to Valerie Fridland and Agnes-Melinda Kovács for supplying original copies of figures from their publications. The Interlibrary Loan staff at the University of Utah always amazes me with their fast and helpful service.

Many thanks are due to everyone who read and commented on various parts of the manuscript: Scott Liddell, Misha Becker, Rachel Hayes-Harb, Shannon Barrios, Robin Dodsworth, and especially Mark Shoun. As usual, none of these fine people should be held responsible for any remaining shortcomings of the book.

Special thanks to my family for being supportive throughout the whole process. My husband Aaron and I had many useful discussions about practically all of the material here; he also patiently endured rants about chimpanzee research, Hart & Risley, the direction of time, or whatever else I happened to be reading or writing about that day. My older son Graham showed poor planning in being three years old just at the time I was reading about all the fascinating experiments that bilingualism researchers have done with young children. Thanks for playing some silly games with Mommy – and I was so proud when you aced the DCCS task at 3;11. My younger son Jay provided lots of moral support, mostly by napping cutely on me while I was reading. Thank you all!

1 Introduction

In February of 2013, *The Journal of Neuroscience* published an article under the title 'Foxp2 mediates sex differences in ultrasonic vocalization by rat pups and directs order of maternal retrieval'. Stories about the paper quickly made the rounds in the popular media, with eye-catching headlines:

- 'Sorry to interrupt, dear, but women really do talk more than men (13,000 words a day more to be precise)' (MacRae 2013)
- 'Chatty Cathy, listen up: New study reveals why women talk more than men' (Kim 2013)
- 'Brain protein may explain why girls talk more than boys' (Castillo 2013)

Reports like these managed to make *The Huffington Post* look tame by comparison ('Biological evidence may support idea that women talk more than men, study says'). One frequent reaction was that the study was a waste of money: everybody knows women talk more than men; why do we need a scientific experiment to prove it?

Given publicity like this, many readers would be surprised to learn that the study did no such thing. In fact, the authors didn't examine living humans at all; they compared male and female baby mice ('pups'), with the following results:

- Male pups made more vocalizations than females when separated from their mothers.
- Male pups had higher levels of the *FOXP2* protein than females in some regions of their brains.
- Inhibiting the *FOXP2* gene in the pups' brains eliminated the sex difference: males vocalized less, and females vocalized more.
- In a sample of brain tissue from 10 young human children, the girls had somewhat higher levels of the *FOXP2* protein than the boys.

It's a long way from here to 'Science proves why women talk more than men', but the reasoning seems to be something like this: *FOXP2* causes male rats to talk a lot → *FOXP2* does the same thing in all humans → *FOXP2* causes female humans to talk a lot. Obviously, this line of reasoning (which the authors didn't endorse in their paper) assumes that women *do* talk more than men – but the '13,000 words' mentioned in news reports have nothing to do with this study; the number is a zombie statistic, often repeated despite the fact that there is no evidence whatsoever to back it up.

This book is about two things, both neatly illustrated by this story. First, it is about popular beliefs about language: the conventional wisdom on topics from linguistic sex differences to the effects of text messaging. Sometimes, of course, popular opinion has things more or less right – but it's more interesting to examine cases where 'what everyone knows' is wrong, and so we will put a special focus on debunking language myths. Moreover, popular beliefs about language are often responsible for shoddy media coverage of the kind we have just seen. We wouldn't be nearly so interested in the genetics of baby mice if we didn't think it told us something about the battle of the sexes.

Second, this is a book about *how* to study language – not in the sense that it will train you to do linguistic analysis for yourself, but in the sense that it provides a glimpse of the kinds of things linguists do. Linguists now have a large toolkit of techniques for investigating how people use language, and many of them make at least a brief appearance in these pages: syntactic analysis in section 2.2.1, description of speech sounds in section 10.2.1, and ethnographic work in section 8.2.1, for example. But the primary focus of this book is on quantitative studies of behavior, either in the laboratory or in a more natural setting; we will devote a substantial amount of time to analyzing specific studies and understanding their strengths and weaknesses. The goal is for you to become an informed consumer of social science research with an appreciation of how the scientific process works.

Each chapter of this book addresses one language-related topic: sign language, bilingualism, language and thought, and so on. Chapters begin with a general overview of the area, describing popular beliefs about language and comparing those beliefs with what linguists actually know to be true. The last part of each chapter is a case study of a specific question such as 'Do women really talk more than men?' or 'Is it harder to learn a second language as you get older?'[1] We examine in detail several published studies that address the question, evaluating how each study was conducted and what the results appear to mean: What do the results say about the question at hand? Does it seem likely that they would generalize to other situations?

[1] Due to the nature of the material, Chapter 4 ('Chimpanzees can talk to us') and Chapter 6 ('Adults can't learn a new language') are structured somewhat differently. Chapter 8 ('Women talk more than men') has two case studies instead of one.

What potential confounding factors weren't controlled? Along the way, we will get a glimpse into the process of conducting social science research, where careful experiments are extremely difficult to design but are nevertheless crucially important. One of the most important lessons to learn is that despite the definitive-sounding claims that often appear in popular science articles, no one experiment is ever the final word. To be really sure of something, we need converging evidence from a variety of sources.

Each chapter concludes with a section called 'For further reflection' with suggested exercises for stimulating further engagement with the topic. Many of these involve reading popular essays written by non-linguists; there is a great deal of material like this on the internet, but as far as possible I've included only works that have been published in journals (and are therefore accessible through most university libraries) or that are hosted by major media organizations (such as *The New York Times*) whose links are likely to stay current for a while.

The 'For further reading' section at the end of each chapter describes other resources that the interested reader can consult for more information. I've made an effort to emphasize non-technical sources that are appropriate for a general audience, but more challenging material (especially on narrower topics) is included as well. Accompanying notes sketch the content of these references and indicate the level at which they're written.

At a larger scale, this book is organized into three thematic sections. The first explores several types of language use that are widely considered to be something less than 'real' language: non-standard dialects, sign language, and the use of linguistic systems by non-human animals. The overarching question in these chapters is whether these systems appear to be full-fledged languages or not. The second section looks at the process of learning a language and at the consequences of knowing more than one language. The last section brings together four chapters that examine the relationship between how we use language and other aspects of daily life, such as our use of technology or the way we conceptualize the world. Despite these groupings, the chapters largely stand on their own and can be read in any order. (An exception is Chapter 2, which emphasizes the rule-governed nature of language and therefore lays important groundwork for everything that follows. It's also very useful to read Chapter 3, on signed languages, before reading about the ape language experiments in Chapter 4.)

Above all, my hope is that this book will encourage you to think of linguistics as an empirical science, one that requires systematic and technical study. The world is full of self-appointed experts who feel free to make pronouncements on language with little or no supporting evidence. Chapter 2 emphasizes the fact that every native speaker follows a set of complex rules in using his or her language – but the fact that you speak a language doesn't make you an expert on language, any more than the fact that you can walk makes you an expert on biomechanics. It's only through careful investigation that linguists have learned just how rich and fascinating language is; this book offers a small window into how linguists do this and what they have learned.

Further reading

Pinker (1994) is an entertaining and well written overview of linguistics; it is also a sustained argument for the Chomskyan view that language is an innate human ability. Rickerson and Hilton (2006) is a collection of very brief essays on language and related topics, based on a popular NPR series. There are many books that provide a more technical introduction to the field at an undergraduate level; *Language Files* (Mihalicek and Wilson 2011) is an especially broad overview, with lots of problem sets that give students the chance to analyze linguistic data for themselves. Another classic textbook is Fromkin et al. (2013).

Bauer and Trudgill (1998) is a collection of short essays that address popular misconceptions, mostly related to social evaluations of language. Newbrook (2013) catalogues ideas about language that, using a deliberately non-evaluative term, he calls 'non-mainstream' – you or I might call them 'crackpot'. Although the book is dense and Newbrook's rebuttals of these ideas are necessarily brief, the text has plenty of references to more thorough criticisms of various fringe proposals.

Bibliography

Biological evidence may support idea that women talk more than men, study says. *Huffington Post*, February 21 2013. Available at http://www.huffingtonpost.com/2013/02/21/women-talk-more-than-men-study_n_2734215.html.

Bauer, Laurie, and Peter Trudgill, editors. *Language Myths*. Penguin Books, London, 1998.

Bowers, J. Michael, Miguel Perez-Pouchoulen, N. Shalon Edwards, and Margaret M. McCarthy. Foxp2 mediates sex differences in ultrasonic vocalization by rat pups and directs order of maternal retrieval. *The Journal of Neuroscience*, 33(8):3276–3283, 2013.

Castillo, Michelle. Brain protein may explain why girls talk more than boys. *CBS News*, February 22 2013. Available at http://www.cbsnews.com/news/brain-protein-may-explain-why-girls-talk-more-than-boys/.

Fromkin, Victoria, Robert Rodman, and Nina Hyams. *An Introduction to Language*. Cengage Learning, Boston, MA, 10th edition, 2013.

Kim, Eun Kyung. Chatty Cathy, listen up: New study reveals why women talk more than men. Available at http://www.today.com/health/chatty-cathy-listen-new-study-reveals-why-women-talk-more-1C8469360, February 21 2013.

MacRae, Fiona. Sorry to interrupt, dear, but women really do talk more than men (13,000 words a day more to be precise). *Daily Mail Online*, February 20 2013. Available at http://www.dailymail.co.uk/sciencetech/article-2281891/Women-really-talk-men-13-000-words-day-precise.html.

Mihalicek, Vedrana, and Christin Wilson, editors. *Language Files: Materials for an Introduction to Language and Linguistics*. The Ohio State University Press, Columbus, OH, 11th edition, 2011.

Newbrook, Mark. *Strange Linguistics: A Skeptical Linguist Looks at Non-Mainstream Ideas about Language*. Lincom Europa, Munich, 2013.

Pinker, Steven. *The Language Instinct: How the Mind Creates Language*. William Morrow and Company, New York, NY, 1994.

Rickerson, E. M., and Barry Hilton, editors. *The 5 Minute Linguist: Bite-Sized Essays on Language and Languages*. Equinox Publishing, London, 2nd edition, 2006.

Part I

...But is it language?

2 'A dialect is a collection of mistakes'

No language is spoken exactly the same way by everyone who uses it. On one level, there are idiosyncratic differences among individuals. For example, there may be particular words that you tend to use a lot that your friends use less often; the specific shape of your mouth and throat affects the way your voice sounds; and so on.

On another level, different groups of people may use their language in systematically different ways. Speakers are typically aware of some of these differences, and we use the word *dialect* to refer to an identifiable variety of a language. You can probably name some of the dialects of your native language; in American English, for example, it is widely recognized that 'Southern English' (spoken in the southeastern part of the United States) is a distinctive variety, and so is the English spoken in New York City. Great Britain has many of its own varieties of English, and so do Australia and New Zealand. Parisian French is different from the variety spoken in Quebec; European Portuguese is different from Brazilian Portuguese; the Spanish of Argentina is different from the Spanish of Mexico; and on it goes.

It's common to describe dialects in terms of geography, but dialect differences can be associated with any number of social dimensions. In the United States, for example, one very salient variety is African American English (AAE). AAE is associated with differences based on race: it is spoken by many African-Americans (though not by all, and it is spoken by people of other racial backgrounds as well). Social class, age, and other factors all have an impact on the way we speak.

What's interesting is that speakers often have the feeling that various dialects are not merely different from each other; some are actually *better* than others. Southern American English is stigmatized as uneducated, lazy, and backwards; New York English is said to be rude and 'nasal'. Many English speakers believe that there are correct and incorrect ways to speak, and there is a particular variety – 'Standard English' – that gets things right by obeying grammatical rules.[1]

[1] Of course, it's a simplification to talk about a single 'Standard English'. Most obviously, there are different standards in the United States, Great Britain and other English-speaking countries. Interestingly, many Americans feel that British English is better or more 'proper' even than Standard American English!

If this assessment is right, then Standard English is the true embodiment of the language, and non-standard dialects are something less than language. If Standard English follows 'the rules' (whatever those are) and other varieties do nothing more than break those rules, then Southern English and AAE are just collections of mistakes. And if they're just a collection of mistakes, then these non-standard dialects have no place in schools or other official domains.

In this chapter, we will examine the belief that non-standard dialects don't obey grammatical rules. We will focus particularly on AAE – as discussed in the next section, AAE is commonly accused of having no grammar. We will see that *all* varieties of a language, whether standard or not, do in fact obey grammatical rules; non-standard varieties are just obeying rules that happen to be different from the rules of the standard. Our case study at the end of the chapter focuses on the issue of education: what is the best way to teach the standard dialect of a language to students who speak a non-standard dialect? This question was addressed by the Oakland Board of Education in 1996, and their resolution on the issue became a topic of national debate in the United States.

2.1 AAE as a rule-breaker

AAE is one of the most well-known non-standard dialects in the United States. It is also known as *Black English* or *Ebonics*; the latter term became famous during the Oakland Board of Education debate in 1996. The word *Ebonics* was actually coined by a linguist as a word to refer to a whole family of language varieties and practices associated with enslaved Africans. The term has never been widely adopted by linguists, and today it is mostly used as a synonym for AAE (often with negative undertones). Linguists usually use the term *AAE* (or *AAVE*, for *African American Vernacular English*).

AAE is highly stigmatized, and many people believe that it does nothing more than disobey the rules of Standard English. Raspberry (1996) refers to it as 'a language that has no right or wrong expressions, no consistent spellings or pronunciations and no discernable rules'. Mitchell (1979, 164) suggests that there may even be something deliberately subversive about the dialect: 'its blithe disregard of standard grammatical forms is as crafty as it is cocky'. And it isn't hard to find even harsher assessments – for example, in the definitions of 'Ebonics' submitted to Urban Dictionary:

> It... has almost no defined syntactical structure. Also of note is the almost complete lack of conjugation of verbs ("I be", "she be", "thems be", etc)....

> When in doubt... just string random thoughts together and insinuate that they actually mean something.

A form of mental retardation characterised by inability to grasp the basics of human language.

'Ebonics', Urban Dictionary (www.urbandictionary.com)

One of the features of AAE that is most frequently commented on is the behavior of verbs, particularly *be*. Mitchell (1979, 164) sarcastically proposes a program for teaching AAE in schools, in which teachers 'explain... that verb forms that change in the past tense are the result of centuries of prejudice and intolerance'. Raspberry (1996) claims that 'you can say pretty much what you please, as long as you're careful to throw in a lot of "bes" and leave off final consonants'.

Verbs in AAE are indeed different from verbs in Standard English. As it turns out, though, linguists who have studied how people actually use AAE have discovered that it too follows a set of complex grammatical rules, which just happen to be different from the rules of Standard English. In fact, there are some parts of the AAE verb system that are arguably *more* complex than Standard English. In the next section, we will examine some of the systematic grammatical rules that speakers of standard and non-standard dialects alike follow automatically and unconsciously.

2.2 Grammatical rules in standard and non-standard dialects

We're used to thinking of grammatical rules as something you learn in school: 'don't end a sentence with a preposition', 'make sure your subject agrees with your verb', and so on. Linguists distinguish between *prescriptive* rules like these, which tell people how they *should* speak; and *descriptive* rules, which describe how people actually *do* speak. As it turns out, these prescriptive rules only scratch the surface of what's going on when people use language: the descriptive rules that linguists discover when they study how people actually speak are much more complex and interesting than what's taught in most high school English classes.[2]

2.2.1 My *in Standard English*

Words like *my*, *your*, and *her* in English indicate possession. (Of course, what 'possession' actually means depends on the context: *my book* could be a book I own, a book I wrote, a book I have chosen to do a report on, or any other

[2] Not only that, but the most common prescriptive rules are a hodge-podge of several different things. Some, such as 'don't use double negatives', are an attempt to describe an aspect of Standard English grammar that is different from the grammar of some non-standard dialects. Others, such as 'don't split an infinitive', were invented in the eighteenth century based on a misguided analogy with Latin.

book that is appropriately associated with me.) You may have been taught in school that *my* and words like it are 'possessive adjectives': special adjectives that indicate the possessor of the noun they modify. Thus, *my books* are books that belong to me, just as *red books* are books that are red.

But if we examine *my* more closely, we discover that it actually doesn't behave very much like an adjective at all. Native English speakers follow very specific rules when they use *my*, but those rules are different from the ones that apply to adjectives. For example, an adjective like *red* can appear between words like *the* or *a* and the noun, as in examples (1a) and (2a).

(1) a. The red books are on the table.
b. *The my books are on the table.

(2) a. A red book is on the table.
b. *A my book is on the table.

The asterisks in examples (1b) and (2b) mean that native English speakers think there's something strange about these sentences; these sentences are not something they would ever say. Linguists call strange-sounding sentences like these *ungrammatical*. These examples illustrate one rule that native English speakers follow when they use *my*: it cannot appear between *the*/*a* and a noun.

There are further differences between words like *my* and words like *red*. It's possible for *red* to appear alone after the verb *be*, in what is known as *predicate position*; we can describe the color of a book with a sentence like (3a). But *my* cannot do the same thing; a sentence like (3b) is ungrammatical. (To describe the owner of the book, we would have to say something like *The book is mine*, using a different word.)

(3) a. The book is red.
b. *The book is my.

Another difference between the two involves the behavior of nouns. In English, some nouns (called *count nouns*) seem to refer to individual countable things, while other nouns (called *mass nouns*) do not. *Book* is a count noun; we can talk about *one book*, *two books*, *three books*, and so on. *Rice* is a mass noun; even though rice is made up of small, discrete pieces, we can't talk about *one rice*, *two rices*, and so on. (Instead, English speakers have to say something like *one grain of rice*.) One restriction on singular count nouns in English is that they cannot appear by themselves; they must be preceded by a word like *the* or *a*.

(4) a. The book is on the table.
b. A book is on the table.
c. *Book is on the table.

An adjective like *red* is not enough; even the phrase *red book* requires another word to stand before it. (*The red book* or *a red book* is fine.) But *my book* can stand on its own; in fact, as we saw above, adding *the* or *a* before *my book* creates an ungrammatical sentence.

(5) a. *Red book is on the table.
b. The red book is on the table.
c. My book is on the table.
d. *The my book is on the table.

Finally, it's possible to emphasize the redness of something by using a word like *very*, as in example (6a). But it's not possible to emphasize my ownership of something in the same way, as in example (6b). *My* is similar to *the* in this way: **very the* is impossible too.

(6) a. These are very red books.
b. *These are very my books.
c. *These are very the books.

All these examples suggest that *my* is not an adjective at all; in fact, it's the same kind of word as *the* and *a*. These latter words are often called *articles*, but linguists use the word *determiners* to refer to the larger class of words that includes *the*, *a*, *my*, *your*, and many other words. *My* has all the same properties as other determiners in English:

- It is impossible to have more than one determiner in a noun phrase; this is why **the a book* and **the my book* are ungrammatical.
- A determiner cannot appear by itself in predicate position; this is why **These books are the* and **These books are my* are ungrammatical.
- A singular count noun must have a determiner before it; this is why *The book is red* and *My book is red* are acceptable, but **Book is red* is not.

If you try substituting words like *your* or *our* into the examples above, you will find that they, too, behave like determiners and not adjectives.

As it turns out, then, native speakers of English obey strict rules: *red* is an adjective, a type of word that follows one set of rules; *my* and *the* are determiners, a type of word that follows a different set of rules. And native speakers do this despite the fact that many of them have been taught something completely different about these words! All this goes to show that even though native speakers can identify *which* sentences of their language are grammatical or ungrammatical, they would usually be hard-pressed to explain *why*. Rules about determiners and adjectives operate below the level of consciousness: English speakers obey them in their daily language use without ever having been taught them explicitly, and indeed the vast majority of speakers couldn't explain how they know which sentences are grammatical and which are not. Over and over again, linguists have found that speakers unconsciously obey complex grammatical rules that they have never been explicitly taught and often can't even describe.

2.2.2 *Regularities in AAE*

Consonant deletion

One common complaint about AAE is that its speakers 'leave off final consonants' (Raspberry 1996). It's true that sometimes the final consonant of a word in Standard English is omitted in AAE – but as Green (2002) describes in detail, saying that AAE just leaves off the last consonant is too simplistic. First, this consonant deletion happens only in words that end in more than one consonant: that is, to words that end in a *consonant cluster*. For example, the final *t* sound of *fast* might be omitted in AAE, leaving *fas*. But the final *s* sound of *pass* would not be omitted; this word would not be pronounced as *pa*.[3]

In addition, not every final consonant in a consonant cluster can be deleted. It's acceptable in AAE to omit the final consonants of the words in (7), but not the words in (8).

(7) a. mask → mas
  b. adopt → adop
  c. bold → bol

(8) a. paint ↛ pain
  b. jump ↛ jum

The reason deletion is forbidden in (8) appears to be that the final two consonants in *paint* and *jump* are different with respect to a feature that linguists call *voicing*. The *n* of *paint* and the *m* of *jump* are *voiced*: they are pronounced with vibrating vocal folds. (To feel this, try putting your finger on your throat and saying *mmm*: you should be able to feel the vibration.) By contrast, *t* and *p* are *voiceless*: they are pronounced without vibrating vocal folds. Green (2002, 110) calls the AAE rule the *voicing generalization*: if the two consonants in the cluster have different values of voicing, deletion is impossible. In (7), both consonants in each cluster have the same value of voicing; *s*, *k*, *p*, and *t* are all

[3] An exception to this generalization, of course, is the final *-s* on plurals and third-person singular verbs. Omitting this marker is part of a separate pattern, related to the fact that plurals and verb agreement work differently in AAE; see Green (2002) for an overview.

voiceless, while *l* and *d* are both voiced. Therefore, the final consonant can be omitted in these words.

In addition to the voicing generalization, there are further restrictions on consonant deletion in more complex words. If a suffix that starts with a consonant is added to a word that ends in a consonant cluster (where both consonants have the same voicing), then the consonant immediately before the suffix can still be deleted, even though it isn't technically at the end of the word.

(9) a. friend+ly → frienly
b. soft+ness → sofness

But if the suffix starts with a vowel, then both consonants of the cluster are retained.

(10) a. accept+able → acceptable
b. expect+able → expectable

Why should this be? One reason may be that languages in general tend to avoid consonants that aren't immediately next to a vowel, partly because being next to a vowel makes the consonant much easier to hear. In a word like *friendly*, the *d* is sandwiched between two other consonants and is an obvious target for deletion. In a word like *acceptable*, the *t* is next to a vowel, so there's no reason to delete it. What we see, then, is that speakers of AAE aren't just deleting consonants at random; they are following a grammatical pattern, one that actually improves the words from a perceptual point of view.

We will look at one more complication in the pattern of consonant deletion. It's not quite true that final consonants are never deleted before a suffix that starts with a vowel; some suffixes, such as *-er* and *-ing*, allow deletion to happen anyway.

(11) a. cold+er → coler
b. spend+ing → spening
c. soft+er → sofer

To understand what's going on here, let's look at a similar pattern in Standard English. The words *hymn*, *damn*, *condemn*, and *solemn* are spelled with an *mn* cluster at the end, but these words are actually pronounced with just *m*. When certain vowel-initial suffixes are added, the *n* appears even in pronunciation.

(12) a. hymn+al → hymnal
b. damn+ation → damnation
c. solemn+ity → solemnity

But with other vowel-initial suffixes, the *n* is still missing.

(13) a. damn+ing → daming
b. condemn+ing → condeming
c. hymn+ing → hyming[4]

One way of understanding this pattern is to say that rules may apply either before or after suffixes are attached to a word. Some suffixes, such as *-al* and *-ation*, appear to attach 'early', before many rules have applied. Other suffixes, such as *-ing*, attach 'late', after most or all of the rules have applied. If *-ation* attaches to *damn* before the rule applies that says 'delete *n* if it comes after *m* at the end of a word', then the *n* of *damn* is protected from deletion in *damnation*. But if *-ing* attaches after the rule applies, then by the time *-ing* is added to *damn*, it's too late: the *n* has already been deleted.

(14)

	'damnation'	**'damning'**
Stem	damn	damn
Add *-ation*	damn+ation	—
Delete *n*	—	dam
Add *-ing*	—	dam+ing
Pronunciation	damnation	daming

Turning back to the AAE pattern, we can explain the difference between (10) and (11) in a similar way. The suffix *-able* is added to the word early, before the final consonant of *accept* or *expect* can be deleted. Suffixes like *-er* or *-ing* are added late, after the final consonants of *cold* and *spend* have already been deleted.

All this means that AAE speakers are following a rule much more complicated than 'delete the last consonant of the word'. Speakers are sensitive to subtle properties of how the word is pronounced and what its internal structure is.

Aspectual be

Consider the following story.

(15) Bruce has a box of toys he keeps in the garage. If there is no car in the garage, he plays with the box of toys there. Sometimes John comes over and he and Bruce play with the toys from the box in the garage.

[4] This is not an actual word, of course, but we can test its behavior in the intuitions of native English speakers. For example, suppose you wanted to coin a new verb *hymn* meaning 'to sing a lot of hymns'. Given this new verb, if you said *The chorus spent the whole day hymning*, would you pronounce the underlined word as *hyming* or *hymning*? Most native English speakers would say *hyming*.

> But, today, Bruce has to move his box of toys to the porch because he is keeping a box of John's baseball stuff in the garage.
> *Question: What box be in the garage?*

Another salient feature of AAE is the use of *be* where Standard English would use *is* or *are*. This isn't because speakers don't know how to conjugate verbs; instead, *be* is actually a distinct grammatical marker in AAE: it indicates that the action happens regularly or habitually. This use of the word is known as *aspectual be* or *habitual be*; it is also known as *invariant be*, because *be* with this meaning never takes another form such as *is* or *are*. Aspectual *be* is a systematic property of AAE grammar; for example, the sentence *Bruce running* means something like 'Bruce is running right now', while the sentence *Bruce be running* means something like 'Bruce usually runs'.

This means that in AAE, the correct answer to the question *What box be in the garage?* is *Bruce's toys* (which are usually in the garage), not *John's baseball stuff* (which happens to be there right now). Green and Roeper (2007) told this story and others like it to four- and five-year-old children in Louisiana; they found that the black children were more likely to say *Bruce's toys*, while the white children were more likely to say *John's baseball stuff*. In other words, the black children had learned one set of grammatical rules, while the white children had learned a different set.

One difficulty AAE speakers face is that aspectual *be* looks so similar to the Standard English verb *be*. A Standard English speaker who hears aspectual *be* will probably conclude (1) that it means the same thing as *is* or *are*, and (2) that the speaker doesn't know how to use verbs correctly. Not only are both of these conclusions false, but they can lead to misunderstanding, as in the following anecdote recounted by Ross (1997):

> While sitting in an office waiting to be escorted to a classroom, [Noma LeMoine] observed a white teacher entering the room with an African-American child. It appeared the teacher wanted to telephone the child's parents.
>
> "Bobby, what does your mother do?" the teacher asked.
>
> "She be at home," Bobby replied.
>
> "You mean she *is* at home," the teacher said.
>
> "No she ain't," Bobby offered, "'cause she took my grandmother to the hospital this morning."
>
> The teacher snapped. "You know what I meant. You aren't supposed to say, 'She be at home.' You say, 'She is at home.'"
>
> But Bobby, incredulous, could only reply, "Why you trying to make me lie? She ain't at home."
>
> Ross (1997, 31)

Aspectual *be* is a characteristic of AAE grammar that is arguably more complicated than that of Standard English. Obviously, Standard English speakers can say that something happens usually or habitually, but (at least in the present tense) their language has no dedicated grammatical marker for this: the speaker has to use adverbs or other tools to express that meaning (e.g., *Bruce usually runs*). AAE, by contrast, has a specific grammatical marker *be* for describing habitual action. In other words, AAE consistently makes a grammatical distinction that Standard English does not.

Not only does aspectual *be* mean something different in AAE from Standard English *be*, but it also obeys different grammatical rules. In Standard English, the way to form a yes-no question from a sentence with a form of *be* is to move *be* to the beginning of the sentence, as in example (16). If the sentence contains a different verb (other than a modal), *do* is used instead, as in example (17).

(16) a. They are running.
b. Are they ___ running?

(17) a. They run.
b. Do they run?

AAE has the same pattern for non-aspectual uses of *be*; for example, the question corresponding to *Dee was here* is *Was Dee here?* But for aspectual *be*, the rules are different: *do* appears in yes-no questions with aspectual *be*, as shown in (18). This means that AAE speakers systematically treat aspectual *be* differently from other forms of *be*.

(18) a. They be running.
b. Do they be running?

These patterns demonstrate that using *be* in AAE is not ignorant, lazy, or perverse. Rather, AAE speakers are following a set of complex grammatical rules in marking habitual action.

Stressed BIN

Stressed *BIN* is another grammatical marker in AAE that Standard English lacks. Stressed *BIN* looks similar to Standard English *been*, but it is always stressed; in addition, like aspectual *be*, it has a specific grammatical meaning.

(19) Someone asked, 'Is she married?' and someone else answered, 'She BÍN married'. Do you get the idea that she is married now?

Rickford (1983) presented scenarios like the one in (19) to 50 people, 25 black and 25 white. The black respondents overwhelmingly answered 'yes'; very few of the white respondents did. In AAE, stressed *BIN* marks actions that happened in the remote past, or states that began in the remote past. The meaning of *She BIN married*, then, is 'she has been married for a long time'; the answers of the black respondents show that this is how they interpreted the sentence. But in Standard English, a sentence like *She has been married* just means 'she was married at some point in the past'; in the context of the conversation in (19), the implication is that she isn't married anymore, or else the speaker would have said so. This explains why most of the white respondents answered 'no'.

Like aspectual *be*, then, stressed *BIN* is a grammatical marker in AAE. It has its own rules of question formation: where *do* is used to form questions with aspectual *be*, *have* is used with stressed *BIN*.

(20) a. They BIN running.
'They have been running for a long time.'
b. Have they BIN running?

To sum up, AAE has its own set of complex grammatical rules. In particular, the verbal system of AAE is just as complex as that of Standard English; speakers of AAE are obeying regular rules when they speak, but those rules happen to be different from the rules of Standard English. So why is there a persistent belief that AAE is nothing more than a bunch of mistakes?

One reason may be the close similarity between AAE and Standard English. As noted above, aspectual *be* looks a lot like the Standard English word *be*, so many people assume that aspectual *be* actually *is* Standard English *be*, used incorrectly. Similarly, speakers of Standard English usually interpret stressed *BIN* as though it were Standard English *been*.

Another reason may be the fact that many speakers of AAE also have some knowledge of Standard English. It's common for someone who speaks a non-standard dialect to speak the standard too; the person's speech will be more standard or more non-standard depending on the situation. In fact, even people who speak only the standard dialect command a range of styles; speech becomes more or less formal as the occasion requires. When a speaker of Standard English listens to a speaker of AAE who sometimes says *They are running* and sometimes says *They be running*, it's easy to assume that the person 'knows the rules' but sometimes makes mistakes. The situation is made even more complicated by the fact that speakers are capable of *code-switching* – switching between different dialects very quickly, within a single conversation or even within a single sentence. The speaker may appear to be using non-standard forms haphazardly and irregularly, when what the speaker is actually doing is switching between two different grammatical systems.

There is one final point to be made here. Linguists argue that no variety of a language is *linguistically* superior to any other; every dialect of every language follows regular grammatical rules and is capable of fulfilling the communicative needs of its speakers. This is true even for languages and dialects that are widely thought to be crude or unsophisticated: as soon as linguists start studying what speakers actually do, we discover that these languages are just as rule-governed as any other. (This situation for AAE in the United States is similar in many ways to that of creole languages around the world; see section 5.2.1 for more discussion.)

But linguists also recognize that not all dialects of a given language are *socially* equal. Standard English is no better or worse than AAE on linguistic grounds, but it is much more highly valued than AAE in many social situations. Whether we like it or not, it's a fact of life that a person who speaks Standard English will find it much easier to excel in the academic world or get certain kinds of jobs than a person who speaks only AAE. Thus, there are good pragmatic and ethical arguments for helping speakers of non-standard dialects learn Standard English too, while acknowledging that it's only by historical accident that this particular variety is the prestigious one. This is the issue at the heart of the Ebonics controversy, to which we now turn.

2.3 Case study: What is the best way to teach the standard dialect to speakers of a non-standard dialect?

2.3.1 Background: The Oakland Ebonics controversy

In December of 1996, the Oakland Board of Education adopted a resolution on methods of formal English instruction for African-American students. Commentators reported that African-American children in Oakland were going to be taught a language called 'Ebonics' instead of English, and the result was a national outcry. The board was accused of dumbing down the curriculum, of giving up on Standard English, and of inventing a new language in order to get access to federal money for bilingual education.

In reality, the Oakland Board of Education never proposed teaching AAE as a second language to students of any race. (Some of the most ridiculous commentary on the issue assumed that there was a plan to teach Ebonics *to* African-American children – but the whole point was that African-American children *already* spoke this variety.) Rather, the plan was to give students explicit instruction in the differences between AAE and Standard English *in order to help the students learn Standard English*. The resolution was inspired by scholarly research suggesting that for students who speak a non-standard dialect, one of the best ways to teach the standard dialect is to acknowledge the non-standard explicitly in the classroom.

One reason people had such strong reactions to this issue is the persistent belief that the standard variety of a language is 'correct' and non-standard varieties are a collection of mistakes. (Or, as an acquaintance of mine once put it, 'Isn't Ebonics just English spelled wrong?') Another factor in the backlash was the fact that the original text of the resolution included several cases of unfortunate wording, including a reference to Ebonics as 'genetically-based' and an insistence that Ebonics is an African language and not a variety of English.

The question of whether specific features of AAE originated in Africa, the Americas, or elsewhere is extremely complex, and the issue is a matter of ongoing research to this day. But to the broader question – is AAE a dialect of English or a separate language? – linguists can give no definitive answer. Globally and historically, decisions about where to draw the line between languages and dialects are based just as much on politics as they are on purely linguistic considerations. The languages that we call 'Chinese' and 'Arabic', for example, are actually collections of mutually unintelligible dialects. Under other circumstances, these dialects would probably be considered separate languages, but for now they are counted as belonging to the same language for political and social reasons. Conversely, some languages that we consider to be different, such as Swedish and Norwegian or Hindi and Urdu, are so similar that speakers of the different languages can understand each other very well. Again, the reasons these varieties are called languages rather than dialects are political and social, not linguistic.

In this section, we will investigate the merits of the Oakland Board of Education's actual proposal: to teach Standard English by giving students explicit instruction in the differences between the standard and their native dialect. There are many reasons an institution might want to try this approach: to encourage students to take pride in their dialect, for example, or to give teachers a more accurate understanding of their students' linguistic abilities. Our focus, though, will be on the narrow question of whether this kind of instruction actually improves students' ability to use the standard dialect. In other words, can this approach really accomplish what the Oakland Board of Education said it would?

2.3.2 Learning to read in rural Sweden: Österberg (1961)

Piteå is an isolated rural area in northern Sweden with a distinctive local dialect. Standard Swedish is taught in schools, and the local dialect is a source of embarrassment to children and adults alike, especially when they interact with outsiders. Österberg (1961) compared two methods of teaching children in Piteå to read: one in which students were taught to read Standard Swedish from day one, and another in which students were taught to read in their own dialect first before switching to the standard.

The study involved a total of 331 first-grade students and their teachers. Before the start of the 1957–1958 school year, all of the teachers involved in the study were trained to teach students to read in the dialect of Piteå rather than Standard Swedish. The teachers were then assigned to two groups: half, group 'R', taught reading in Standard Swedish; the other half, group 'D', spent the first 10 weeks of the school year teaching students to read in their native dialect, and then transitioned to the standard. Aside from the dialect used in instruction, both groups used the same teaching methods and had comparable reading materials (the materials in the Piteå dialect were created specifically for the experiment). Österberg took great care to make sure that the two groups of teachers and their students were as similar as possible; he controlled for factors such as teacher age, experience, student school readiness, and so on.[5]

Students took several standardized reading tests at the end of the school year, all in Standard Swedish. Table 2.1 summarizes students' scores on Reading Test I, which involved reading single words in a list. The students in group D, who received dialect instruction, had better scores on average than the students in group R. Thus, students who initially learned to read in their native Piteå dialect were actually *better* at reading Standard Swedish than the students who spent the entire year using Standard Swedish. (Interestingly, though, this difference was statistically significant for the girls but not for the boys.)

There were statistically significant differences between the two groups for some of the other reading tests as well, and in every case, group D performed better than group R. (The difference was always statistically significant for girls, but not always for boys – a pattern that suggests that the girls may have benefited more from dialect instruction than the boys. But even when the difference was not statistically significant for boys, the results trended in the right direction: the average score for boys in group D was slightly better than the average score for boys in group R.) Österberg concluded that students learned Standard Swedish better after learning to read in their native dialect first, despite the fact that group D actually spent *less* time using Standard Swedish than group R!

These results are encouraging, but naturally there is reason to be cautious before we apply them to AAE in the United States. First, groups D and R showed statistically significant differences on only a few of the nine tests of

[5] One of the factors Österberg explored was whether students had received any reading instruction before they arrived at school. Interestingly, Österberg worried that the parents' teaching would be 'technically inferior' and actually harmful to the children's learning! This perspective seems very odd to us today, since it's now widely believed that children gain an advantage when their parents teach them to read at home. See Chapter 5 for discussion of the culture-specific nature of beliefs about child-rearing and language acquisition.

Table 2.1 *Means (M) and standard deviations (SD) for scores on Reading Test I (reading of single words), adapted from Table 24 of Österberg (1961). An asterisk indicates a statistically significant difference between groups D and R.*

Groups	M	SD
Girls		
D (N = 84)	23.0	6.17
R (N = 86)	19.3	6.85
t	3.70*	
Boys		
D (N = 74)	21.3	6.94
R (N = 87)	19.4	7.36
t	1.67	
All		
D (N = 158)	22.2	6.54
R (N = 173)	19.4	7.11
t	3.73*	

reading and writing. The effect of dialect instruction was real, but it was also relatively small. In addition, this study doesn't tell us how long these benefits last, or what would happen if students received dialect instruction continuously throughout their education, or whether dialect instruction has any benefit if it begins after students have already learned to read the standard dialect.

The situation in Piteå is also different from the situation of AAE in several important respects. Piteå is an isolated, homogeneous community, and the vast majority of students and teachers are native speakers of the dialect. What would change if the methods used here were taken to an inner-city school in the United States where some students are native speakers of AAE, some are native speakers of other varieties of English, and some are not native speakers of English at all? What difference does it make if the teacher is not a native speaker of the non-standard dialect?

2.3.3 *Comparing the local dialect with the standard: Yiakoumetti (2006)*

Cyprus has a distinctive local dialect of Greek. Standard Greek is expected in formal contexts, but many Cypriots aren't fully fluent in the standard variety. Yiakoumetti (2006) studied whether explicit instruction in the differences between Cypriot Greek and Standard Greek would encourage students to use more Standard Greek in school.

The study involved a total of 182 11-year-old students from four schools. For three months, half of the students received 45 minutes of instruction

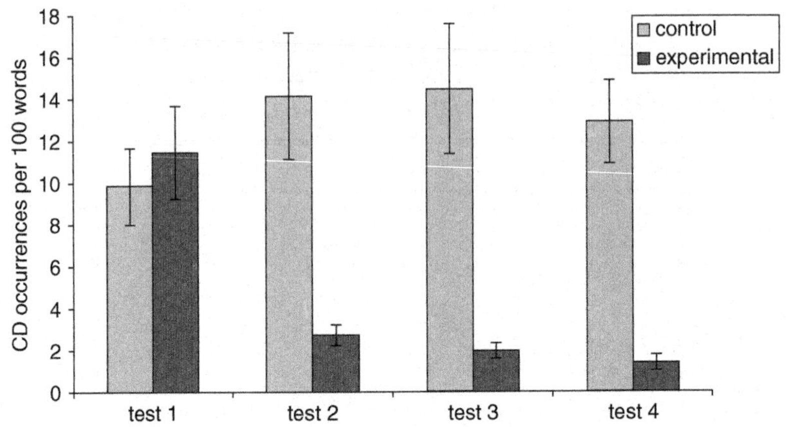

Figure 2.1 Frequency of Cypriot Greek dialect features in students' essays. Test 1 took place at the beginning of the experiment, test 2 in the middle, test 3 at the end, and test 4 three months later. Androula Yiakoumetti, A bidialectal programme for the learning of Standard Modern Greek in Cyprus, *Applied Linguistics* 2006, 27, 2, 295–317, Figure 5. Reprinted by permission of Oxford University Press.

every day on the differences between Cypriot Greek and Standard Greek. The instruction included practice identifying the differences between the two dialects and using the standard in contrast to Cypriot Greek. The other half of the students, the control group, received no special instruction. To assess whether this practice actually affected students' speech, Yiakoumetti assessed students' performance on two separate writing assignments and their speech in a three-minute oral interview.

Figure 2.1 shows how often students used Cypriot features in one of the writing assignments, a geography essay. On the first test, before the students had received any special instruction, both groups performed about the same. But on the later tests, the experimental group used much less Cypriot Greek in their writing, while the control group used more; Yiakoumetti reports that both of these changes are significant at $p < .001$. The results for the other writing assignment and the oral interview were similar. It seems, then, that explicitly comparing their native dialect to standard Greek was effective in helping students use more Standard Greek in their schoolwork.

Because these students had already been educated in the standard dialect for several years, this study makes a nice complement to Österberg's, where students received instruction in the local dialect in their very first year of school. Thus, this study demonstrates that an intervention of this type can be effective for older students as well. In addition, the type of instruction used here is more similar to the kinds of proposals that have been made in the United States than the instruction in Österberg's study was. The students in Cyprus were trained to identify differences between Cypriot Greek and Standard Greek, rather than reading extended texts in their native dialect as the students in Piteå did. Programs that encourage students to compare the grammatical structures of AAE and Standard English are in the same spirit.[6]

On the other hand, this study has its own limitations. It's encouraging that the experimental group continued to do well even at the last test, three months after the end of the study; but it would be useful to know how long the effect lasted. In addition, for assessing students' speech (as opposed to their writing), a three-minute interview is very short. Is it possible that the students were able to concentrate enough for those three minutes to switch to Standard Greek, but that they wouldn't be able to do this for a longer period of time?

Despite these limitations, Yiakoumetti's results give further support to the idea that talking about students' non-standard dialect in the classroom is more likely to help them than to harm them.

2.3.4 Comparing AAE and the standard in college: Taylor (1989)

Taylor (1989) reports the results of her efforts to teach Standard English by explicitly comparing it with AAE. Taylor, an English professor at Aurora University (located near Chicago), started 'Project Bidialectalism' after she noticed that many of her African-American students were bright but struggled to express themselves in Standard English. She met weekly with two groups of students; one group received instruction using standard teaching methods, while the other group was taught using 'Contrastive Analysis': explicit instruction in the differences between Standard English and AAE, inspired by approaches to foreign language instruction.

As part of Contrastive Analysis, Taylor used several different techniques to help students analyze the differences between AAE and Standard English. Some of the exercises were drills such as the following that asked students to compare the two dialects or to produce forms in Standard English.

(21) Change the following sentences to express negation:

a. The actors should always look directly at the audience.

b. He knew everybody from the St. Louis area.

[6] Some educators have tried using 'dialect readers' written in AAE, and anecdotal and experimental evidence suggests that they're helpful. But programs with dialect readers often face strong resistance from parents and teachers, and for that reason they've been infrequently used. See Rickford and Rickford (1995) for an overview.

(22) Identify standard English or black English features, included in parentheses:

a. I know my husband (love, loves) me.
b. The entire family gathered into my (sister, sister's) room.

Other exercises involved memorizing and performing passages from AAE literature or translating passages from AAE into Standard English. Taylor encouraged students to talk about the social setting of AAE, especially their own daily experience with language; she also drew parallels between her students' experiences and her own as a speaker of a non-standard dialect of German (and as a non-native speaker of English). Taylor encouraged her students to see their use of AAE features as dialect interference, not mistakes, and as something common to any bidialectal or bilingual situation.

To evaluate whether Contrastive Analysis was effective, Taylor and a colleague compared two writing samples for each student: a pre-test writing sample from the beginning of the instructional period and the final writing project from the end. Overall, she found that the students who were instructed using Contrastive Analysis reduced the number of AAE features in their writing by 59.3%, while the students who were instructed using traditional methods actually *increased* the number of AAE features in their writing by 8.5%.

Taylor's study has its limitations; the number of students involved was small[7], and she doesn't report any tests of statistical significance. However, the study is notable because it involves AAE and because the participants were college students, not elementary-school children. Taylor's results provide further evidence that something like Contrastive Analysis is genuinely effective in teaching students how to use Standard English.

2.3.5 *General conclusions*

All the studies we've seen show that an effective way to teach the standard dialect of a language to speakers of a non-standard dialect is to give students explicit instruction in the differences between the two varieties. These studies, and others like them (see 'Further reading' below), suggest that the Oakland Board of Education was on the right track: rather than ignore the fact that many students are AAE speakers, it's better to acknowledge the situation and teach students explicitly how the standard is different from their native dialect.

[7] In fact, it's not clear how many students were actually involved in the project. Taylor (1989, 100) refers to '20 student-participants' but doesn't specify whether there were 20 students total or 20 in each group.

One thing that's especially encouraging is the variety of studies that all arrive at the same conclusion. These experiments were conducted in different languages, with students of different ages, using different teaching methods, and for different lengths of time. They all have their own limitations, but together they suggest that explicit instruction in dialect differences is likely to be effective in a wide variety of situations.

2.4 Summary

- Every variety of a language, whether standard or not, follows grammatical rules.
- These rules operate below the level of conscious thought: speakers obey them even if they can't explicitly describe the rules they are following.
- African American English is not just a collection of mistakes. AAE verbs, for example, follow complex grammatical rules, which happen to be different from the rules of Standard English.
- In 1996, the Oakland Board of Education proposed giving students explicit instruction in the differences between AAE and Standard English in order to help them learn Standard English. The board never proposed teaching 'Ebonics' as a second language.
- Several studies have shown that explicit instruction in dialect differences is an effective way to help speakers of a non-standard dialect learn the standard.

For further reflection

(1) Read Wiens (2012). Do you think Wiens is right to use 'grammar' (that is, adherence to the rules of Standard English) in determining whether or not to hire people at his company? Do you think there is ever a situation where it is, or is not, appropriate to make a hiring decision based on the person's command of Standard English?

(2) Read Dong (1992), a classic analysis of certain obscene and profane English words. 'Dong' (actually a pen name of the linguist James McCawley) argues in some detail that *fuck* in the sentence *Fuck you* is not a verb. Do an informal survey of two or three native English speakers: Ask them if they think *fuck* in *Fuck you* is a verb. Then test whether they agree with Dong's grammaticality judgments: Do they think sentences like *I said to fuck you* are grammatical or ungrammatical? Do the beliefs of the people you surveyed match their actual behavior when it comes to the grammatical status of the word *fuck*? What does this tell

you about the relationship between explicit knowledge about grammar and the rules people actually follow?

(3) Read Morse (1973). Which of Morse's observations about AAE and other non-standard dialects are correct? Which are inaccurate?

(4) In the late 1980s, there was heated public discussion in Great Britain about the proper way to teach English grammar to students. Read the analysis of the controversy in Cameron (1995) and compare it to the Oakland debate. In what ways did the two controversies involve some of the same concerns? In what ways were they different?

Further reading

Green (2002), an undergraduate-level textbook, is a general overview of AAE with particular attention to grammatical structures. Mufwene et al. (1998) and Rickford (1999), also surveys, are collections of technical scholarly papers with somewhat more emphasis on the social and historical dimensions of AAE.

Two accessible essays on the grammatical rules of AAE, in the context of the Ebonics debate, are Rickford (1997) and Pullum (1999). The Linguistic Society of America adopted a formal resolution in response to the controversy, which is available on the Society's website (see references below). Nunberg (1997) reviews media coverage of the Oakland school board resolution and linguists' response.

Other studies on methods for teaching Standard English to speakers of AAE include Schierloh (1991), Fogel and Ehri (2000), Maddahian and Sandamela (2000), Wheeler and Swords (2004), and Sweetland (2006); see Rickford (2005) for an overview. There are similar studies on teaching Standard English to speakers of English-based creoles; Kephart (1992) and Siegel (1997) are examples. Siegel (2006) is a highly accessible overview of the issue of including non-standard varieties (including creoles) in the classroom.

Bibliography

Cameron, Deborah. *Verbal Hygiene*, chapter 4: Civility and its discontents: Language and 'political correctness', pages 116–165. Routledge, London, 1995.

Dong, Quang Phuc. English sentences without overt grammatical subject. In Arnold M. Zwicky, Peter H. Salus, Robert I. Binnick, and Anthony L. Vanek, editors, *Studies out in Left Field: Defamatory Essays Presented to James D. McCawley on His 33rd or 34th Birthday*, pages 3–10. John Benjamins Publishing Company, Amsterdam, 1992.

Fogel, Howard, and Linnea C. Ehri. Teaching elementary students who speak Black English Vernacular to write in Standard English: Effects of dialect transformation practice. *Contemporary Educational Psychology*, 25(2):212–235, 2000.

Green, Lisa, and Thomas Roeper. The acquisition path for tense-aspect: Remote past and habitual in child African American English. *Language Acquisition*, 14(3):269–313, 2007.

Green, Lisa J. *African American English: A Linguistic Introduction*. Cambridge University Press, Cambridge, 2002.

Kephart, Ronald. Reading Creole English does not destroy your brain cells! In Jeff Siegel, editor, *Pidgins, Creoles, and Nonstandard Dialects in Education*, number 12 in Occasional Papers, pages 67–86. Applied Linguistics Association of Australia, Queensland, Australia, 1992.

Linguistic Society of America. LSA resolution on the Oakland 'Ebonics' issue. Linguistic Society of America, January 1997. Available at http://www.linguisticsociety.org/about/what-we-do/resolutions-statements-guides/lsa-res-ebonics.

Maddahian, Ebrahim, and Ambition Padi Sandamela. Academic English Mastery Program: 1998–99 evaluation report. Los Angeles Unified School District Research and Evaluation Unit, Publication No. 781, March 2000.

Mitchell, Richard. *Less than Words Can Say*, chapter 13: Hydra, pages 156–165. Available at http://www.sourcetext.com/grammarian/less-than-words-can-say/13.htm.

Morse, J. Mitchell. The shuffling speech of slavery: Black English. *College English*, 34(6):834–843, 1973.

Mufwene, Salikoko S., John R. Rickford, Guy Bailey, and John Baugh, editors. *African-American English: Structure, History, and Use*. Routledge, London, 1998.

Nunberg, Geoffrey. Double standards. *Natural Language and Linguistic Theory*, 15(3):667–675, 1997.

Oakland Board of Education. Resolution of the Board of Education adopting the report and recommendations of the African-American task force; a policy statement and directing the Superintendent of Schools to devise a program to improve the English language acquisition and application skills of African-American students. No. $597-0063, December 1996. Original resolution available at http://linguistlist.org/topics/ebonics/ebonics-res1.html.

Österberg, Tore. *Bilingualism and the First School Language – An Educational Problem Illustrated by Results from a Swedish Dialect Area*. Västerbottens Tryckeri, Umeå, 1961.

Pullum, Geoffrey K. African American Vernacular English is not Standard English with mistakes. In Rebecca S. Wheeler, editor, *The Workings of Language: From Prescriptions to Perspectives*, chapter 3, pages 39–58. Praeger Publishers, Westport, CT, 1999.

Raspberry, William. To throw in a lot of 'bes,' or not? A conversation on Ebonics. *The Washington Post*, December 26 1996.

Rickford, John R. *African American Vernacular English: Features, Evolution, Educational Implications*. Number 26 in Language in Society. Blackwell, Oxford, 1999.

Rickford, John R. Carrying the new wave into syntax: The case of Black English BÍN. In Ralph W. Fasold, editor, *Variation in the Form and Use of Language: A Sociolinguistics Reader*, pages 98–119. Georgetown University Press, Washington, DC, 1983.

Rickford, John R. Suite for ebony and phonics. *Discover Magazine*, December 1997. Available at http://discovermagazine.com/1997/dec/suiteforebonyand1292.

Rickford, John R. Using the vernacular to teach the standard. In J. David Ramirez, Terrence G. Wiley, Gerda de Klerk, Enid Lee, and Wayne E. Wright, editors, *Ebonics: The Urban Education Debate*, New Perspectives on Language and Education, pages 18–40. Multilingual Matters, Clevedon, GB, 2nd edition, 2005.

Rickford, John R., and Angela E. Rickford. Dialect readers revisited. *Linguistics and Education*, 7(2):107–128, 1995.

Ross, Randy. Why 'Black English' matters. *Education Week*, January 29 1997.

Schierloh, Jane McCabe. Teaching Standard English usage: A dialect-based approach. *Adult Learning*, 2(5):20–22, 1991.

Siegel, Jeff. Keeping creoles and dialects out of the classroom: Is it justified? In Shondel J. Nero, editor, *Dialects, Englishes, Creoles, and Education*, ESL & Applied Linguistics Professional Series, chapter 2, pages 39–67. Lawrence Erlbaum Associates, Mahwah, NJ, 2006.

Siegel, Jeff. Using a pidgin language in formal education: Help or hindrance? *Applied Linguistics*, 18(1):86–100, 1997.

Sweetland, Julie. *Teaching Writing in the African American Classroom: A Sociolinguistic Approach*. PhD thesis, Stanford University, 2006.

Taylor, Hanni U. *Standard English, Black English, and Bidialectalism: A Controversy*. American University Studies. Peter Lang, New York, NY, 1989.

Wheeler, Rebecca S., and Rachel Swords. Codeswitching: Tools of language and culture transform the dialectally diverse classroom. *Language Arts*, 81(6):470–480, 2004.

Wiens, Kyle. I won't hire people who use poor grammar. Here's why. Harvard Business Review Blog Network, July 20 2012. Available at http://hbr.org/2012/07/i-wont-hire-people-who-use-poo.

Yiakoumetti, Androula. A bidialectal programme for the learning of Standard Modern Greek in Cyprus. *Applied Linguistics*, 27(2):295–317, 2006.

3 'Sign language is skilled charades'

When I was a small child I used to play with the girl next door. She didn't understand anything I tried to tell her, but it didn't matter. We played together all the time, using simple gestures to communicate. I thought something was wrong with her, but I adapted easily to her limitation.

One day when I was about four, I went inside her house. As I stood there, her mother came downstairs. Nothing happened between her and the girl that I could see. Then I saw her mother point at the doll house in the hallway. The girl ran and moved the doll house back into her room, as if she had just been told to do so. I was astounded. I knew it was different, something different. I knew they had communicated, in a form I couldn't see. But how? I asked my mother about what I had seen.

'They are called "hearing",' she explained. 'They don't sign. They are hearing. They are different. We are Deaf. We sign.'

I asked if the family next door are the only ones, the only hearing people.

My mother shook her head. 'No', she signed, 'it is us that are alone'.

I was very surprised. I naturally assumed everyone was like me.[1]

This childhood experience of Sam Supalla, recounted in Perlmutter (1986, 515), vividly illustrates the fact that sign language is a living language for many people, just as spoken language is for many others. When hearing people think and talk about language, we usually mean *spoken* language – and it's easy to understand why, because the majority of human languages are in fact spoken. But it's also true that deaf individuals use sign as a medium for communication that is every bit as rich and expressive as speech.

Nor is sign limited to people who are deaf. Until the twentieth century, for example, a sizeable proportion of the population on Martha's Vineyard (a small island off the coast of Massachusetts) was deaf. The community used their own sign language – different from American Sign Language (ASL) – which was known by deaf and hearing individuals alike. Martha's Vineyard isn't unique; there are similar situations in small communities around the world, some of

[1] With kind permission from Springer Science+Business Media: *Natural Language and Linguistic Theory*, No nearer to the soul, 4, 1986, 515–523, David Perlmutter.

which are described in Perlmutter (1986). Apparently, once the number of deaf people reaches critical mass, the entire community will adopt signing as a second language.

But in most parts of the world, deaf people make up a tiny proportion of the population. The result is that most hearing people don't personally know anyone who is deaf and have no first-hand experience with signing. In this context, there are two very interesting widespread beliefs about the nature of sign:

1. Signing is a visual representation of the surrounding spoken language. People who know ASL are signing 'in English'; people who know French Sign Language are signing 'in French', and so on.
2. Sign is a universal language, because it's basically pantomime that draws pictures in the air.

These two beliefs are obviously incompatible: if sign language is universal, how could it be a direct representation of so many different (and mutually unintelligible) spoken languages? In addition, both beliefs suggest that signing is something less than a language: either it's just a derivative representation of spoken language, or it's an elaborate game of charades. Neither view predicts that sign language would have its own, independent grammatical structure.

As we will see, it turns out that *both* ideas are false. Along the way, we'll take a closer look at some of the things linguists have learned about the structure of sign language and how it is related to spoken language.

3.1 Signed languages versus spoken languages

For centuries, linguists paid virtually no attention to signed languages; they thought there was nothing to analyze. This changed in 1960, when William Stokoe of Gallaudet University published the first serious linguistic analysis of ASL. Since then, linguists have made enormous progress in understanding how ASL and other signed languages work. Okrent (2011) sums up the state of the field at the end of the 1970s: 'There was still a long way to go, but among linguists two things had become clear: (1) sign language was not spoken language; (2) sign language was just like spoken language!'

In this section, we will examine some of the ways in which signed languages are, and are not, like spoken languages. We will also look at some of the opposition that signed languages have historically faced, particularly the oralist philosophy that was prevalent in the nineteenth and twentieth centuries.

3.1.1 *Signed language is not spoken language*

When we say that signed languages aren't the same as spoken languages, we're usually talking about the first myth mentioned above. Contrary to popular belief, ASL is *not* a signed version of English, nor is any other natural signed language a direct 'translation' of the spoken language around it.

One of the easiest ways to demonstrate the differences between signed and spoken languages is to compare their rules for word order: the word order of a signed language isn't necessarily the same as the word order of the spoken language(s) around it. In English, for example, the subject comes before the verb: *The boy fell*, not **Fell the boy*. In ASL, it's possible for the subject to come after the verb, but only in certain circumstances: if the subject is a full noun phrase, it must come before the verb; if it's a pronoun, it may come after. Thus, *FALL BOY[2] isn't grammatical in ASL, but FALL PRO is (where PRO represents an ASL pronoun). The latter sentence means something like 'He fell down, he did' (Liddell 2003, 59).

A striking example of differing word order in signed and spoken languages is Al-Sayyid Bedouin Sign Language (ABSL). This is a very young language; it's used in an isolated community in southern Israel that has a significant number of deaf individuals, the first of whom were born in the early twentieth century. One interesting and well-documented aspect of ABSL is its basic sentence structure. In English, the object of a verb comes after the verb; for example, we say *I read books*, not **I books read*. The same is true in the spoken languages of the area, Hebrew and the local dialect of Arabic. But in ABSL, the object comes *before* the verb. This regular, rule-governed word order couldn't have been borrowed from any of the local spoken languages; it must have emerged independently within the signing community.

Signed and spoken languages can also differ in their vocabulary. For example, ASL has different signs for addressing one person versus more than one person; Standard English has just one word *you*, and listeners have to rely on the context to figure out how many people are being addressed. On the other hand, English has pronouns that distinguish among males, females, and inanimate objects (*he*, *she*, *it*), but ASL doesn't. What's interesting is that in both of these examples, ASL has a property that is also shared by some spoken languages other than English. Spanish and many other languages have separate pronouns for 'you' (one person) and 'you' (more than one person); Turkish and Mandarin Chinese don't distinguish between 'he' and 'she'. In other words, ASL is doing things that many spoken languages do, but it couldn't have borrowed those patterns from English.

[2] In writing, it is conventional to represent a sign with its closest translation in a spoken language, printed in capital letters.

Signed languages often borrow words from the spoken languages around them, but they may end up using those words differently. For example, Israeli Sign Language (ISL) has a sign that we can translate roughly as 'already'; in addition to moving the hands, this sign involves mouthing the Hebrew word *kvar*, which also means 'already'. ISL has obviously borrowed this word from spoken Hebrew, but today ALREADY and *kvar* have very different uses. The ISL sign ALREADY always means that the action has been completed, whereas the Hebrew word *kvar* can mean that the action is ongoing or isn't finished yet. Meir and Sandler (2008, 99) illustrate the differences between the two:

(1) 'Did you do your homework?'

a. ALREADY, ALREADY. (ISL)
'I've already done it.'

b. *Kvar.* (Hebrew)
'Not yet, but soon; I'll do it in a minute.'

(2) a. BOOK INDEX$_a$ – I ALREADY READ THREE-DAY. (ISL)
'It took me three days to read this book.'

b. *ani kvar kore et ha-sefer ha-ze shlosha yamim.* (Hebrew)
I already read ACC the-book the-this three days
'I've been reading this book for three days already (and haven't finished yet).'

Not only are signed languages structurally different from the spoken languages around them, but signed and spoken languages may not even occupy the same geographical areas. The most famous example is ASL and British Sign Language (BSL), which are not related to each other and aren't mutually intelligible, despite the fact that they're both used in English-speaking countries. (Because sign language isn't the same everywhere, linguists sometimes refer to *signed languages* rather than *sign language*, emphasizing the fact that there are many different signed languages just as there are many different spoken ones.)

The fact that signed languages aren't equivalent to spoken ones has been recognized for a long time. In fact, attempts to 'fix' signed languages to make them more like spoken ones go back to the earliest days of deaf education. The Abbé de l'Épée, a pioneering eighteenth-century educator, learned the signed language of the deaf community in Paris and was one of the first to use signs to teach deaf students. But Épée was dissatisfied with the differences between French and his students' native system of signs, so he modified the system to make it correspond more closely to spoken French. This new system was very unnatural for the students; they followed it as required in the classroom, but used their own signed language among themselves. Today, there are many similar systems for mimicking a spoken language in sign, but they are no more natural now than they were then. These systems are used for various educational purposes, but deaf communities do not adopt them as a native language. ASL is distinct from Signed English.

3.1.2 Oralism and negative views of signed language

The hundred years or so after the founding of Épée's school in Paris were a kind of golden age in the history of deaf education. Signing was encouraged and respected (even if educators sometimes tried to 'improve' the students' language); and, for the first time in history, large numbers of deaf people were able to get an education and participate in the larger society as never before.

It was during this period that deaf education was established in the United States. Thomas Gallaudet traveled to Europe to learn how to teach deaf children; when educators in Great Britain refused to share their methods with him, he went to Paris and studied for several months at Épée's school. Gallaudet returned to the United States with Laurent Clerc, who was a deaf graduate of the school; they founded the Connecticut Asylum for the Deaf and Dumb (now the American School for the Deaf), where Clerc's signed language became a model for deaf students from around the country. (This is why ASL is related to French Sign Language but not to BSL.) ASL flourished for over half a century: the school hired many deaf teachers, and its graduates went on to found schools in other parts of the country, bringing ASL with them.

Everything changed toward the end of the nineteenth century with the rise of the educational philosophy known as *oralism*. Oralists believed that the best way to help deaf students was to teach them to speak and read lips; only this approach, they believed, would allow students to participate fully in the broader hearing society. Oralism was an international phenomenon; an influential meeting of deaf educators in Milan in 1880 officially endorsed oralism to the exclusion of all other methods, and this approach had a powerful effect around the world for many decades. Oralism also got a boost from its many prominent advocates, including Alexander Graham Bell – to this day, the Alexander Graham Bell Association for the Deaf and Hard of Hearing promotes oral methods.

Oralism effectively forced ASL and other signed languages underground. The number of deaf teachers in deaf schools plummeted, and signing was often forbidden outright; students from oralist schools recall being punished for signing, or forced to wear gloves that tied their hands together. Today, drastic measures like these seem unnecessary and cruel – but at the time, oralists were acting with good intentions. One problem with the oralist approach is that lip-reading is extraordinarily hard, and many students just can't do it. (Learning to speak is similarly difficult for congenitally deaf students.) Educators thought they could motivate their students to try harder if spoken language was their only option.[3]

This opposition to signing wasn't just a practical one; many oralists believed that signed languages were inherently inferior to spoken ones anyway. The following excerpt from an 1898 report by an oralist educator illustrates the kinds of beliefs that were common at the time.

> [ASL] is simply an extension of signs and gestures which are commonly understood by all men. It requires several years of diligent application and constant use for an intelligent person to acquire a familiar, or working acquaintance with this form of sign language. Deaf mutes acquire it, however, with comparative ease, and generally become devotedly attached to this means of communication.
>
> In practical use this form of sign language relates to ideas rather than to words and bears no marked resemblance to any other language. It does not require the use of any sign corresponding to the verb 'to be,' omits symbols of time relations, all the finer distinctions expressed by prepositions, distinctions between adverbs and adjectives, and, in fine, possesses an extremely limited 'vocabulary' which is used with such a disregard of grammatical relations as to render this form of communication practically a grammarless language.... These signs even when limited to a definite signification are used generally and habitually in an inverted order, and any attempt at a word for word translation produces an indescribable jargon....
>
> This language fails to express ideas which are not of an exceedingly simple character, and it is utterly unfitted to convey with accuracy scientific definitions, philosophical distinctions, or even the elementary facts of science. This language not only fails to meet these higher requirements, but it tends to unfit the minds of those dependent upon it for the successful prosecution of many very important studies.
>
> Gordon (1898, 45–46)

The first sentence of this passage shows that Gordon sees sign language as essentially pantomime: its gestures are 'commonly understood by all men'. (Oddly, he immediately goes on to acknowledge that it takes several years to become proficient in this language – a contradiction that he doesn't seem to notice.) The rest of the passage shows that educators were well aware that ASL isn't just a signed version of English, and that this is part of the reason they opposed it.

[3] Sadly, many deaf children today who receive cochlear implants are put in a similar situation. Cochlear implants require extensive training and therapy (and may fail anyway); well-meaning medical professionals often recommend that implanted children be completely isolated from sign language on the grounds that children who sign won't be motivated to learn spoken language. The tragic result is that the child may end up with *no* native language. See Humphries et al. (2012) for a forceful argument that all children with cochlear implants should learn a signed language in addition to any speech training they receive.

In retrospect, of course, it's easy to see that many of the features Gordon complains about are perfectly ordinary even in spoken languages; they just happen to be different from the way English works. There are spoken languages, such as Russian, that either lack a verb meaning 'to be' entirely or omit it in many contexts, just like ASL. English has a suffix *-ly* that distinguishes some adjectives and adverbs, but ASL doesn't and neither does German. ASL verbs aren't marked for tense (the time when the event occurs), but they are marked for aspect (information about the structure of the event, such as the difference between a completed event and an event that occurs repeatedly); the same is true of Mandarin Chinese.

As for the claim that ASL can't express complex ideas, that is simply false. ASL today is used in college-level courses, high-quality academic research, and any number of professional careers. It's true that ASL has to acquire new technical vocabulary every time it expands into a new domain. But this is true of spoken languages too; English went through a similar process in the Middle Ages as it gradually replaced Latin and French as the language of government, law, and education. English speakers suddenly had to invent or borrow the words they needed to talk about these things (and ended up borrowing a huge number of words from French and Latin); ASL speakers do the same thing. In addition, ASL has highly developed art forms including storytelling, poetry, and theater. Signed languages are every bit as rich and expressive as spoken languages.

3.1.3 Signed language is just like spoken language

The influence of oralism began to decline in the middle of the twentieth century, although even today it is still very strong. Schools for the deaf started relaxing their restrictions on signing, and ASL and the Deaf community[4] began to get more national exposure in the United States. A bilingual production by the National Theatre of the Deaf was televised by NBC in 1967; deafness was portrayed in major motion pictures such as *Children of a Lesser God*; the popular children's television show *Sesame Street* included a Deaf character for several decades. In March of 1988, a student-led protest at Gallaudet University attracted national attention and led to the appointment of the school's first deaf president.

It was in this context that William Stokoe published his pioneering linguistic analysis of ASL in 1960, and other linguists soon followed. What became clear very quickly was that signed languages, just like spoken languages, are made

[4] 'Deaf' with a capital 'D' refers to the distinct community and culture with which many deaf individuals identify themselves; 'deaf' with a small 'd' refers to the physical condition of deafness. It is possible to be deaf but not Deaf.

up of discrete parts that are combined according to regular grammatical rules. We've already seen some examples of this: word order in ABSL, pronouns in ASL, and ALREADY in ISL all involve grammatical structure.

Not only do signed languages follow regular rules, but those rules are often strikingly similar to the kinds of rules we find in spoken languages – even in patterns that, at first glance, look very different from the kinds of constructions familiar from European languages. In ASL, for example, a negated sentence (e.g., 'I didn't read it') doesn't necessarily include a separate negative word such as NOT. Instead, a headshake during the sentence can be enough to signal negation (Veinberg and Wilbur 1990). The ASL headshake conveys negation *simultaneously* with the rest of the sentence; this stands in contrast to English words like *not*, which are arranged *sequentially* in the sentence.

Layering grammatical markers simultaneously in this way is a common strategy in signed languages, possibly because the visual modality makes this easier to do. But spoken languages can have simultaneous constructions too. Consider the following examples from Chiquihuitlán Mazatec, an Oto-Manguean language spoken in Oaxaca:

(3) Negation in Chiquihuitlán Mazatec (Jamieson 1982, 165–167)

a. (i) bu^{1}ja^{1} 'I return'
   (ii) bu^{2}jã^{21} 'I don't return'

b. (i) hba^{3}nka^{1} 'I harvest'
   (ii) hba^{2}nkã^{21} 'I don't harvest'

c. (i) bu^{3}ta^{3}ja^{1} 'I study'
   (ii) bu^{3}ta^{2}jã^{21} 'I don't study'

d. (i) hi^{3}nta^{1}ja^{1} 'I shout'
   (ii) hi^{3}nta^{2}jã^{21} 'I don't shout'

Chiquihuitlán Mazatec is a tone language; the pitch of a word carries lexical and grammatical information. In these examples, the raised numbers show the tone contours associated with each vowel (1 is the highest tone and 4 the lowest). We can see that the negative forms of these verbs don't have any extra suffix that marks negation; instead, they are distinguished by their tone pattern: the last two syllables of a negative verb have a 2–21 pattern. In addition, the last vowel of the negative verbs is *nasalized* (as indicated by the tilde), with air escaping through both the mouth and nose. Both the tone change and the nasalization are expressed simultaneously with the rest of the verb. Thus, simultaneous grammatical markers may indeed be more common in signed languages, but they occur in both signed and spoken languages.

Beyond formal linguistic analysis, there are other reasons to believe that signed and spoken languages are fundamentally similar. In hearing people, language processing and visual-spatial processing occur in different parts of the brain; in native signers, sign language is processed in the language-related areas of the brain, not the visual-spatial areas. Hearing people experience language impairments (known as *aphasias*) when the language-processing part of the brain is damaged; damage to those same areas has similar effects on native signers, but signing doesn't seem to be affected when the visual-spatial area of the brain is damaged. Finally, children who are learning a signed language go through the same developmental stages as children who are learning a spoken language. All these pieces of evidence converge to suggest that, on some level, signed and spoken languages are fundamentally the same thing.

3.1.4 Then again, maybe signed language is different from spoken language after all

The first linguists who devoted serious attention to signed languages discovered that they were similar to spoken languages in ways no one had expected. Over the next several decades, there was a strong emphasis in sign language research on documenting the parallels between signed and spoken languages. Not only was this a genuinely new discovery, but it was also seen as a way to foster respect for languages that had long been considered inferior or primitive. In addition, all the tools of linguistic analysis up to that point had been developed for spoken languages, so it was only natural that linguists would use the tools and concepts they were already familiar with as they turned their attention to signed languages.

But now that ASL has been firmly established as a real, full-fledged language, linguists have begun to reconsider ways in which signed and spoken languages might be systematically different. After all, signed and spoken languages use very different channels for communication – vision versus hearing – and it wouldn't be surprising if we discovered that signers and speakers exploit the advantages of each channel in order to communicate as effectively and efficiently as possible.

Some patterns in signed languages clearly follow grammatical rules but have *no* obvious parallel in spoken languages. One of the most striking examples is how the two types of languages handle pronouns. In spoken languages, a pronoun such as English *he* can refer to any male person who is sufficiently salient in the conversation; speakers rely on context to understand exactly who *he* is. Signed languages exploit the visual, three-dimensional nature of signing to keep track of the people and other entities being talked about. The first time a signer mentions John, for example, she can sign his name and then point to a particular place in front of her. Later in the conversation, if she wants to refer to John, she can just point back to that same spot. If the signer also wants to talk about Mary, she can sign Mary's name and point to a different location, which will then be available for referring to Mary. This kind of system is common to many signed languages; it's hard to imagine how a spoken language could achieve something similar.

3.2 Iconicity in signed and spoken languages

We have seen that signed and spoken languages are both full-fledged, expressive languages that are fundamentally similar on many levels, although in some ways the two language types may work differently because they exploit the unique strengths of their respective modalities. In the rest of this chapter, we will explore one of the most salient differences between signed and spoken languages, one that has sometimes been claimed to make them fundamentally different from each other: *iconicity*.

A sign is *iconic* if the form of the sign is related to the idea it describes. The ASL sign TREE is iconic: the forearm is held vertically, like the trunk of a tree, and the fingers are spread like branches or leaves. The BSL sign DINNER is iconic too: the signer's two hands move up and down in a way that resembles the action of eating with a knife and fork.

Signed languages have many iconic signs, and this is one reason so many people think signing is just an elaborate form of pantomime. It's also one of the reasons sign has been viewed as fundamentally different from speech. In spoken languages, the vast majority of words have no inherent connection to their meanings whatsoever: there's nothing about the sounds of the words *tree* or *dinner* that tells us they ought to have the meanings they do. These words have fixed meanings only because English speakers have implicitly agreed that we will use those particular sounds in those orders to refer to those ideas. Ferdinand de Saussure, one of the fathers of modern linguistics, proposed that the *arbitrariness of the sign* is one of the foundational principles of human language.

Our case study at the end of this chapter explores whether signed languages really are as much like pantomime as they appear to be at first glance. First, though, we will briefly ask whether the difference between the two types of language is as basic as it seems. Can we find examples of arbitrariness in signed languages, or of iconicity in spoken ones?

The answer to both questions is yes. First of all, even iconic signs involve some degree of arbitrariness. There may be many ways to create a visual representation of an object or idea, and different signed languages can adopt different iconic signs for the same object. Figure 3.1 shows the sign for TREE in three different signed languages. The ASL sign, as noted above, uses the forearm and hand to represent the trunk and branches of the tree. In Danish Sign Language, the signer 'traces' the rounded top of the tree and then the straight trunk underneath. In Chinese Sign Language, the hands indicate the rounded shape of the trunk and move upward to show its length. In other words, the

(a)

(b)

(c)

Figure 3.1 Signs for TREE in American Sign Language (a), Danish Sign Language (b), and Chinese Sign Langauge (c). Ursula Bellugi and Edward S. Klima, Two faces of sign: Iconic and abstract, *Annals of the New York Academy of Sciences* 1976, Figure 6. Reprinted by permission of John Wiley & Sons, Inc.

signer is not creating an iconic sign from scratch every time he or she needs to convey the idea of a tree. ('Let's see – how can I draw a tree in the air? I think I'll do this to represent the trunk, and this to represent the branches...') Rather, each signed language adopts a different convention for referring to a tree, and that conventional sign must be used consistently by anyone who wants to communicate in the language.

Second, many signs are iconic, but many are not. Plenty of concepts are hard to represent visually; signs for abstract ideas, for example, are often highly arbitrary. Even signs for physical objects don't have to be iconic, as in the ASL sign SHOE, which involves bumping two fists together.

Finally, iconicity isn't exclusive to signed languages; spoken languages can have iconic words too. The most obvious example is onomatopoeia, in words for animal sounds (*tweet*, *ribbit*) or other noises (*swish*, *thump*). As in signed languages, these words are simultaneously iconic and conventional: a rooster says *cock-a-doodle-doo* in English but *quiquiriquí* in Spanish.

In fact, it turns out that the sounds of spoken languages can be associated with non-auditory properties of things too. Suppose you were told that some language has the words *mal* and *mil*, and that one of these words means 'small' and the other means 'large'. Most people guess that *mal* means 'large' and *mil* means 'small'; for some reason, the sound of the *a* vowel 'feels bigger' than the sound of the *i* vowel. Of course, this doesn't mean that every word in spoken language that refers to size has the 'right' vowel: even the English word *small* has the 'big' vowel *a*. But associating *a* with bigness and *i* with smallness somehow feels right, and this association may help explain some generalizations across languages, such as the fact that many languages have a marker with the *i* vowel that indicates smallness (e.g., English *-ie*, Spanish *-ito*). Apparently words in spoken languages aren't quite so arbitrary as previously thought.

All this means that both signed and spoken languages are partly iconic and partly arbitrary; thus, if the two are different, it is a difference of degree rather than kind. In the next section, we will consider whether users of signed languages appear to be influenced by the iconic nature of so many signs.

3.3 Case study: Are signed languages just pantomime?

Many signs are iconic, and adults learning a signed language for the first time may rely on the iconic nature of those signs to help them remember which signs mean what. But just because the signs are iconic doesn't mean native signers necessarily perceive them that way. It's possible to use the ASL sign TREE, for example, without noticing that the sign resembles the shape of a tree. Speakers of spoken languages know thousands of words without necessarily knowing where those words came from; for example, English has borrowed a huge number of words from French and Latin, but it's possible to be a fluent English speaker without knowing the origins of these words. Even if an English speaker does know that *liberty* was borrowed from French, it's unlikely that she thinks about the origin of the word every time she uses it. Similarly, it could be the case that native signers use the signs of their language as arbitrary symbols without necessarily thinking about their iconic nature. Alternatively, it could be that signers *do* notice that signs are iconic, and that this aspect of signed language causes it to be used in a way that is fundamentally different from spoken languages. (A third possibility, of course, is that the truth lies somewhere in the middle.) In this section, we will look at evidence from a variety of sources on whether iconicity matters in everyday signing.

3.3.1 Anecdotal evidence from historical change

Many signed languages have existed for long enough that they have changed over time. One source of anecdotal evidence on the role of iconicity in signed languages has to do with how iconic signs change. It turns out that there are many examples of signs that were iconic when they were first adopted into a language, but gradually became less so. These examples suggest that once a sign becomes a conventional part of the language, speakers are free to treat it as a more or less arbitrary symbol and aren't bothered if the sign becomes less iconic over time.

In ISL, for example, the sign CAMERA used to involve two hands positioned as though they were holding a camera; one hand would make a motion with the fingers as though pushing the button to take a picture. But there's a general preference in signed languages for symmetrical signs, and CAMERA has changed accordingly. Today, both fingers move during the sign, despite the fact that cameras don't actually work this way (Meir and Sandler 2008, 54).

Similar to the tendency for signs to become symmetrical is the tendency for signs to be produced at the center of the body instead of off to one side. Many ASL signs related to emotions, such as FEEL and LOVE, used to be produced on the left side of the chest, over the heart. Today, these signs are produced at the center of the chest, further away from the heart – even though it's the heart, not the breastbone, that we associate with emotions (Frishberg 1975, 704–705).

Examples like these suggest that signers don't depend on the iconic nature of these signs in order to communicate. Once everyone in the signing community agrees on what a sign means, it becomes less important that the sign be an accurate depiction of the real world. The sign is free to change, as long as the agreement about the meaning of the sign remains.

3.3.2 Children's acquisition of ASL pronouns: Petitto (1987)

Another line of evidence on the role of iconicity in sign comes from children who are acquiring a signed language as a native language. One question we might ask is whether their development is affected by iconicity. Do children learn iconic signs more easily than non-iconic ones? Do they make mistakes that suggest that they're treating sign as a form of pantomime?

Petitto (1987) studied pronouns in two Deaf girls who were learning ASL as a first language. Personal pronouns in ASL are highly iconic: ME is signed by pointing at yourself, and YOU[5] by pointing at the person you're talking to. Both hearing and deaf children learn to point at a very young age, and Petitto was interested in the relationship between ordinary pointing and pointing in ASL. She followed the girls from the time they were six months old until they were a little over two. She made videotapes of them at various ages engaged in ordinary play with a parent; she also played games with them that were designed to elicit lots of pronouns.

Petitto discovered two ways in which the girls' development strongly resembled the development of hearing children learning a spoken language. First, she observed that although the girls used non-linguistic pointing just as hearing children do, both girls went through a phase (starting a little after one year) during which they consistently avoided pointing to people, even though they frequently pointed in other contexts. This behavior is parallel to the linguistic development of hearing children, who often avoid pronouns entirely at around the same age and use proper names for everyone instead. In other words, the

[5] Following the original paper, I translate these signs as ME and YOU. In the years since, many linguists have argued that ASL and other signed languages don't make the same person distinctions that spoken languages do; see Cormier et al. (2013, 236–238) for an overview.

Deaf girls had learned that pointing has a linguistic function in ASL, and they avoided the pointing pronouns just as hearing children avoid spoken ones.

Second, once the girls *did* start to produce ME and YOU, they made mistakes. Hearing children sometimes confuse *me* and *you*; they're especially likely to refer to themselves as *you*, possibly because that's what everyone else calls them! The Deaf girls did the same thing: they sometimes referred to themselves with the ASL sign YOU, despite the fact that this sign involves pointing to the other person. Petitto describes an example in which one of the children asked for food by signing EAT YOU WANT EAT – as with hearing children, the result was a confused mother and a frustrated child!

This study is obviously a small one, and it's impossible to draw firm conclusions from just two children. In addition, although both speaking and signing children use YOU to mean 'me', it would be instructive to learn whether one group tends to make the mistake more often than the other. Overall, though, these results provide intriguing evidence that children acquiring ASL don't interpret YOU as an iconic pointing gesture: it's an arbitrary symbol of the language, and just as difficult to learn as spoken-language pronouns.

3.3.3 Children's mistakes in forming signs: Meier et al. (2008)

Another study of children's acquisition of ASL was conducted by Meier et al. (2008). As in spoken language, children learning a signed language make mistakes not just by using the wrong word, but also by producing the right word incorrectly. If children treat ASL as a form of pantomime, then we might expect them to make errors by producing signs in a form that is more iconic than the standard ASL version – in a sense, they might overzealously 'act out' the meaning of the sign. On the other hand, if children treat signs as arbitrary symbols, we would expect their mistakes to be no more or less iconic than the correct signs.

Meier et al. collected several hours of videotaped interaction for four Deaf children between 8 and 17 months. Every sign produced by each child was shown to an adult Deaf signer, who rated the sign in terms of how iconic it was relative to the target adult-like sign. Table 3.1 summarizes the results; for each child, the percentage of that child's signs are given that were rated as much less iconic than the adult sign, somewhat less iconic, and so on. The majority of the children's signs were rated just as iconic as the target adult forms; only a few signs (4.3% of the total) were rated as *more* iconic. A large proportion of the children's productions were actually *less* iconic than the adult forms – in fact, the less iconic signs significantly outnumbered the more iconic signs ($p < .002$ for each child).

Meier et al. argue from these results that the children weren't making mistakes by overzealously pantomiming instead of producing the conventional

Table 3.1 *Iconicity of children's signs relative to adult signs as a percentage of each child's total number of signs; raw counts are given in parentheses. Richard P. Meier, Claude E. Mauk, Adrianne Cheek, and Christopher J. Moreland, The form of children's early signs: Iconic or motoric determinants?,* Language Learning and Development *2008, Table 1. Reprinted by permission of Taylor & Francis Ltd., www.tandfonline.com.*

Child	Much Less Iconic	Somewhat Less Iconic	Neutral	Somewhat More Iconic	Much More Iconic
Caitlin ($n = 45$)	20.0 (9)	0.0	80.0 (36)	0.0	0.0
Katie ($n = 238$)	10.1 (24)	18.1 (43)	63.4 (151)	7.1 (17)	1.3 (3)
Noel ($n = 113$)	28.3 (32)	13.3 (15)	52.2 (59)	6.2 (7)	0.0
Susie ($n = 209$)	25.4 (53)	29.7 (62)	42.1 (88)	2.4 (5)	0.5 (1)
Mean Percentage	20.9	15.3	59.4	3.9	0.4
SD	8.0	12.3	16.2	3.3	0.6

ASL signs; if they were, we should see a bias toward productions that are more iconic than the adult targets, rather than the opposite. The rest of their paper presents evidence that many of these errors are just the result of the fact that children are still learning motor control and aren't yet skilled enough to produce every sign correctly.

One weakness of this argument is that if children have trouble producing the signs they want to make, it's possible that they really are trying to produce more iconic signs, but their motor skills are still so poor that adults can't see this. In other words, maybe the children are trying to do more pantomime, but they aren't very good at it. Another difficulty with studying children's productions is that a sign that appears iconic to an adult may not be iconic for a child. For example, the ASL sign MILK involves opening and closing one hand, as though the signer were milking a cow. But children this young, especially in an urban or suburban setting, may not know that this is where milk comes from.

This doesn't mean that the study was poorly conducted; it's difficult to imagine what Meier et al. could have done differently, since the children were clearly not at an age where they could answer a question like 'What were you trying to show when you made that sign?' And the study certainly doesn't provide any evidence that children *do* treat ASL signs as iconic. The authors looked for evidence of iconicity in an obvious place and failed to find it.

3.3.4 Aphasia in BSL: Marshall et al. (2004)

As noted above, one line of evidence for the fundamental similarity between sign and speech comes from aphasia: damage to the language-processing areas of the brain results in similar impairments in both signed and spoken languages. As it turns out, aphasia can also tell us something about the role of iconicity in signed languages.

Marshall et al. (2004) present a case study of a British man they call 'Charles'. Charles was congenitally deaf and used BSL; he had a stroke at 54 that left him with a kind of aphasia called *anomia*, meaning that he had trouble remembering words. To compensate for his language difficulties, Charles frequently used pantomime to communicate. Because Charles' ability to pantomime was not affected by his stroke, we might expect that he would be able to remember iconic signs, even if he couldn't remember non-iconic ones. Interestingly, Marshall et al. found that this was not the case: they showed Charles 40 pictures (20 depicting the meaning of a highly iconic sign and 20 that weren't iconic at all) and found that he was no better at remembering the iconic signs than the non-iconic ones (about 50% accuracy for each group; at $p > .5$, the difference between the two groups was not statistically significant).

Although a case study is limited because the amount of data involved is so small, these results suggest that Charles' brain treated BSL signs as names, not non-linguistic gestures, even when the signs were very similar to something a person might act out in pantomime. Unfortunately for Charles, this meant that his stroke impaired all of his signing, even as it left his ability to pantomime intact.

3.3.5 Matching signs and pictures: Ormel et al. (2009)

So far, we've seen studies of whether iconicity matters in very young children acquiring a signed language or in brain-damaged adults. What about ordinary language use by fluent individuals? One experiment that addresses this question is Ormel et al. (2009), who studied students who were bilingual in Sign Language of the Netherlands (SLN) and in written Dutch. In Ormel et al.'s experiment, 40 students between 8 and 12 years old were asked to watch a series of signs on a computer screen. Each sign was shown together with a picture; the subjects' task was to press a key indicating whether or not the picture showed the meaning of the sign. In some cases, the sign was highly iconic – for example, HOUSE, in which the hands show the outline of the roof of a house. In other cases, the sign wasn't iconic at all.

The results are summarized in Table 3.2. Not surprisingly, the older students (in 5th and 6th grades) had lower reaction times; that is, they responded faster overall. Most interesting for our purposes is the fact that both groups of students were faster, and more accurate, when they saw iconic signs. In other words, students were able to match signs to their pictures faster – and they made fewer mistakes – when those signs were iconic than when they were not.

Table 3.2 *Reaction times (in milliseconds) and accuracy by grade and strong/weak iconicity. Ellen Ormel, Harry Knoors, Daan Hermans, and Ludo Verhoeven, The role of sign phonology and iconicity during sign processing: The case of deaf children,* Journal of Deaf Studies and Deaf Education *14(4): 2009, 436–448, Table 2 (adapted).*

Factors and conditions	Grade	Reaction times	Accuracy
Condition 1: Strong	3rd/4th grade	1871 (455)	.92 (.05)
Condition 2: Weak	3rd/4th grade	1959 (367)	.83 (.09)
Condition 1: Strong	5th/6th grade	1542 (378)	.93 (.06)
Condition 2: Weak	5th/6th grade	1680 (384)	.81 (.11)

Ormel et al. report that the difference between strongly and weakly iconic signs was significant for both measures ($p < .05$ for reaction time and $p < .01$ for accuracy).

What this experiment suggests is that iconicity isn't all-or-nothing. There may indeed be ways in which the fact that many signs are iconic simply doesn't matter during the day-to-day use of a signed language, or during the process of learning it. But this doesn't necessarily mean that iconicity *never* matters; apparently, it gives a small boost to signers in matching signs to their meanings. Although the benefit is real, it's also small: notice that the difference between the strongly and weakly iconic signs in both groups is only about a tenth of a second (100 milliseconds). Iconic signs may speed language processing by a very small amount, but whether this is enough to make a practical difference in everyday life remains to be seen.

3.3.6 General conclusions

We have seen several pieces of evidence that signed languages are more than pantomime, and that iconicity may even be irrelevant for many aspects of signing. Signs may become less iconic over time; children make mistakes that suggest they're ignoring the iconic properties of signs; aphasia can leave a signer able to gesture but unable to sign. On the other hand, iconicity *does* seem to matter in some domains; for example, iconic signs seem to be processed just a little bit faster than non-iconic ones. Other studies on this topic (see 'Further reading' below) are similarly mixed: there is some evidence that children acquiring signed languages learn iconic signs a little faster than non-iconic ones; processing studies similar to Ormel et al. (2009) find evidence for an iconicity effect in some types of tasks but not others.

All this leaves us with the conclusion that signed languages are highly conventionalized – they aren't just an elaborate game of charades – but signers do sometimes exploit the fact that there's a useful connection between the shapes of many signs and their meanings. Some researchers have suggested that both signed and spoken languages use iconic symbols when they can, but it's easier to create an iconic symbol using gesture than using sound. (We all know what a tree looks like, but what distinctive sound does a tree make?) In other words, spoken languages would be happy to be more iconic, if only they could be!

3.4 Summary

- Signed languages are complete, fully expressive languages that follow grammatical rules.
- Signed languages are not equivalent to the spoken languages around them. The grammatical rules of ASL are different from the grammatical rules of English.
- Signed languages are fundamentally similar to spoken languages on many levels: they have similar kinds of grammatical rules, are processed similarly in the brain, and are acquired similarly by children.
- Signed languages have a long history of being regarded as something less than language. At times, signed languages have been actively suppressed.
- Many signs are *iconic* – directly connected to their meanings in some way. But signed languages are not pantomime, and there is evidence that iconicity is irrelevant to many aspects of how signed languages are used.

For further reflection

(1) Interview someone you know who is involved in the Deaf community – for example, a Deaf person, a family member, or a teacher or interpreter. What role does sign language play in the person's life? What does the person believe sign language is and how it relates to spoken languages? How do these beliefs affect the way the person chooses to use signed and/or spoken languages in his or her daily life?

(2) Starting in the 1990s, a number of companies began marketing products that encourage parents to teach signs to hearing infants and toddlers. Look through the material on the websites of one or two of these companies, and summarize what you find. What exactly are parents being encouraged to do? What claims do these companies make about the benefits of 'baby sign'? Do you think any of these claims are plausible? Why or why not?

(3) Thompson et al. (2012) and Baus et al. (2013) both present experimental evidence that the iconicity of a sign has some effect on how it is learned or processed. Read one of these papers, and evaluate the evidence. Are you convinced? Why or why not?

Further reading

Lane (1984) is a classic, detailed history of deafness in general and ASL in particular. Padden and Humphries (1990) gives an insider's perspective on Deaf culture. Perlmutter (1986) is a good sketch of signed languages around the world, and Groce (1985) is a detailed history of sign language on Martha's Vineyard.

Meier (1991) is a brief popular summary of arguments for the fundamental similarity of signed and spoken languages. Campbell et al. (2008) is a technical review of the literature on how signed and spoken languages are processed in the brain.

There are a number of books written for non-linguists that give an overview of the linguistic structure of signed languages: Valli and Lucas (2001) for ASL, Sutton-Spence and Woll (1999) for BSL, Johnston and Schembri (2007) for Australian Sign Language (Auslan), and Meir and Sandler (2008) for ISL. The last chapters of the latter two books include thoughtful discussion on the role of iconicity in signed languages and whether there are important differences between signed and spoken languages. Sandler et al. (2005) is a technical report on word order in ABSL.

There are many studies on the role of iconicity in sign. Orlansky and Bonvillian (1984), Meier (1987), and Thompson et al. (2012) investigate the acquisition of iconic signs and grammatical devices. Other studies of whether and how iconicity affects language processing include Poizner et al. (1981), Arendsen et al. (2010), and Baus et al. (2013).

Humphries et al. (2012) is a forceful argument, accessibly written, that all deaf children should learn a signed language, even those who also receive cochlear implants. Johnston et al. (2005) and Nelson et al. (2012) review the existing literature on the claimed benefits of 'baby sign'. Pizer et al. (2007) is a thoughtful discussion of how baby sign relates to middle-class parenting practices and ideologies.

Bibliography

Arendsen, Jeroen, Andrea J. van Doorn, and Huib de Ridder. Acceptability of sign manipulations. *Sign Language & Linguistics*, 13(2):101–155, 2010.

Baus, Cristina, Manuel Carreiras, and Karen Emmorey. When does iconicity in sign language matter? *Language and Cognitive Processes*, 28(3):261–271, 2013.

Bellugi, Ursula, and Edward S. Klima. Two faces of sign: Iconic and abstract. *Annals of the New York Academy of Sciences*, 280:514–538, 1976.

Campbell, Ruth, Mairéad MacSweeney, and Dafydd Waters. Sign language and the brain: A review. *Journal of Deaf Studies and Deaf Education*, 13(1):3–20, 2008.

Cormier, Kearsy, Adam Schembri, and Bencie Woll. Pronouns and pointing in sign languages. *Lingua*, 137:230–247, 2013.

Frishberg, Nancy. Arbitrariness and iconicity: Historical change in American Sign Language. *Language*, 51(3):696–719, 1975.

Gordon, J. C. Illinois Institution for the Education of the Deaf and Dumb. In Joseph H. Freeman, editor, *Twenty-Second Biennial Report of the Superintendent of Public Instruction of the State of Illinois*, pages 41–50. Phillips Brothers, Springfield, IL, 1898.

Groce, Nora Ellen. *Everyone Here Spoke Sign Language: Hereditary Deafness on Martha's Vineyard*. Harvard University Press, Cambridge, MA, 1985.

Humphries, Tom, Poorna Kushalnagar, Gaurav Mathur, Donna Jo Napoli, Carol Padden, Christian Rathmann, and Scott R. Smith. Language acquisition for deaf children: Reducing the harms of zero tolerance to the use of alternative approaches. *Harm Reduction Journal*, 9(16), 2012. Available at http://www.harmreductionjournal.com/content/9/1/16.

Jamieson, Carole Ann. Conflated subsystems marking person and aspect in Chiquihuitlán Mazatec verbs. *International Journal of American Linguistics*, 48(2):139–167, 1982.

Johnston, J. Cyne, Andrée Durieux-Smith, and Kathleen Bloom. Teaching gestural signs to infants to advance child development: A review of the evidence. *First Language*, 25(2):235–251, 2005.

Johnston, Trevor, and Adam Schembri. *Australian Sign Language: An Introduction to Sign Language Linguistics*. Cambridge University Press, Cambridge, 2007.

Lane, Harlan. *When the Mind Hears: A History of the Deaf*. Random House, New York, NY, 1984.

Liddell, Scott K. *Grammar, Gesture, and Meaning in American Sign Language*. Cambridge University Press, Cambridge, 2003.

Marshall, Jane, Jo Atkinson, Elaine Smulovitch, Alice Thacker, and Bencie Woll. Aphasia in a user of British Sign Language: Dissociation between sign and gesture. *Cognitive Neuropsychology*, 21(5):537–554, 2004.

Meier, Richard P. Elicited imitation of verb agreement in American Sign Language: Iconically or morphologically determined? *Journal of Memory and Language*, 26(3):362–376, 1987.

Meier, Richard P. Language acquisition by deaf children. *American Scientist*, 79(1):60–70, 1991.

Meier, Richard P., Claude E. Mauk, Adrianne Cheek, and Christopher J. Moreland. The form of children's early signs: Iconic or motoric determinants? *Language Learning and Development*, 4(1):1–36, 2008.

Meir, Irit, and Wendy Sandler. *A Language in Space: The Story of Israeli Sign Language*. Lawrence Erlbaum Associates, New York, NY, 2008.

Nelson, Lauri H., Karl R. White, and Jennifer Grewe. Evidence for website claims about the benefits of teaching sign language to infants and toddlers with normal hearing. *Infant and Child Development*, 21(5):474–502, 2012.

Okrent, Arika. 30 years of linguistics at Gallaudet. Language Log, October 25 2011. Available at http://languagelog.ldc.upenn.edu/nll/?p=3524.

Orlansky, Michael D., and John D. Bonvillian. The role of iconicity in early sign language acquisition. *Journal of Speech and Hearing Disorders*, 49:287–292, 1984.

Ormel, Ellen, Harry Knoors, Daan Hermans, and Ludo Verhoeven. The role of sign phonology and iconicity during sign processing: The case of deaf children. *Journal of Deaf Studies and Deaf Education*, 14(4):436–448, 2009.

Padden, Carol, and Tom Humphries. *Deaf in America: Voices from a Culture*. Harvard University Press, Cambridge, MA, revised edition, 1990.

Perlmutter, David M. No nearer to the soul. *Natural Language and Linguistic Theory*, 4(4):515–523, 1986.

Petitto, Laura A. On the autonomy of language and gesture: Evidence from the acquisition of personal pronouns in American Sign Language. *Cognition*, 27(1):1–52, 1987.

Pizer, Ginger, Keith Walters, and Richard P. Meier. Bringing up baby with baby signs: Language ideologies and socialization in hearing families. *Sign Language Studies*, 7(4):387–430, 2007.

Poizner, Howard, Ursula Bellugi, and Ryan D. Tweney. Processing of formational, semantic, and iconic information in American Sign Language. *Journal of Experimental Psychology: Human Perception and Performance*, 7(5):1146–1159, 1981.

Sandler, Wendy, Irit Meir, Carol Padden, and Mark Aronoff. The emergence of grammar: Systematic structure in a new language. *Proceedings of the National Academy of Sciences*, 102(7):2661–2665, 2005. Available at http://www.pnas.org/content/102/7/2661.full.

Sutton-Spence, Rachel, and Bencie Woll. *The Linguistics of British Sign Language: An Introduction*. Cambridge University Press, Cambridge, 1999.

Thompson, Robin L., David P. Vinson, Bencie Woll, and Gabriella Vigliocco. The road to language learning is iconic: Evidence from British Sign Language. *Psychological Science*, 23(12):1443–1448, 2012.

Valli, Clayton, and Cecil Lucas. *Linguistics of American Sign Language: An Introduction*. Gallaudet University Press, Washington, DC, 3rd edition, 2001.

Veinberg, Silvana C., and Ronnie B. Wilbur. A linguistic analysis of the negative headshake in American Sign Language. *Sign Language Studies*, 68:217–244, 1990.

4 'Chimpanzees can talk to us'

If a rabbit defined intelligence the way man does, then the most intelligent animal would be a rabbit, followed by the animal most willing to obey the commands of a rabbit.

Robert Brault, *A Robert Brault Reader*, rbrault.blogspot.com

If you want to get a sense of what the apes may have experienced in some of the studies described below, do exercise (1) under 'For further reflection' before *reading this chapter.*

People use language with animals all the time. We talk to dogs, cats, horses, dolphins, parrots – any animal we have the opportunity to interact with. Much of this speech is used for commands, of course: we tell dogs to *sit* or *fetch* and instruct horses on when to go or stop. But our use of language with animals isn't restricted to giving orders; it's common, for example, for people to talk to their pets they way they would talk to another human.

And animals respond. Dogs, horses, and other animals can be trained to obey commands given in human language. Parrots repeat words and phrases they hear humans using around them. Many pet owners swear that their pets understand English. People have to be careful about using words like *walk* or *vet* around their dogs because they know what kind of reaction they'll get.

In this chapter, the crucial question that we will ask is whether this behavior really involves *language* in a meaningful way. When a dog responds to the command to *sit*, does that dog understand the meaning of the word in a linguistic sense? Or has it simply learned 'when I hear those sounds, if I sit, I'll get a reward'? When the dog's owner talks about her bad day and the dog comes over to comfort her, is the dog a language user or just an expert at reading the owner's body language?

Dogs and dolphins don't talk back, of course. Human voices sound the way they do because of the particular shape of the human mouth and throat; we can't expect a dog to make human sounds, just as humans can't exactly recreate a dog's bark. Even great apes, who are more anatomically similar to humans, don't have the physiological equipment necessary for human speech. Viki, a chimpanzee who was raised like a human child during the 1940s, eventually learned to approximate four spoken words (*mama*, *papa*, *cup*, and *up*), but only with intensive training by her caretakers. For a long time, the failure of chimpanzees like Viki to learn to speak was taken as evidence that animals simply could not learn language.

But the fact that other animals cannot produce human speech doesn't mean they can't use human language. Maybe Viki failed, not because she was innately incapable of using language, but because she didn't have the appropriate tools to make words: in other words, she needed something other than *spoken* language. In the second half of the twentieth century, researchers have suggested two types of systems that might give apes a better chance of learning to use human language: word-like symbols represented in some physical way that apes can manipulate, and sign.

There were several famous experiments in the 1960s and 1970s in which researchers tried to teach these two kinds of systems to great apes (mostly chimpanzees). These experiments aroused a great deal of interest and were widely reported in the popular media, and many people today believe it to be an established fact that 'monkeys can learn sign language'. In this chapter, we'll take a detailed look at the most well-known studies and ask what they really show us about animals' ability to use human language: What exactly did the researchers do? What kind of environment were the apes in, and what tasks were they asked to perform? In what ways does their behavior resemble human language (or not)?

As we will see, the great apes who participated in these experiments were extremely intelligent and used their trainers' systems in impressive ways. But when we look more closely at their behavior, it turns out that what the apes were doing is different in some fundamental ways from what humans do with language. This doesn't mean these animals are stupid or inferior to human beings. Rather, the more we learn about how language works, the more it appears to be a species-specific form of communication. Great apes and other animals are certainly able to communicate, but it's misleading to say that they use the same system humans do – and that human system is the thing we call 'language'.

4.1 First-generation studies with artificial languages

4.1.1 Sarah

In the 1960s, David Premack set out to study the intelligence of chimpanzees, particularly their linguistic abilities. His lab eventually acquired five chimpanzees, all of whom were born in Africa and taken from their mothers by hunters, and some of whom had had previous owners. Most of the published reports on Premack's experiments focus on Sarah, who performed the best of any of the chimps – possibly because all the others seemed to suffer from physical and/or mental problems.

Sarah's language consisted of colored pieces of plastic, which were backed with metal and could be attached to a magnetized board. Each piece of plastic represented a word, and Sarah earned rewards by writing 'sentences': lining up the words vertically in the correct order, from top to bottom. (Although the final arrangement of the words had to be in a certain order, Sarah did not have to add them in the correct sequence, and she frequently didn't.)

In general, whenever Sarah was taught a new construction, her training proceeded in three phases. First came 'errorless trials', in which Sarah had just one word and was required to place it on the board. Next came 'choice trials', in which Sarah had to choose the correct word(s) from among a set of alternatives; all of these choice trials involved examples that she had previously encountered in errorless trials. Last were 'transfer trials', in which Sarah had to extend the construction she had learned to new words. Sarah eventually achieved around 80% accuracy on nearly every construction she was trained on.

Some of Sarah's tasks mixed plastic words and real objects. For example, the trainer might lay out two objects on the table with a 'question' word between them; Sarah had to choose one of two plastic pieces to substitute for the question word – either *same-as* if the two objects were the same, or *different-from* if they were not. On other trials, the question word took the place of one of the objects rather than the relationship between them; given the sentence *(stamp) same-as ?*, Sarah would replace the question word with another stamp, rather than a different object such as a paperclip.

Sarah learned several relationships between words and objects, including *name-of*, *color-of*, *shape-of*, and *size-of*; the trainers were careful make the symbols arbitrary by making sure, for example, that the piece of plastic meaning *apple* (a blue triangle) didn't look like an actual apple. Sarah learned these constructions very successfully and could complete various tasks related to them. For example, not only could Sarah correctly replace *?* with *apple* in trials such as *? name-of (apple)*, she could also replace *?* with the correct relation (e.g., *color-of*) in trials such as *red ? (apple)*. She was eventually able to learn new names for objects just by seeing a trainer use them in a *name-of* construction; after seeing the sentence *brown color-of fudge*, she used *brown* correctly for other brown objects.

Other constructions required Sarah to make a connection between the words and some situation in the lab. Some trials were essentially commands, such as *Sarah insert apple dish*, that Sarah was required to perform. On other trials, Sarah had to produce a sentence that corresponded to something her trainer had done: for example, *blue on green* if the trainer placed a blue card on top of a green card.

What should we make of all this? Sarah obviously learned *something*; she performed well on many different tests, some of considerable complexity. The crucial question for our purposes is whether Sarah's behavior looks like human language, or something else. But as it turns out, there are many ways in which Sarah's behavior does *not* resemble human language. The problem, essentially, is the artificial nature of Sarah's environment and her training regimen. Almost all of Sarah's contact with the 'language' involved highly constrained training or testing situations; this is very different from the language input that a human child receives. The tasks Sarah performed look a lot more like puzzle-solving than natural language use.

Sarah's behavior looks even less like language when we consider the fact that Sarah's training sessions always involved a single construction type, and she always responded by choosing words or performing actions from a limited set of alternatives, often just two. Sarah's 80% accuracy is less impressive when we consider the fact that she would be tested on the same construction up to 20 times in a row: *? name-of (apple)*, *? not-name-of (banana)*, *? name-of (orange)*, and so on. This is not what normal language use looks like in humans.

Premack himself has stated in some of his writings that he was interested in chimpanzees' intelligence, not their linguistic abilities per se, and that this is why he didn't try to make Sarah's training more natural. But some of the constructions Premack attempted to teach Sarah, such as a word meaning 'to be' or a plural agreement marker, look suspiciously linguistic. In addition, he devotes a non-trivial amount of space in his writing to the question of what properties a system has to have in order to count as a language, and some of his publications on the project have titles such as 'Language in chimpanzee?' (Premack 1971) and 'Teaching language to an ape' (Premack and Premack 1972).[1] One gets the sense that it's entirely appropriate to view this experiment as an attempt to teach language to an ape, and that is exactly how later researchers have viewed it.

4.1.2 Lana

The methods Premack used with Sarah inspired a group of researchers at the Yerkes National Primate Research Center in Atlanta, Georgia. They thought using a language-like system with a physical basis was a good idea, but they knew that training a chimpanzee on such a system was extremely time-consuming and had the potential for human error. (For example, Premack tried to teach Sarah some constructions with non-English word order, such as *Mary apple Sarah give*. But Sarah's trainers often forgot and used the English word order, so Sarah's input was inconsistent.)

The researchers at the Yerkes center designed a fully automated system that was controlled by a computer; this laboratory became the home of Lana, a

[1] Not to mention his wife's book on the project, *Why Chimps Can Read*!

Figure 4.1 Lana at her lexigram keyboard. Susan M. Essock, Timothy V. Gill, and Duane M. Rumbaugh, Language relevant object- and color-naming tasks, *Language Learning by a Chimpanzee: The LANA Project*, Duane M. Rumbaugh, ed., 1977, Figure 1. Reprinted by permission of Elsevier.

female chimpanzee born in captivity. Lana's room had a window, a movie projector, and food and drink dispensers, all of which were controlled by the computer. Lana communicated with the computer and with her trainers by pressing buttons on a keyboard, as shown in Figure 4.1; each button had a symbol, called a *lexigram*, with a specific meaning. In order to obtain rewards (such as food or a movie), Lana had to press the correct lexigrams in the correct order.

Lana's trainers believed that the computerized system improved on Premack's methods in several ways. Because the system was automated, Lana would have to use the language to fulfill all her basic needs; training could occur 24 hours a day instead of only when a trainer was present. The computer was programmed with a set of grammatical rules that Lana had to follow precisely in order to obtain rewards, and it kept a perfect record of everything Lana and her trainers ever said.

The system of lexigrams that Lana learned was called *Yerkish* in honor of the center's founder. Each lexigram consisted of abstract shapes superimposed on a colored background. There was a row of video monitors above the keyboard; when Lana pressed a lexigram key, the first monitor displayed an image of the lexigram she had pressed; when she pressed another lexigram, the next monitor

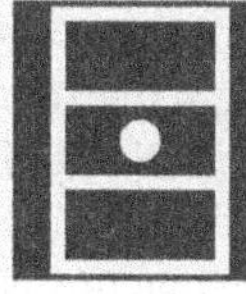

Figure 4.2 Example of a Yerkish sentence: *please machine give milk period.*

displayed that lexigram; and so on until she pressed the *period* lexigram, which marked the end of the sentence. A second row of monitors displayed messages from Lana's trainers; even when they were in the same room, communication between Lana and her trainers was exclusively in Yerkish.

The researchers assigned an English translation to every word, but it's important to remember that this is just a convenient representation for lexigrams. Lana was dealing with visual symbols, not listening to (or producing) English words. For example, every request that Lana made, either of the machine or of one of her trainers, had to be prefixed with a special lexigram that the researchers translated as *please*. (Figure 4.2 illustrates how Lana could request milk from the machine.[2]) As the researchers themselves point out, this doesn't mean Lana was being polite; in all likelihood, *please* meant no more to her than 'the symbol I push first in order to get something'.

Not surprisingly, the majority of Lana's 'utterances' were requests: *please machine open window period, please Tim tickle Lana period*, and so on. Lana also had sessions with human trainers in which she answered questions. Like Sarah, Lana learned relations like *name-of* and *color-of*; in response to questions such as *? what name-of this period*[3] (where the object to be named was visible to Lana inside the machine), Lana would be required to produce a sentence such as *apple name-of this period.* In a more complex task, Lana would be presented with two objects of different colors and types, and have to answer a question such as *? what name-of this which-is red period*; in the presence of a blue M&M and a red umbrella, the required response was *umbrella name-of this which-is red period.* Lana also answered yes-no questions such as *? blue color-of this period.*

In many ways, Lana's training was restricted like Sarah's; she had to be trained intensively on specific constructions and responded correctly in order to

[2] The color-coding scheme, basic shapes, and examples of a few lexigrams are given in publications such as von Glaserfeld (1974). To my knowledge, no complete list of Lana's lexigrams has ever been published. Lexigrams given here and in the online supplemental material are taken directly from publications, if possible; others are borrowed from lexigrams with similar meanings on a chart that was posted on the website of the Iowa Primate Learning Sanctuary. (The website has since moved and the chart is no longer available.)

[3] A special lexigram, translated *?* by the researchers, was used at the beginning of questions.

get a reward. However, the design of the experiment allowed Lana much more initiative than Sarah had in making requests and interacting with the trainers. To a degree that wasn't possible with Sarah, Lana had the potential to engage in *conversations*.

Rumbaugh and Gill (1977) argue that this is exactly what happened, and that Lana produced novel utterances that demonstrated her ability to use language creatively. In one striking instance, for example, Lana didn't know the word for *orange (fruit)*; she described it as *apple which-is orange (color)*. (Distinct lexigrams were used for *orange* the fruit and *orange* the color.) By themselves, examples like these suggest that Lana used Yerkish in a language-like way. But when we see Lana's novel utterances in context, they start to look less like creative use of language and more like one in a series of haphazard attempts to get what she wants. The following conversation gives the context of *? Tim give apple which-is orange.*

(1) TIM: ? What color of this.
LANA: Color of this orange.
TIM: Yes.
LANA: ? Tim give cup which-is red.
TIM: Yes. *(Tim gives Lana a red cup, which she discards.)*
LANA: ? Tim give which-is shut.
LANA: ? Shelley give.
TIM: No Shelley.
LANA: Eye.
LANA: ? Tim give which-is orange.
TIM: What which-is orange.
LANA: ? Tim give apple which-is green.
TIM: No apple which-is green.
LANA: ? Tim give apple which-is orange.
TIM: Yes. *(Tim gives Lana the orange.)*
(Rumbaugh and Gill 1977, 178–179)

On the one hand, Lana's utterances aren't completely random; the fact that she uses the lexigrams *apple* and *orange* in the presence of this unfamiliar orange-colored fruit is surely no coincidence. But it's not clear that Lana is actually trying to *describe* the fruit, or that she's using Yerkish grammar to do so; it seems just as likely that she is pasting together short strings from her training until she hits on a combination that gets her what she wants. Timothy Gill eventually started a systematic program of refusing normal requests in order to elicit novel expressions from Lana; the results are described in Gill (1977). Lana's behavior in these conversations often looks a lot like desperation ('What do you want from me??'); it's hard not to suspect that Lana was trying every string she could think of until she happened to produce one that corresponded to an appropriate English expression (and thus was acceptable to her trainer).

These examples underscore how important it is to avoid relying on a few anecdotal examples when arguing that an ape has learned language. If the ape is doing nothing more than producing random strings, some of those strings are bound to be meaningful just by coincidence. And if the ape has memorized a few formulas and re-uses parts of them (so that the strings aren't entirely random), then the chances are even greater that he or she will say something meaningful by accident. The fact that even random processes can generate apparently meaningful output is well known, and a popular way to describe this is to say that if a thousand monkeys sat at keyboards for eternity, they would eventually produce the complete works of Shakespeare.[4] Lana is *literally* a monkey at a keyboard.[5]

It seems premature, then, to use these few apparently meaningful constructions to conclude that Lana learned language. Without more systematic evidence that Lana used language in novel and human-like ways, we can't rule out the possibility that her novel productions were just lucky guesses.

There are a number of other ways in which Lana's use of language was very different from humans'. Although she had the opportunity to converse freely with her trainers, the vast majority of her utterances were either direct requests or part of an attempt to get something she wanted. Young children who are learning to speak do make a lot of requests, but they also very quickly begin to use language to comment on the world around them. Even at the one-word stage, a child who has learned to say *ball* does so not just for requests ('Give me the ball!') but also to make observations ('Look at this ball I have!') and for other social purposes. Lana simply didn't do this.

In addition, Lana's productions overwhelmingly consisted of stock sentences (e.g., *please machine give Lana X period*). Lana's trainers had to force Lana to use novel expressions by putting her in situations where her usual sentences didn't work; she typically did not do this on her own. Again, this behavior stands in stark contrast to that of human children, who clearly do *not* have to be forced to use new grammatical structures as they develop.

The studies with Lana, like those with Sarah, clearly show that a chimpanzee is capable of using a complex language-like system to get what she wants. Because Lana had more freedom with her language than Sarah did, her results

4 This story is meant as a memorable illustration, not a literal claim. 'Monkeys at keyboards' are supposed to represent a process that generates random letters; real monkeys, of course, would be unlikely to do this. In 2003, a computer was placed inside a monkey enclosure in a zoo in Great Britain; the monkeys typed several pages of the letter 's' and urinated on the machine (BBC News 2003).

5 Lana is of course an ape, not a monkey, but her situation is clearly in the spirit of the popular idea.

also suggest what chimpanzees do *not* do: they don't use language to comment on things, and they don't apply the rules of the language creatively except when forced to do so. Ultimately, the most plausible conclusion is that both Sarah and Lana were expert pattern-learners, but they never learned to use language the way humans do.

4.2 First-generation studies with sign

One criticism of the ape language studies is that many lacked the social context within which human children acquire language. Both Sarah and Lana, for example, constructed very specific sentences to get rewards such as food. Although human children are occasionally asked to do similar things ('Say please!'), by and large their emerging use of language serves a social purpose. In fact, if a human child were raised like Sarah or Lana, we would call that child abuse.

Another weakness of the Sarah and Lana studies is the physical nature of the language medium. It's certainly easier for a chimpanzee to manipulate objects or push buttons than to make human sounds; again, though, we might wonder whether a human child would learn language normally if that language consisted of pieces of plastic or symbols on a keyboard.

Several groups of researchers have undertaken projects that attempt to address these shortcomings. The three studies we turn to now all involve some form of signing – ostensibly ASL, although in practice the apes were taught signs borrowed from ASL with English word order, not true ASL. Because sign is physically accessible to apes and exists as a natural form of human language, it represents one of the best opportunities for an ape to acquire human language the way a child might. The researchers on these projects also made an effort to give the apes a rich social environment.

4.2.1 Washoe

Allen and Beatrice Gardner were aware of the previous failed attempts to teach language to chimpanzees like Viki, and they thought it might be possible to succeed by using signing instead of speech. They acquired an infant chimpanzee, whom they named Washoe, and raised her in a trailer in their backyard. Washoe was accompanied by one or more signing human companions throughout the day; in addition to formal training, her activities included daily rituals for food and hygiene, games, and other highly social activities.

Initially, the Gardners hoped Washoe would imitate their signs spontaneously the way a human child does. Although it seems that Washoe did produce a few imitations on her own (for example, she began signing SWEET around dessert time), it became clear that the research staff would make little progress unless they took a more active approach. They encouraged Washoe to sign by physically molding her hands into the correct shapes, and they adopted routines in which Washoe had to sign in order to receive a reward (for example, she was eventually required to sign SWEET in order to get dessert).

When Washoe first began to sign, the research staff kept daily logbooks of every sign Washoe produced. When this became too much to handle, they switched to a checklist system: each day, the researchers checked off every sign they saw Washoe produce. Eventually, even that was too much, and the Gardners instituted daily vocabulary drills to check whether Washoe still remembered all the signs she knew. The vast majority of the Gardners' data on Washoe comes from these written logs, although in later years some trainers narrated audio tapes of training sessions.

The Gardners also kept track of Washoe's multi-sign combinations. The following examples illustrate the types of combinations Washoe produced:

(2) Some of Washoe's multi-sign combinations (Gardner and Gardner 1971, 176)

a. PLEASE TICKLE MORE
b. COME ROGER TICKLE
c. OUT OPEN PLEASE HURRY
d. YOU ME IN
e. YOU ME GREG GO
f. YOU NAOMI PEEKABOO
g. YOU TICKLE ME WASHOE
h. YOU ME DRINK GO
i. YOU ME OUT LOOK
j. HUG ME GOOD

To interpret Washoe's utterances, the Gardners used a method from studies of child language acquisition known as 'rich interpretation'; the basic idea is to use whatever contextual information is necessary to make sense of the utterance. The Gardners adapted a scheme that had been invented by Roger Brown to study two-word sentences in children; they classified Washoe's two-sign combinations into categories such as 'agent-action' (ROGER[6] TICKLE) and 'possessive' (YOU HAT). The Gardners found that 78% of Washoe's two-sign combinations fit into one of their categories, similar to the 75% that Brown found for young children. On this basis, they claimed that Washoe's linguistic abilities were comparable to those of very young children; this is one of the pieces of evidence that has been used to argue that chimpanzees have the same linguistic ability as two-year-olds.

6 'Roger' in Washoe's productions is Roger Fouts, one of her trainers – not Roger Brown, who wasn't part of the project.

Rich interpretation is a valuable tool for understanding emergent language, but it's also vulnerable to one of the most difficult problems in ape language research: the danger of overinterpretation. The analysis just described is essentially a measure of how many two-word or two-sign utterances can be given a reasonable interpretation by an adult human; whether the meanings we assign reflect what the chimpanzee (or child) was actually doing is another matter. Humans are expert language users, and it's all too easy to interpret apes' behavior through human lenses, even when other explanations are possible.

For example, one of Washoe's best-known combinations is WATER BIRD, which she signed in the presence of a swan on a lake. Before we conclude that Washoe was creating a novel (and very apt) description of a creature she had no word for, we need to be able to rule out some other possibilities. It could also be that Washoe was responding separately to the water and the bird, or even that this production was a coincidence. Similarly, Lucy (a home-raised chimpanzee who received some language training) famously signed CANDY DRINK for watermelon. But this feat looks less impressive when we learn that Lucy was being asked to name unfamiliar foods, and that her entire food-related vocabulary at the time consisted of the signs FOOD, FRUIT, DRINK, CANDY, and BANANA (Fouts 1997, 156).

The interpretation problem is even more basic than assigning meanings to sign combinations; just determining what signs the ape made in the first place turns out to be a non-trivial task. In fact, some of the gestures that were counted as signs by the research staff probably weren't actual signs at all. The Gardners did make an effort to ensure that random gestures were not mistakenly counted as signs; before a sign could be listed as part of Washoe's vocabulary, for example, it had to be observed by three different trainers on separate days. But the hearing trainers (who weren't native signers) may still have been too generous in what they counted as a sign, as suggested by the recollections of a Deaf assistant who worked with some of Washoe's successors:

> The hearing people were logging every movement the chimp made as a sign. Every time the chimp put his finger in his mouth, they'd say, 'Oh, he's making the sign for *drink*,' and they'd give him some milk. For part of the day, I was supposed to just sign to the chimp about things he knew, things around the place that he knew the signs for. I signed my head off... but mostly the chimp didn't seem to notice....
>
> They always held up their arms so you could tickle them under the armpits.... O.K., a few days later, I look in the log book and see the sign *more: arms held over head, fingers touching....*
>
> When the chimp scratched itself, they'd record it as the sign for *scratch*.
>
> (Neisser 1983, 214–215)

As we saw in the previous chapter, many ASL signs do resemble the kinds of gestures that one might make to mime an action, but ASL itself isn't pantomime. The Deaf assistant's story suggests that the hearing research assistants failed to make this distinction: the chimpanzees were credited with linguistic ability because their ordinary gestures happened to vaguely resemble ASL signs, not because they were actually using language. The problem is made worse by the fact that the trainers frequently accepted productions that only partially resembled ASL signs. It's reasonable to allow the chimpanzees some leeway since their hands aren't precisely the same as human hands, but the danger is that this practice will seriously overcount the number of signs the chimpanzee actually meant to produce.

In fact, some of the chimpanzees' most frequent 'signs' were gestures that occur naturally in the wild; the most notable was a begging gesture that the Gardners translated as COME or GIMME, depending on the context. The Gardners believed these natural gestures were actually an asset to their research project; this is all well and good if the goal is to communicate with the chimpanzee by any means necessary, but not if the goal is to assess whether the chimpanzee can learn human language.

What should we take away from the Washoe project? One the one hand, the Gardners were undoubtedly pioneers; at the time they started their project, no one believed it was possible to teach language of any sort to a chimpanzee. Within four years, Washoe had learned hundreds of signs and become a national sensation; today, almost no one denies that Washoe was able to communicate with her trainers.

On the other hand, there remain some deep differences between the way Washoe used signs and the way humans do. Perhaps most striking is the fact that Washoe's utterances were overwhelmingly attempts to get something she wanted; the multisign utterances in (2), for example, all appear to be requests of some kind. Despite the fact that Washoe's environment was stimulating and richly social, she never seemed to sign just for the sake of conversation. This is very much like Lana's behavior, but unlike that of human children. The recurring theme of these studies is that apes can learn some kind of communication system, but they simply don't do the same things with language that humans do.

4.2.2 Koko

Koko the gorilla is possibly the most famous subject of any of the ape language projects. Born in 1971 in the San Francisco Zoo, Koko has received intensive language instruction and interaction with humans since she was about one year old – mostly with Francine Patterson, who is still her primary companion. Koko now lives in a trailer in the Santa Cruz mountains, and her surroundings are similar to Washoe's: toys and implements of daily life, accompanied by intense social interaction. Like Washoe, Koko has attracted a great deal of attention in the popular media; she was the subject of a PBS television special, and the Gorilla Foundation (the organization that funds Koko's living arrangements) sells a variety of Koko-related merchandise, including a children's book about Koko's pet kitten.

Unlike the Washoe project, where signing was used exclusively and speech was forbidden, Koko's trainers sign and speak simultaneously. Their goal is to give Koko as many opportunities as possible to understand what is being said to her, whether aurally or visually. As a result, though, Koko's input is not ASL, but a series of ASL signs in English word order.[7] Koko, of course, signs but doesn't speak.

Patterson's claims about Koko's linguistic abilities go far beyond those that have been made for the other ape language projects. Koko is said to know over 2,000 signs and many English words; Patterson also claims that Koko uses language in extremely sophisticated ways, including puns and wordplay. This project has been one of the most severely criticized of the ape language studies, in large part because the amount of popular attention it has received is vastly out of proportion to the number and quality of scientific publications describing Koko's behavior.

Unfortunately, many of Patterson's claims don't exactly inspire confidence. Some accounts suggest problems similar to those of the Washoe project: non-linguistic gestures interpreted as ASL signs.

> One of Koko's favorite early games was one in which her companion would blow on the window in order to make it foggy so they could draw on it. At the beginning of the second month of the project, Koko indicated that she wanted to play the game in the following way (request action): Koko signed *there* toward the window. When her companion carried her to the window, Koko pointed to her own *mouth*. Next she touched the *mouth* of her companion (equivalent to *mouth-you*, modulated by signing on the other's body) and then pointed *there* toward the window again. Koko repeated the sequence twice and ended with a question modulation (seeking and holding eye contact with the final sign), because her companion didn't at first understand what she wanted.
>
> (Patterson et al. 1988, 45–46)

Koko's intent is clear, but it is not at all obvious that she is actually using language: the entire scene can easily be understood as a sequence of non-linguistic pointing gestures. In fact, many signs that are given different translations by

[7] In fact, this is almost certainly true of all of the ape language projects, even though researchers have usually attempted to use pure ASL. Fluent signers have worked on some of these projects, but they have provided only a small proportion of the apes' input.

researchers in the ape language projects (e.g., THAT, THERE, and words for various body parts) involve straightforward pointing. There is evidence in human ASL users that pointing signs are not exactly the same thing as ordinary pointing (see section 3.3.2) – but there's no guarantee that the same is true of Koko and her colleagues.

Conversations that are claimed to demonstrate humor or other sophisticated uses of language are equally unimpressive. Patterson has suggested that in the following conversation, Koko is insulting Cindy (a research assistant) by calling her a nut and threatening to scratch her with her nails.

(3) KOKO: Time nails nut.
KOKO: Fruit.
KOKO: Key key time.
CINDY: No, not yet key time.
KOKO: Yes time come time nut.
CINDY: No, not time!
KOKO: Yes time.
CINDY: No time.
KOKO: Nails...
CINDY: Why?
KOKO: Time!
CINDY: Oh!
(Patterson 1980, 552)

Because Koko is exposed to spoken English as well as ASL-derived signs, Patterson claims that Koko's signing can be influenced by the sounds of the corresponding English words. These claims sometimes border on the truly fantastic:

> Koko used a gesture that resembled *on* in its articulation but which was used in contexts where the standard meaning for the word was inappropriate. Only after studying the context of the utterances in which the gesture occurred (i.e., Koko impatiently awaiting goods or services that were slow in coming), and after realizing that the phrase 'come on' was voiced to Koko frequently, did researchers realize that her sign was, indeed a request to 'come-on'.
>
> (Patterson and Cohn 1990, 112–113)

In a very real sense, Koko has had the best opportunity of any ape to learn language: her training has lasted far longer than any of the other ape language projects, and she lives in a stable, stimulating, highly social environment. There's no doubt that she knows many signs and uses them to communicate with her human companions. But despite all this, there are deep and clear differences between what Koko does with her signs and what humans do with language. She has done an excellent job making use of the system of communication adopted by her companions, but she simply hasn't learned to use language the same way humans do.

4.2.3 Nim Chimpsky

The achievements of Washoe, Sarah, and other apes inspired Herbert Terrace, a Columbia University psychologist, to try his own project. Terrace was interested in the linguistic abilities of non-human animals because of the light they might shed on some ideas about language promoted by Noam Chomsky. Chomsky had challenged the widespread idea that language is learned just like any other behavior; he argued that language is unique to humans, and that a large part of humans' ability to use language is hard-wired in the brain rather than learned. If Terrace could succeed in teaching language to a chimpanzee, he could show that Chomsky was wrong.

Terrace acquired an infant chimpanzee in 1973, whom he playfully named Nim Chimpsky. Nim was fostered by a human family in New York City for almost two years; he also received formal training in a small room on the Columbia campus. In 1975, Nim moved to a suburban mansion and was cared for by student volunteers; he remained there for two more years and continued to receive classroom instruction at Columbia.

Project Nim was ambitious and chaotic. Nim was born unexpectedly, before Terrace had a chance to apply for grants to support the project. Terrace accepted Nim anyway on the assumption that he would be able to obtain money quickly, but his grant proposals were repeatedly rejected, and the project had no stable funding until 1976. Terrace was able to pay a few full-time teachers, but Nim required 24-hour supervision. For years, Nim was taught by a rotating cast of volunteer teachers and companions, and he repeatedly grew attached to teachers who later had to leave him. Teaching Nim at Columbia was exhausting – so much so that the researchers reserved a quiet room where teachers could go lie down after a two-hour session. Keeping up with Nim and coordinating his teaching schedule were such time-consuming tasks that very little data was analyzed until after the project was over.

The researchers on the project had high hopes for Nim's abilities. Nim learned over 100 signs and produced many combinations; in addition, he tended to produce signs in a consistent order. This consistent order suggested to Terrace that Nim may have acquired grammatical rules; for example, he was more likely to sign the sequence adjective-noun than noun-adjective.

When the project ran out of funding and ended in 1977, Terrace sent Nim back to the center where he was born and began a more thorough analysis of the data. Terrace had begun the project certain that he could teach language to a chimpanzee – but when he and his collaborators published the results of their study in *Science* (Terrace et al. 1979), they stunned the scientific community by arguing that Nim had *not* learned language.[8] Going further, Terrace and his colleagues argued that none of the other apes (particularly Washoe) had learned language either. This 'conversion' of a prominent scientist persuaded many people, and money for ape language projects quickly dried up.

There were many aspects of Nim's signing that led Terrace to conclude that it wasn't language, some of which we've seen in the other ape language studies. The vast majority of Nim's multi-sign combinations were requests for food or play and were extremely repetitive: PLAY ME NIM, SWEET NIM SWEET, BANANA ME NIM ME, and so on. Terrace et al. (1979) report that Nim's longest utterance was GIVE ORANGE ME GIVE EAT ORANGE ME EAT ORANGE GIVE ME EAT ORANGE GIVE ME YOU.

Even more important was Terrace and colleagues' analysis of Nim's conversational interaction. They argued that a large proportion of Nim's utterances were simply imitations of what the trainer had just signed; further, they analyzed the available video of Washoe and argued that she was doing the same thing. In other words, Nim and Washoe weren't using language creatively; to the extent that they were producing human-like utterances, they were doing so only because they were repeating their trainers' sentences, not constructing new ones of their own.

Human children imitate the adults around them, too, but they're more likely to expand on what's been said to them rather than repeat it verbatim; and as they grow older, children imitate less and less frequently. Terrace et al. found that Nim's behavior was strikingly different: he imitated more often than he expanded, and he showed no sign of imitating less often as time went on.

Nim's tendency to imitate was part of a larger problem: he just didn't seem to understand the rules of conversation, something that even young children learn very quickly. Nim interrupted his teachers at an astonishing rate – the numbers given in Terrace et al. (1979, 897) suggest that at least half of Nim's utterances interrupted a teacher – and he frequently signed at the same time as his teachers, showing little regard for the turn-taking that characterizes human conversation.

Like Washoe and other apes before him, then, Nim learned to communicate as a way to get what he wanted from his human companions. Laura Petitto, one

[8] Terrace himself didn't reach this conclusion until after the project was over, although some accounts (Neisser 1983, 225–227) suggest that other members of the research staff had suspicions much earlier. Pullum (2011) notes the dishonest title of Terrace's popular book on the project (*Nim: A Chimpanzee Who Learned Sign Language*) and suggests that 'the publisher would not have gone with an honest one like "Nim, A Chimpanzee Who, Like Every Other Chimpanzee, Never Learned Sign Language".'

of Nim's teachers, later described how Nim managed the constrained world he lived in:

> Learning the signs didn't mean a thing to him. He hated it. He hated the whole thing, but he knew I wanted him to do it. He knew it was important to me, and he used it to manipulate me. I mean, he used the whole signing situation as a tool....
>
> If he didn't know a sign, sometimes he'd give me his hands. Just bring them over and hold them up for me to shape. His attitude was, It's your game, let's get it over with.
>
> Neisser (1983, 222–224)

What Nim and the other apes did *not* learn to do was to use language the way humans do: to combine nouns, verbs, and adjectives using a consistent and coherent grammar; to comment on the world around them; to engage in reciprocal conversation, with turn-taking. Whatever they were doing, it was not the thing that we call human language.

4.3 Second-generation studies

The early ape language studies focused on vocabulary and syntax: researchers tried to show that apes could learn a substantial number of words, and that they could combine these words in regular ways. But, as we've seen, critics have suggested that there are more fundamental questions that need to be answered first: Do the apes actually understand that signs (or lexigrams) are *symbols*? And can they use language socially, the way humans do, not just as a tool to satisfy their needs? The second generation of ape language studies addressed these concerns.

4.3.1 Washoe's successors: Loulis and company

After working with Washoe for four years, the Gardners sent her to Oklahoma. Not long afterward, they acquired several more infant chimpanzees and trained them with a similar regimen. The idea was to learn whether chimpanzees living together would sign with each other – in other words, would they spontaneously use language for social purposes? These younger chimpanzees (Moja, Tatu, and Dar) later joined Washoe and her adopted son, Loulis; the entire group eventually ended up at Central Washington University under the care of Roger Fouts.

Fouts and his team were careful to incorporate signing into everyday social routines, and they made a special effort to document signing among the chimpanzees (particularly when no humans were present). In addition, to see whether chimpanzees could independently hand the signs down from one generation to the next, they completely forbade signing in Loulis' presence for the first several years of his life.

Some of the harshest critics of the ape language projects (e.g., Umiker-Sebeok and Sebeok 1981) have argued that Washoe and other chimpanzees are merely responding to their trainers' unintentional nonverbal cues – essentially, that they're highly trained circus animals, not language users. Fouts' observations pretty conclusively lay that criticism to rest; the research team showed that the chimpanzees *did* in fact sign to each other without human prompting, sometimes signing even when no humans were present at all. Most spectacularly, Loulis learned a large number of signs from Washoe without any human intervention; in fact, Washoe sometimes seemed to be teaching Loulis explicitly, molding his hands into the correct shapes.

For these chimpanzees, then, signing clearly has some degree of social function; they weren't mindlessly mimicking their trainers.[9] But the chimps' utterances are still highly repetitive; Rivas (2005, 412) records examples such as FLOWER HURRY FLOWER HUG GO FLOWER BOOK FLOWER GIMME FLOWER GIMME FLOWER HUG HURRY DRINK GIMME. Unlike human children, the chimpanzees don't add grammatical complexity as their utterances get longer. In addition, a large proportion of the chimps' 'signs' are actually gestures that occur naturally in the wild, including COME/GIMME (noted above) and HURRY – Fouts and Fouts (1989) report that in a 15-hour sample of Loulis' interaction with other chimpanzees, fully 65% of the 206 signs he produced were HURRY.

4.3.2 Lana's successors: Sherman, Austin, and Kanzi

Although the team that worked with Lana was initially enthusiastic about her performance, some researchers questioned whether what Lana was doing was really language. Sue Savage-Rumbaugh, in particular, observed that Lana didn't seem to understand that her lexigrams had *meanings*; rather, she used them as tools to get what she wanted:

> [Lana] tried unusual combinations of lexigrams, seemingly in order to catch the experimenter's interest. Combinations that were successful were remembered and used on other occasions. She readily learned to form requests that would cause people to move about in space. However, she could not use... a preposition such as *out* to describe the state of an individual or object. *Out* was a word to be used when Lana wanted another

9 O'Sullivan and Yeager (1989) showed that even Nim Chimpsky did much less imitating when he was engaged in a more relaxed and social way, as opposed to being drilled. It's been suggested that Nim failed to learn language *only* because his training was regimented and insufficiently social – but this criticism is overstated; Nim's classroom was indeed a sterile and artificial environment, but he also had plenty of unstructured social time with his trainers and other companions.

> individual to move "out." If a bowl of chow was placed outside her room and she was asked "?where bowl," her responses were at chance.
>
> Savage-Rumbaugh et al. (1980, 59)

In other words, Lana didn't see *out* as a descriptive word any more than you see the act of turning a doorknob as a word that means 'open'. Savage-Rumbaugh had also worked with Lucy, and was equally skeptical of the signing projects:

> During the preparation of tea... [Lucy's] teachers were instructed to repeatedly stop and mold Lucy's hands into the sign for "tea." Thus the signing of "tea" became as much an aspect of getting the tea made as did the acts of heating water, stirring, etc.
>
> Savage-Rumbaugh (1986, 344)

The idea that a symbol 'stands for' something – so obvious to humans – apparently doesn't come easily to chimpanzees. Savage-Rumbaugh et al. (1978) describe how Sherman and Austin, two of Lana's successors, learned lexigrams in task-specific ways. For example, they learned to use lexigrams to request specific tools for retrieving food (e.g., a key to open a locked box); however, even after they were proficient at this requesting task, they couldn't name those same tools when shown them by the experimenter (although they had already been trained to name other objects, such as foods). In other words, the tool lexigrams were part of a ritual for obtaining tools, not words that referred to things.

Through carefully designed training regimens, Savage-Rumbaugh and her team eventually managed to guide Sherman and Austin to a more symbol-like use of lexigrams. The researchers have built up a plausible case that Sherman and Austin now understand lexigrams as a means of conveying information; for example, they can use the tool lexigrams to request tools *from one another*. The researchers' most spectacular success has been with Kanzi, a bonobo (a species closely related to chimpanzees) who apparently learned lexigrams spontaneously as an infant while watching his mother being trained. After the team discovered that Kanzi was beginning to use lexigrams on his own, they adopted a policy that he would receive no formal training of the kind given to Lana, Sherman, and Austin; instead, lexigrams were incorporated into natural social interactions. Kanzi now commands a large number of lexigrams and can use them for an array of functions – requesting, naming, responding to requests, and so on.

Savage-Rumbaugh and her team don't claim that Kanzi has 'learned language' (although they have argued that Kanzi has created a kind of primitive syntax). Instead, Savage-Rumbaugh is interested in what apes like Kanzi can teach us about the basic building blocks of language. What skills are necessary for a creature to understand a symbol? What kinds of social interaction are necessary for those skills to emerge? Which of these skills can be learned by species other than *Homo sapiens*?

4.4 Language, communication, and human uniqueness

At the end of the day, it seems that none of the extreme claims about the ape language studies turn out to be quite right. On the one hand, charges that the apes' behavior is exclusively cued or imitation overreach; the weight of the evidence suggests that at least some of the apes engage in genuine communication. On the other hand, we now see that early assessments that apes are linguistically equivalent to two-year-old human children were far too optimistic; there are deep differences between the species, not least the fact that even the most successful studies haven't succeeded in producing apes who talk just for the sake of making conversation.[10] The popular idea that there are 'talking apes' who communicate just like humans is simply false.

And so, despite all the controversy that surrounds ape language projects to this day, there are two things that nearly everyone can agree on: apes can learn to communicate with humans, but no one would confuse a transcript of an ape's conversations with a transcript of a human child learning to speak (or sign). The question, then, is whether we should say that the thing these apes learned to do counts as 'Language'. In other words, where is the boundary between 'Language' and 'Not Language'?

To think about what's really at stake in all this, imagine a group of bees discussing bee dances – the movements performed by bees that allow other bees to find a food source. Suppose the bees start arguing about whether any other species has bee dances. One bee observes that no other species has been observed to dance in the same way bees do; therefore, bee dances must be unique to bees. Another bee replies that there are other species, such as humans, with very complex societies; obviously they must have *some* sort of bee dance in order to maintain these social groups. A third bee reports that some humans have been seen watching bee dances and gone straight to the appropriate food source; they clearly understood the message, so humans must be capable of bee dances. A fourth bee responds that humans may be able to figure out the meanings of bee dances, but they have never been seen doing bee dances themselves, and infant humans who grow up around bees never learn to do bee dances naturally. A fifth bee accuses the other bees of melissocentrism: isn't it insulting to say that no other species is sophisticated enough to use this valuable tool? A sixth bee wants to go back to the beginning and define exactly

[10] Lyn et al. (2011) argue that Kanzi and some other apes who received similar training do in fact spontaneously comment on things, but rarely – only 5.4% of the apes' utterances in the researchers' database, compared to 40.4% of utterances in a similar analysis of children.

what true 'Bee Dance' is; only then will it be possible to properly test whether any other species has it.

The real answer, of course, is that only bees have bee dances; it's a species-specific form of communication. Certainly other species (such as humans) can learn *about* bee dances, and even learn to interpret some of them; but no human will ever 'use' bee dances the way bees do. But saying that only bees have bee dances doesn't mean that they are the only species that can think or communicate, or that their type of communication is superior to all others; it's just different.

Similarly, there is a form of communication – what linguists call 'language' – that is apparently specific to humans. Other species can learn parts of the system – the meanings of some words, or possibly some of the rules for putting words together – but no other species uses this system the way humans do. The very fact that non-human animals do *not* naturally use this system makes it all the more impressive that Washoe, Nim, and others learned as much as they did, just as it's a testament to human intelligence that we have learned something about bee dances despite not being bees ourselves.

In fact, there's even a hint of anthropocentrism in the insistence that other species ought to be able to learn language. Some people who argue for the linguistic abilities of non-human animals do so out of a desire to give them respect and dignity. It's odd, then, to ask these creatures to prove their worth by doing something so distinctively human. Few people today would argue that a human being with a language impairment is less valuable for that reason; to insist that animals must use language is, perversely, to hold them to a higher standard.

4.5 Summary

- Non-human apes cannot speak, but several apes have been trained to communicate with humans using a language-like system – either physical symbols or signs from ASL.
- With intensive training, apes can learn individual words and formulas for combining them. These words are not necessarily learned as symbols (as opposed to routines for satisfying the apes' needs), but there is evidence that apes may be able to learn the symbolic function of words under the right circumstances.
- Apes' utterances are repetitive, often imitative, and overwhelmingly consist of requests. In these respects, apes' behavior is very different from that of human children.
- There are fundamental differences between the ways humans use language and the ways apes do. As far as we can tell, human language is a system that is unique to our species.

For further reflection

(1) Go to www.cambridge.org/kaplan and download the file 'Learning Yerkish', which has examples of the kinds of Yerkish sentences used with Lana. Try to guess the meanings of the lexigrams you see; then look at the translation key to check your guesses. Were some lexigrams more difficult than others? Based on your experience, do you think these translations are reasonable representations of what the lexigrams may have come to mean for the chimpanzee subjects?

(2) In 1998, AOL hosted 'Koko's first interspecies web chat'. Selected questions from audience members were relayed by the AOL moderator over the phone to Patterson, who signed the questions to Koko. Patterson then translated Koko's responses for the AOL moderator, who typed them in for the online audience. Read the transcript of the chat, available at www.cambridge.org/kaplan. Which of Koko's answers appear to be genuine and appropriate responses to the questions she was asked? Which ones might have been overinterpreted?

(3) *Project Nim* is a 2011 documentary on the life of Nim Chimpsky. Watch the documentary; then read the commentary in Singer (2011) and the reply to Singer in Seidenberg (2011). The film and these two blog posts illustrate some of the non-linguistic issues that arise when people consider the question of whether other species can learn language. Reflect on the motivations of the various people involved in the project: what factors might have made these individuals more or less likely to interpret Nim's behavior as language-like?

Further reading

The history of ape language research is a fascinating one full of colorful personalities, both human and chimpanzee (and gorilla). There are several non-technical books that tell the stories of specific projects: Hayes (1951) for Viki, Temerlin (1975) for Lucy, Fouts (1997) for Washoe and friends, Patterson and Linden (1981) for Koko, Terrace (1979b) for Nim Chimpsky, and Savage-Rumbaugh and Lewin (1994) for Kanzi.

The Sarah project is described briefly in Premack (1971) and Premack and Premack (1972), and more extensively in Premack (1976b). Rumbaugh (1977) is a collection of papers on the Lana project.

Gardner and Gardner (1969) is an early overview of the Washoe project; Gardner and Gardner (1971) provides a more detailed account. Work with Washoe's successors is described in Gardner and Gardner (1978) and Gardner et al. (1989).

Koko's behavior has been reported in popular outlets such as *National Geographic* (Patterson 1978). Transcripts of some of Koko's conversational interactions are published in Patterson (1980) and Patterson et al. (1988).

The most important scientific publication resulting from the Nim project is Terrace et al. (1979). Terrace (1979a) summarizes the researchers' conclusions for a general audience.

Kanzi's history and training are described in Savage-Rumbaugh et al. (1986) and Savage-Rumbaugh et al. (1993).

Petitto and Seidenberg (1979) and Seidenberg and Petitto (1979) are somewhat technical critiques of the ape language experiments; Wallman (1992) is a critical book-length treatment of the same topic. Neisser (1983) has a chapter on the ape language experiments from the perspective of the Deaf community, including interviews with some of the people involved in the projects. Anderson (2004) is a more general overview of animal communication.

Bibliography

Anderson, Stephen R. *Doctor Dolittle's Delusion: Animals and the Uniqueness of Human Language*. Yale University Press, New Haven, CT, 2004.

BBC News. No words to describe monkeys' play. *BBC News*, May 9 2003. Available at http://news.bbc.co.uk/2/hi/3013959.stm.

Essock, Susan M., Timothy V. Gill, and Duane M. Rumbaugh. Language relevant object- and color-naming tasks. In Rumbaugh (1977), chapter 10, pages 193–206.

Fouts, Roger. *Next of Kin: What Chimpanzees Have Taught Me about Who We Are*. William Morrow and Company, New York, NY, 1997.

Fouts, Roger S., and Deborah H. Fouts. Loulis in conversation with the cross-fostered chimpanzees. In Gardner et al. (1989), chapter 9, pages 293–307.

Gardner, Beatrice T., and R. Allen Gardner. Two-way communication with an infant chimpanzee. In Schrier et al. (1971), chapter 3, pages 117–184.

Gardner, R. Allen, and Beatrice T. Gardner. Teaching sign language to a chimpanzee. *Science*, 165(3894):664–672, 1969.

Gardner, R. Allen, and Beatrice T. Gardner. Comparative psychology and language acquisition. *Annals of the New York Academy of Sciences*, 309(1):37–76, 1978.

Gardner, R. Allen, Beatrix T. Gardner, and Thomas E. Van Cantfort, editors. *Teaching Sign Language to Chimpanzees*. State University of New York Press, Albany, NY, 1989.

Gill, Timothy V. Conversations with Lana. In Rumbaugh (1977), chapter 12, pages 225–246.

Hayes, Cathy. *The Ape in Our House*. Harper & Brothers, New York, NY, 1951.

Lyn, Heidi, Patricia M. Greenfield, Sue Savage-Rumbaugh, and Kristen Gillespie-Lynch. Nonhuman primates do declare! A comparison of declarative symbol and gesture use in two children, two bonobos, and a chimpanzee. *Language & Communication*, 31(1):63–74, 2011.

Marsh, James. Project Nim. Lionsgate Home Entertainment, 2012.

Neisser, Arden. *The Other Side of Silence: Sign Language and the Deaf Community in America*. Gallaudet University Press, Washington, DC, 1983.

O'Sullivan, Chris, and Carey Page Yeager. Communicative context and linguistic competence: The effects of social setting on a chimpanzee's conversational skill. In Gardner et al. (1989), chapter 7, pages 269–279.

Patterson, Francine. Conversations with a gorilla. *National Geographic*, 154(4):438–465, October 1978.

Patterson, Francine G. Innovative uses of language by a gorilla: A case study. In Keith E. Nelson, editor, *Children's Language*, volume 2, chapter 9, pages 497–561. Gardner Press, New York, NY, 1980.

Patterson, Francine G. P., and Ronald H. Cohn. Language acquisition by a lowland gorilla: Koko's first ten years of vocabulary development. *Word*, 41(2):97–143, 1990.

Patterson, Francine, and Eugene Linden. *The Education of Koko*. Holt, Rinehart and Winston, New York, NY, 1981.

Patterson, Francine, Joanne Tanner, and Nancy Mayer. Pragmatic analysis of gorilla utterances: Early communicative development in the gorilla Koko. *Journal of Pragmatics*, 12(1):35–54, 1988.

Petitto, Laura A., and Mark S. Seidenberg. On the evidence for linguistic abilities in signing apes. *Brain and Language*, 8(2):162–183, 1979.

Premack, Ann J. *Why Chimps Can Read*. Harper & Row, New York, NY, 1976a.

Premack, Ann James, and David Premack. Teaching language to an ape. *Scientific American*, 227:92–99, October 1972.

Premack, David. Language in chimpanzee? *Science*, 172(3985):808–822, 1971.

Premack, David. *Intelligence in Ape and Man*. Lawrence Erlbaum Associates, Hillsdale, NJ, 1976b.

Pullum, Geoffrey K. Nim: The unproject. Language Log, August 16 2011. Available at http://languagelog.ldc.upenn.edu/nll/?p=3369.

Rivas, Esteban. Recent use of signs by chimpanzees (*Pan troglodytes*) in interactions with humans. *Journal of Comparative Psychology*, 119(4):404–417, 2005.

Rumbaugh, Duane M., editor. *Language Learning by a Chimpanzee: The LANA Project*. Communication and Behavior. Academic Press, New York, NY, 1977.

Rumbaugh, Duane M., and Timothy V. Gill. Lana's acquisition of language skills. In Rumbaugh (1977), chapter 9, pages 165–192.

Savage-Rumbaugh, E. Sue. *Ape Language: From Conditioned Response to Symbol*. Animal Intelligence. Columbia University Press, New York, NY, 1986.

Savage-Rumbaugh, E. Sue, Duane M. Rumbaugh, and Sally Boysen. Linguistically mediated tool use and exchange by chimpanzees (*Pan troglodytes*). *The Behavioral and Brain Sciences*, 1(4):539–554, 1978.

Savage-Rumbaugh, E. Sue, Duane M. Rumbaugh, and Sarah Boysen. Do apes use language? *Sigma Xi, The Scientific Research Society*, 68(1):49–61, 1980.

Savage-Rumbaugh, E. Sue, and Roger Lewin. *Kanzi: The Ape at the Brink of the Human Mind*. Wiley, New York, NY, 1994.

Savage-Rumbaugh, E. Sue, Kelly McDonald, Rose A. Sevcik, William D. Hopkins, and Elizabeth Rubert. Spontaneous symbol acquisition and communicative use by pygmy chimpanzees (*Pan paniscus*). *Journal of Experimental Psychology: General*, 115(3):211–235, 1986.

Savage-Rumbaugh, E. Sue, Jeannine Murphy, Rose A. Sevcik, Karen E. Brakke, Shelly L. Williams, and Duane M. Rumbaugh. Language comprehension in ape and child. *Monographs of the Society for Research in Child Development*, 58(3–4), 1993. Serial No. 233.

Schrier, Allan Martin, Harry Frederick Harlow, and Fred Stollnitz, editors. *Behavior of Nonhuman Primates: Modern Research Trends*, volume 4. Academic Press, New York, NY, 1971.

Seidenberg, Mark. Seidenberg on Singer and Nim. Language Log, August 27 2011. Available at http://languagelog.ldc.upenn.edu/nll/?p=3390.

Seidenberg, Mark S., and Laura A. Petitto. Signing behavior in apes: A critical review. *Cognition*, 7(2):177–215, 1979.

Singer, Peter. The troubled life of Nim Chimpsky. *The New York Review of Books*, August 18 2011. Available at http://www.nybooks.com/blogs/nyrblog/2011/aug/18/troubled-life-nim-chimpsky/.

Temerlin, Maurice. *Lucy: Growing Up Human*. Science and Behavior Books, Palo Alto, CA, 1975.

Terrace, H. S. How Nim Chimpsky changed my mind. *Psychology Today*, 13(6):65–76, 1979a.

Terrace, H. S., L. A. Petitto, R. J. Sanders, and T. G. Bever. Can an ape create a sentence? *Science*, 206(4421):891–902, 1979.

Terrace, Herbert S. *Nim: A Chimpanzee Who Learned Sign Language*. Alfred A. Knopf, New York, NY, 1979b.

Umiker-Sebeok, Jean, and Thomas A. Sebeok. Clever Hans and smart simians: The self-fulfilling prophecy and kindred methodological pitfalls. *Anthropos*, 76(1/2):89–165, 1981.

von Glaserfeld, Ernst. The Yerkish language for non-human primates. *American Journal of Computational Linguistics*, 1974. Microfiche 12.

Wallman, Joel. *Aping Language*. Themes in the Social Sciences. Cambridge University Press, Cambridge, 1992.

Part II

Language learning

5 'Children have to be taught language'

The process of learning a first language is commonplace in one sense and deeply mysterious in another. It's commonplace because everyone does it. A newborn infant knows almost nothing about the language being spoken around her, but around the time of her first birthday she will start saying her first words. Somewhere between the ages of one and two she will start putting two words together, and sometime after her second birthday she will produce sentences of increasing complexity, all the while learning new words at an incredible rate.

But learning a first language is mysterious because so much of it happens at such a young age. We don't remember doing it ourselves, and the children who are learning now can't tell us much about what they're doing. Researchers who study how children learn language have to come up with creative experimental techniques to explore what their young subjects know.

Learning to talk does more than help young children express what they want (and respond to instructions); speaking is an important part of becoming a full member of the community. This may explain why many people have strong beliefs about first-language acquisition – how children do it, how adults can help, and what the process means for children's eventual place in the world. In this chapter, we'll see that these beliefs are highly culture-specific, and that some beliefs about language acquisition common in western cultures are either based on uncertain evidence or simply wrong.

This chapter focuses especially on the idea that parents teach language to their children explicitly. Mainstream middle-class western parenting practices put a high value on the parent's role as a teacher, and this includes teaching language; parents are expected to train their children on words for colors, shapes, animal sounds, and so on. One question we will explore is whether the parent-as-language-teacher is a universal model of child-rearing: do all cultures include language teaching in a parent's duties? As it turns out, different societies have very different ideas about how children are supposed to learn language.

Parents' role in child language acquisition isn't just theoretically interesting; it also has important real-world consequences. If language must be taught, then it's possible to teach it badly. And if a parent teaches badly, then the child will grow up with an impoverished language. And if the child's language is deficient, then the child will probably do poorly in many areas of his life – school, work, and so forth. And if some children are disadvantaged by inadequate parenting, then the solution is to train their parents to be better language teachers. As we will see, there is a body of linguistic research that makes precisely this argument, and over the past few years several programs have been founded in the United States to combat the 'language gap' by changing parents' behavior. But there's another body of linguistic research that challenges the idea that a first language has to be explicitly taught, and it turns out that many of our ideas about 'good' parental talk are inextricably tied up with culture-specific beliefs about how to raise children. There are no easy answers to the educational and economic disparities in the United States, but a healthy dose of caution is in order before we rush out to fix what we perceive to be other people's bad parenting.

5.1 Culture-specific beliefs about language acquisition

The following interaction between a mother and her three-month-old daughter illustrates a way of talking to babies that feels very natural to many westerners.

(1) A mother-infant interaction, quoted in Ochs and Schieffelin (1984, 282)

ANN: *(smiles)*
MOTHER: Oh what a nice little smile!
MOTHER: Yes, isn't that nice?
MOTHER: There.
MOTHER: There's a nice little smile.
ANN: *(burps)*
MOTHER: What a nice wind as well!
MOTHER: Yes, that's better, isn't it?
MOTHER: Yes.
MOTHER: Yes.
ANN: *(vocalizes)*
MOTHER: Yes!
MOTHER: There's a nice noise.

The mother does several interesting things here. First, she speaks directly to the infant, even though the child clearly can't talk back yet and doesn't understand what the mother is saying anyway. Second, she interprets the infant's behaviors (a smile, a burp) as social acts, and responds to them as though they were part of the conversation. In other words, the mother is helping the infant participate in a social interaction to a degree that the child would be incapable of on her own.

This way of interacting with an infant seems utterly natural to many people, so much so that it's hard to imagine how else you would talk to a baby. Many people are surprised to learn that societies vary widely in what they believe about how adults and infants should interact. As it turns out, many of the practices that are common in western cultures – speaking directly to infants, using a specialized 'baby-talk', treating babies' actions as a meaningful part of the conversation, and so on – are far from universal.

In fact, you don't even have to travel outside the United States to find communities with dramatically different child-rearing practices. Heath (1983) documents the socialization of young children in two rural North Carolina communities. One of these, which she calls 'Trackton', is a low-income African-American community where patterns of adult-child interaction are strikingly different from those in nearby white communities. Heath describes how adults rarely, if ever, speak directly to preverbal infants, and no one thinks babies need explicit teaching in order to learn how to talk. Adults don't interpret babies' vocalizations as language or listen breathlessly for first words; they don't engage infants in spoken interaction or help babies hold up their end of the 'conversation'.

> Adults respond incredulously to queries such as "Did you hear him say *milk*?" They believe they should not have to depend on their babies to tell them what they need or when they are uncomfortable. Adults are the knowing participants; children only "come to know." Thus, if asked, community members explain away their lack of response to children's early utterances; they do not repeat the utterance, announce it as a label for an item or event, or place the "word" in an expanded phrase or sentence. To them, the response carries no meaning which can be directly linked to an object or event; it is just "noise."
>
> Heath (1983, 76)

At first glance, this description might suggest that Trackton babies are raised in a linguistically impoverished environment. How will they learn to talk if adults never speak to them? How do they learn to improve on their imperfect early utterances if they never get any feedback and adults don't even seem to recognize that they are trying to talk?

But Heath emphasizes that babies in Trackton are constantly surrounded by language. Adults don't speak to babies directly, but babies are always in the company of adults and hear adults speaking *to each other*. Infants in Trackton aren't isolated from the larger community or excluded from adult settings; they are right there in the thick of things. You could even argue that the linguistic environment of Trackton babies is *richer* than that of babies raised in mainstream middle-class households: instead of hearing a simplified baby-talk register most of the day, they listen to a non-stop stream of adult conversation in an environment rich with the kinds of social cues that they will need to master in order to participate fully in the community.

In fact, just as the child-rearing practices of Trackton seem odd to many middle-class Americans, mainstream middle-class child-rearing practices seem odd to residents of Trackton. There is no baby-talk in Trackton; when adults do speak to young children, they don't raise the pitch of their voice, use special diminutive words, or simplify their syntax. If an older child uses some form of baby-talk (while playing or while addressing a younger child), adults reprimand the child for not speaking properly. Many middle-class parents see baby-talk as a way to help infants learn an easier version of adult language; to Trackton residents, baby-talk is just a form of childishness. If children are going to learn the adult language of the community, there's no reason to teach them anything else.

Trackton residents also don't engage children in the kinds of question-and-answer sessions that many parents see as a teaching tool. Middle-class parents and caregivers often ask questions they already know the answers to in order to test their children's knowledge: 'What color is that book?' 'How many cars do you see?' 'What sound does a dog make?' To Trackton residents, this is a ludicrous attempt to teach children what they must learn for themselves. Heath quotes one Trackton resident describing how she expects her grandson Teegie to discover the world on his own:

> He gotta learn to *know* 'bout dis world, can't nobody tell 'im. Now just how crazy is dat? White folks uh hear dey kids say sump'n, dey say it back to 'em, dey aks 'em 'gain 'n 'gain 'bout things, like they 'posed to be born knowin'. You think I kin tell Teegie all he gotta know to get along? He just gotta be keen, keep his eyes open.... Ain't no use me tellin' 'im: 'Learn dis, learn dat. What's dis? What's dat?'
>
> Heath (1983, 84)

Thus, even within the United States, there are striking differences between communities regarding how adults view and interact with infants.

Not surprisingly, we see even more variation when we take a global view. The practices in Samoa described by Ochs (1982) seem just as odd to many middle-class westerners as the practices in Trackton, but for different reasons. Ochs describes a society in which young children are believed to have very little control over their actions – so little, in fact, that they cannot function socially. Because young children aren't expected to respond appropriately to social interaction, there's no point in talking to them. The result is that adults in Samoa don't interact directly with infants, just as adults in Trackton don't, but the reasoning is different. Adults in Samoa simply don't expect children to behave in socially appropriate ways; this includes the social functions of language, but it extends to many other types of behavior as well. By contrast, adults in Trackton *do* expect children to behave socially, and they often interpret infants' nonverbal behaviors as social reactions to other people. But Trackton adults see no reason to try to teach language to preverbal children; this is something for children to discover on their own.

A further consequence of the worldview described by Ochs is that Samoan adults don't see infants' early vocalizations as a developing form of language. As discussed in further detail below, it's common for middle-class western caregivers to respond to a child's utterance ('Ball!') by expanding it ('Yes, that's a very nice ball! Do you want to go play with the ball?'). In a sense, these expansions represent what the adult thinks the child *meant* to say (but couldn't). This kind of interaction is foreign to Samoan caregivers because it attributes a degree of linguistic competence to children that Samoan caregivers don't believe the children have.

These differences in how children are spoken to in various social groups are interesting for plenty of reasons; among other things, they tell us something about how children learn language. There is a popular belief among middle-class western parents that children must be *taught* to speak correctly, either by their parents or in school. Many parents believe that explicit instruction ('Can you say *book*?'), question-and-answer sessions ('What color is that book?'), and other interactions like these are necessary, or at least very important, in order for children to learn language. As we have seen, plenty of children around the world *don't* get this kind of training, but they learn to talk anyway.

5.2 The '30-million-word gap'

If children depend on their parents to teach them language, and if there are 'right' and 'wrong' ways to do this teaching, then it's possible that children whose parents were inferior teachers end up with inadequate language skills that leave them unable to succeed in school or in the workplace. In fact, some researchers have argued that this is exactly what happens in many low-income families, and that these language deficits help explain why poor children are less likely to do well in school. One enormously influential study along these lines is Hart and Risley (1995); the authors claim that children from low-income families have smaller vocabularies and lower IQ scores, not because they're poor, but because low-income parents talk to their children much less than high-income parents do.

Extrapolating from their data, Hart and Risley estimate that by age four, children in high-income families have heard about 45 million words, compared to 13 million for children in low-income families. This '30-million-word gap' has become well known in educational circles, and the idea has led to several attempts to get poor parents to talk more. The Thirty Million Words Project at the University of Chicago (which began in 2010) trains parents to say more words to their children, and in 2013 the city of Providence, Rhode Island, obtained a grant to implement a similar program on a citywide scale.

If Hart and Risley are right, then the practical implications are obviously huge: children need the right kind of input to learn language well, and parents who want their children to succeed should do certain things – according to Hart and Risley, they just have to talk more. The theoretical implications are huge too; one major goal of research in child language acquisition is to understand exactly which parts of the acquisition process depend on the child's environment and which don't. In fact, as we will see below, some of the things linguists have learned about child language acquisition suggest that results like Hart and Risley's should be taken with a grain of salt, or at the very least that it's too simplistic to let the take-home message of such research be 'If you don't talk to your children enough (or in the right way), they won't learn language very well'.

5.2.1 Evidence for grammatical rules in young children

As described in Chapter 2, every natural language that linguists have ever studied follows complex grammatical rules, even though speakers usually can't describe what those rules are. This finding contradicts what a lot of people believe about how language works: namely, that speech is naturally chaotic, and children need extensive training and correction in order to follow grammatical rules; people who never get this training, or who simply aren't smart enough, never learn to speak correctly because they don't follow the rules.

In reality, *all* adult speakers follow grammatical rules like the ones discussed in Chapter 2. What's more, there are reasons to believe that this kind of rule-following is present from birth and doesn't have to be taught: even very young children show evidence of systematic and sophisticated grammatical knowledge.

Rule-driven errors in children's speech

One piece of evidence for the rule-governed behavior of young children – perhaps counterintuitively – is their mistakes. Children's early speech is obviously not adult-like, and it takes several years for them to master the language. But even children's mistakes don't look like a failure to use language in a systematic way; they seem to be following rules, but those rules are the wrong ones.

A clear example of this kind of phenomenon is how children handle irregular morphology. In English, for example, nouns typically form plurals by adding *-s*, and the past tense of verbs involves adding *-ed*. But a few English plurals are *irregular* because they don't follow the usual rule (*mice*, *feet*), and many English verbs fail to follow the *-ed* rule (*went*, *saw*, *ate*). Children frequently *overregularize* words like these, producing *foots*, *goed*, *eated*, and so on. The problem isn't that these children failed to learn the plural rule or the past-tense rule, but that they've learned the rules too well! It takes time for children to learn which words do *not* follow the rule and have to be memorized separately.

In other cases, children seem to be following the 'wrong' rule, given the language they are learning. For example, there are a few basic patterns a language can use to form yes-no questions. In some languages, such as Māori, yes-no questions look exactly like ordinary sentences, but pronounced with a special question intonation. (English uses this pattern occasionally, but only in specific kinds of situations, such as responding incredulously to something someone has just said: *John and Mary broke up??*) Other languages have a dedicated word that appears at the beginning of yes-no questions, such as French *est-que*. A third pattern is to move the main verb of the sentence to the beginning in order to form a question: *The book is red* → *Is the book red?*

English follows a version of this last rule, although there are restrictions on which verbs are allowed to move in this way, with the result that most yes-no questions in English start with a form of either *be* or *do*. Children learning English occasionally seem to take one of these words – such as *is* – and misinterpret it as a dedicated 'question word', as though English were following the French rule. Children who do this will produce questions such as *Is this is your book?*, appending *is* to the beginning of a sentence in order to form a question. These children are following a perfectly ordinary grammatical rule, and in fact it's the right rule for languages like French or Hebrew – it just happens to be different from the English rule.

Imperfect input: Evidence from signed languages

In the ordinary case, children learning a language are surrounded by native speakers of that language; this means they get a lot of exposure to the grammatical rules being followed by adults and older children. What happens if a child's language models do *not* follow grammatical rules very well? Does the child conclude that anything goes?

Not at all. This is actually the situation for many deaf children of hearing parents: the child has no access to the parents' native (spoken) language, but the parents aren't native signers. Many hearing parents choose not to sign at all with their deaf children because they want to encourage lipreading and speech; this process is so difficult, though, that the children end up creating a rudimentary 'homesign' system for basic communication with their hearing family members. These homesigns don't have the opportunity to develop into full-fledged languages, but they do show a surprising amount of regularity, much of which seems to be driven by the child.

The results are even more impressive when deaf children's parents *do* use a full-fledged sign language, but aren't native signers themselves. This is almost always the case when hearing parents sign with their deaf children, although it can also happen when a deaf child is born to deaf parents who themselves were raised in an oral environment and therefore aren't native signers. Singleton and Newport (2004) document the case of a deaf child, Simon, in the latter situation. They found that even though Simon's parents used ASL grammatical markers very inconsistently, Simon managed to learn regular patterns anyway. In other words, Simon took his parents' somewhat haphazard input and became a better ASL signer than they were! The behavior of young deaf learners suggests that children are, in a sense, 'looking' for rules to follow: all it takes is some minimal level of linguistic input for children to take the patterns they see (whether consistent or not) and run with them.

Pidgins and creoles

A final piece of evidence for the grammatical sophistication of children comes from pidgin and creole languages. A *pidgin* is a contact language that develops when speakers of different languages need to find a way to communicate, but circumstances don't permit extensive bilingualism. Pidgins can develop as regional trade languages; many pidgins have also come out of multilingual populations brought to work in New World plantations (whether as slaves or as migrant laborers). Pidgins often borrow a large part of their vocabulary from a specific language, known as the *lexifier* language. By definition, pidgins are no one's native language, and so the structure of a pidgin tends to be extremely simple and variable, with speakers often using grammatical structures from their native language when possible. (However, the speakers of a pidgin may also converge on some basic grammatical rules, especially if their native languages have some patterns in common.)

A *creole* is a language that has evolved from a pidgin and has a sizeable number of native speakers. Creoles follow regular grammatical rules and are full-fledged natural languages. Unfortunately, creoles are rarely recognized as complete and independent languages, partly because so much of their vocabulary is recognizably borrowed from another source. Haitian Creole, for example, is a French-lexifier creole spoken by most citizens of Haiti. Until the last few decades of the twentieth century, there was no broad recognition that the creole was even a language in its own right; Haitians (except for the educated elite) were simply thought to be speaking broken French. This is false, of course: the two languages do share a lot of vocabulary, but their grammatical structures are completely different.

Linguists debate where the extra complexity of creole languages come from: what triggers the transition between the variability of a pidgin and the stability and sophistication of a creole? One of the most prominent theories is that the grammatical rules of creoles are essentially invented by children. When a stable community develops around a pidgin, speakers of different languages marry; their children will grow up with the pidgin as their first language. Children, the theory goes, aren't satisfied with the pidgin's lack of rules; through interaction with their peers, communities of children spontaneously converge on a grammar. A creole is born.

Much of the evidence for this hypothesis is indirect, because linguists haven't been around to observe the transition from pidgin to creole in real time. But there is one famous exception: the birth of Nicaraguan Sign Language at a residential school for the deaf established in the late 1970s. Before that time, deaf Nicaraguan children were mostly isolated; the first generation of children at the school (where oralist methods were used and sign language was not taught) brought with them a hodge-podge of homesign systems. Linguists had the good fortune to be able to observe children at the school from a very early date, and they found that the younger children rapidly converged on a full-fledged grammatical system.

5.2.2 Can language acquisition be deficient?

Everything we've seen so far paints a picture in which children learn a first language automatically: all it takes is minimal exposure to a language, and the child's innate language-learning ability will do the rest. If this is all there is to it, then is it even possible for a child to learn language badly or incompletely?

In some circumstances, the answer is clearly 'yes'. One obvious example is children who are linguistically impaired in some way; for example, a small number of children have a condition known as Specific Language Impairment (SLI), which impairs the child's ability to use language but leaves normal intelligence intact. Language difficulties may accompany certain other conditions too, such as autism spectrum disorders.

We also know that it takes some minimum level of exposure to language in order to learn it, even for children. Obviously, a child who never hears language at all (which has happened in extreme cases of abuse) won't learn language; neither will a child whose only exposure to language is through television. The homesign systems of isolated deaf children do have some regular rules, but they aren't as complex as the languages that develop in larger communities.

But all these situations are pretty extreme; the vast majority of children grow up in an environment that is more than rich enough for them to learn language fluently. However, some researchers have asked whether, even among children in ordinary circumstances, different experiences can cause children to learn language more or less well. A lot of this research is driven by concern about how well children do in school; the idea is that maybe some groups do poorly in school (such as children from low-income families) because their language skills are inadequate, and their language skills are inadequate because their parents haven't taught them properly.

The Hart and Risley study mentioned above is by far the most well-known of this research. It was a project of epic proportions: the research team followed 42 children and their families from the age of 7–9 months until they were three years old, recording each child at home for one hour every month. Every utterance that the child produced, and every utterance that was spoken directly to the child, was transcribed and coded. The result was hundreds of hours of audiotapes and thousands of pages of transcripts; the process of collecting, transcribing, and coding the data took six years.

Hart and Risley observed, first, that parents and children from high-income families produced more different words over the course of the study than parents and children from low-income families. Second, parents and children from high-income families simply talked more. They spoke more words during each hour of observation and used a larger number of different words when they did.

Unsurprisingly, Hart and Risley found that children from higher socioeconomic classes had larger vocabularies and performed better on certain tests, both at three and again in the third grade, when some of the children were contacted for a follow-up assessment. Their important claim was that these differences were *not* caused by social class, but by the language input the children had received from their parents. They argued that children whose parents talked more performed better than children whose parents talked less, regardless of class. One important component of their argument was that the correlation between parents' talk and children's achievements could be seen even *within* a single social class. In short, talking to children makes them smarter; children from high-income families do better in school because their parents talked to them more while they were very young.

Many more studies have been done since, and they've mostly come to similar conclusions: the way parents speak to their children in the very early years affects their language development. These later studies have observed children both at their homes and in the lab; they have measured how much parents (usually mothers) talk, how many different words they use, and the kinds of things they say; they have measured how much children talk, how long their utterances are, how many words they know, and so on. The general finding is that children's language looks better when their parents do certain things: talk more, use a wider vocabulary, ask questions instead of giving commands, engage children in intensive interaction, and so on.

The upshot of all this seems to be a contradiction. On the one hand, children are expert rule-learners; except in pathological cases, every child who gets some minimum level of exposure will become a fluent speaker of the language. On the other hand, research in the tradition of Hart and Risley suggests that some children will learn language better than others based on the quality of the input they get from their caretakers. What should we believe?

Part of the answer may be that we're dealing with different things in each case. A child's ability to learn what we might call the 'core' properties of language – the fundamental grammatical patterns that allow us to build words and sentences – is extraordinarily robust. This isn't the kind of thing that Hart and Risley or their successors have assessed; there's no such thing as a child who fails to learn how to form questions in English just because he has a relatively taciturn mother. Instead, these latter studies focus on other aspects of what children known about language and how they use it – things that are arguably more 'peripheral', such as how much they talk, how many words they know, and how well they score on standardized language tests (which, depending on the situation, may not actually measure what the child knows about language; see section 5.2.3 below).

But another part of the answer may have to do with the kinds of differences we saw in section 5.1: beliefs about how parents *should* interact with children, and the kinds of language skills that are valued in children, are by no means universal. In the next section, we will explore how social expectations may influence the results of research like this.

5.2.3 Bias and confounds in language assessment

Look again at the list of things that parents can apparently do to boost their children's language development: talk a lot, directly to the child; use a large vocabulary; treat the child as a conversational partner and engage with her intensively; ask her lots of questions; use indirect requests instead of giving direct commands; and so on. This picture looks suspiciously like the western mainstream middle-class model of parenting – which, as we saw in section 5.1, is far from universal. Not only that, but this is exactly the social group to which researchers on child language acquisition are most likely to belong.

It's possible, of course, that western middle-class society has just happened to hit on the 'right' formula for parenting, at least as far as language is concerned. But we should also take a moment to ask whether, and how much, our findings are influenced by a particular set of cultural assumptions. First, how should we measure a child's linguistic ability? Some of the obvious things we might measure are almost certainly going to be affected by social norms in the child's community. For example, groups differ in how much children are encouraged (or allowed) to talk, especially in the presence of a stranger such as the experimenter; these differences will matter if all we measure is how many words the child says. We run into similar problems if we try to use a checklist to test how many words the child knows: the objects and experiences that are common to many western middle-class children may be foreign to children from other backgrounds.

We also have to consider dialectal variation. For example, Hart and Risley measured children's vocabularies by simply recording every word each child ever said. This looks like an unbiased method for determining how many words a child knows, since the children are not being evaluated against a predetermined list of words. But Hart and Risley in effect *did* check the children's vocabularies against a list: they discounted any words that weren't found in a standard dictionary. Words that are specific to non-standard or regional dialects are often not included in dictionaries of Standard English; this means that children who were learning non-standard dialects may not have gotten credit for all the words they knew. In fact, all six families in the lowest socio-economic group Hart and Risley studied were African-American, and the transcripts reported in Hart and Risley (1995, 81–82, 184–187) suggest that at least some of these families may have spoken African American English (AAE; see Chapter 2). AAE, like all non-standard dialects, contains words that are not found in the standard dialect; Green (2002, 12–33) gives the example of *saditty*, meaning 'conceited', which is not well known outside the AAE-speaking community and unlikely to find its way into a standard dictionary.

Other differences between AAE and Standard English may have further inflated the differences Hart and Risley found. They found that past-tense verbs (e.g., *walk<u>ed</u>*) appeared more frequently in the speech of high-income parents. But tense works differently in AAE; AAE has a rich set of rules for marking information on verbs, including several ways of talking about past time, but many of these rules involve separate words rather than the suffix *-ed* – see Chapter 2 of this book and Chapter 2 of Green (2002) for details. This means that the low-income parents may have talked about the past just as much as the high-income parents, but this would have gone unnoticed because they were using different grammatical rules to do so.

If these ways of measuring children's language are socially or linguistically biased, then maybe the solution is to use standardized language tests instead. Unfortunately, it turns out that standardized tests, too, are biased towards particular groups. It's well documented that African-American children, for example, are placed in special education classes much more often than their white peers. Part of the problem is that the standard tests for assessing linguistic ability, or even general intelligence, yield artificially low scores for African-American children. The reasons for this, discussed in Labov (1976), are essentially the ones we've seen already: these tests assess what children know about Standard English, so children who are learning a different variety of English are at a disadvantage. In addition, these tests make social assumptions that are not universally valid. For example, some children find it perfectly normal for an adult to ask a question that the adult already knows the answer to; their parents have been doing this for years. But for a child whose parents don't do this, it is a completely foreign experience. And so these question-and-answer sessions may help children do better on certain assessments without necessarily improving their linguistic skills. In other words, when you ask your child *What color is the ball?* and *How many cars are there?*, are you teaching her language, or are you training her to take standardized tests?

More generally, bias can show up not just in how we measure things, but in the things we choose to measure in the first place. For example, most of the studies on this topic analyze speech that is specifically addressed to children, but not speech between adults that the child overhears. It seems entirely reasonable that children would pay more attention when they are being spoken to directly, but it's also clear that children 'eavesdrop' as well. (If you doubt this, try swearing within earshot of a two-year-old.) Moreover, we have seen that there are some communities where children are simply not spoken to until they are capable of speaking back; these children obviously manage to at least get started by learning entirely from overheard speech.

Again, this kind of possible bias is particularly obvious in Hart and Risley's study, which relies on many unexamined assumptions about how you ought to speak to a child. Their formal analysis included several measures that attempted to quantify ways in which parents 'added quality to interactions'. 'Feedback Tone', for example, measured how often the parent gave the child verbal affirmation (such as repeating what the child said or offering explicit words of praise) versus explicit disapproval (prohibitions or words such as 'bad'). 'Guidance Style' measured how often the parent gave the child a direction using a question as opposed to a command. Perhaps most striking is the fact that Hart and Risley took these kinds of parenting practices to be self-evidently good: to them, it was obvious that positive feedback and gentle guidance are better than negative feedback and firm guidance:

> The accomplishments and achievements of the higher-SES [socio-economic status] children are hardly surprising when we consider their cumulative experience: 3 years of enriched language and activities, 3 years of being told they were "right" and "good," and 3 years of frequently being chosen as more interesting to listen to and talk to than anyone else.
>
> Hart and Risley (1995, 183)

Frequent affirmation and the use of questions rather than commands may seem self-evidently good to many parents. But if mainstream middle-class parenting were different – if it valued infrequent praise and strict discipline – we could just as easily find an explanation for why *those* practices are obviously good. We might say, for example, that children who are praised all the time become insecure and in need of constant affirmation, or that children who are given firm prohibitions (*Don't*, *Stop*) are more confident in trying new things because they receive clear and loving guidance when they make mistakes. In fact, we may not have to look too far to find ideas like these – at the time of this writing, it's fashionable in the United States to worry that we have raised a generation of narcissists, young people who think they are 'more interesting to listen to and talk to than anyone else'.

Finally, when we focus on middle-class advantages, we run the risk of failing to see the linguistic strengths of other groups. There's a body of research, for example, arguing that many working-class communities in the United States excel at storytelling. Cho and Miller (2003) found that working-class mothers told *three times* as many stories as middle-class mothers during an interview, and Wiley et al. (1998) found that working-class children tell twice as many stories as middle-class children do. Moreover, Wiley et al. observed that working-class adults are much more likely to challenge children on what they have said, while middle-class adults often let factual inaccuracies pass unremarked.

The point here is not that Hart and Risley had it backwards, that the parenting practices they thought were good are actually bad. Rather, the point is that any time we try to study parents and children – including their use of language – our research is inevitably influenced by culture-specific assumptions about the kinds of things parents and children ought to do. It's all too easy to study parents and children in our own culture and conclude that we've learned something about parents and children everywhere.

Where does all this leave us? Despite the potential confounds of all these studies, it's clear that *something* in the environments of very young children matters for their linguistic development; the process of language acquisition is not completely independent of its input. Mainstream middle-class parenting practices promote abilities that allow children to do well on certain kinds of language tests, and these tests in turn are closely associated with the kinds of performance valued by schools. But it's also *not* the case that millions of children fail to learn grammatical rules; children are excellent pattern-finders and will acquire rules given the least opportunity to do so. At the end of the day, designing and interpreting experiments in this area is extremely complex; we have to think carefully about how our results may be influenced by social factors as well as linguistic ones. We may not be able to find the clear or simple answers that parents and policy makers want – but the job of a scientist is to describe reality accurately, no matter how messy it may be.

5.3 Case study: Do parents correct their children's mistakes?

Although Hart and Risley argued that more parental talk leads to larger vocabularies for children, they took pains to acknowledge that all the children they studied were competent users of language by age three: they commanded a wide range of grammatical structures and knew how to use language in socially appropriate ways. More generally, linguists have observed that children around the world seem to learn language in very similar ways, despite the fact that the nature of their parents' interaction with them varies widely.

Some linguists have argued that this uniformity tells us something important about the biological nature of language. One of the most influential proponents of this view is Noam Chomsky, who has argued that children know more about the grammatical rules of their language than they could have possibly learned from their environment. This hypothesis, known as the *poverty of the stimulus*, is one basis of the claim that language is an innate biological phenomenon. Children, on this view, are born knowing a great deal about how language works. They learn fast because they don't have to learn grammar from scratch; they are prepared to encounter a restricted number of grammatical possibilities, and their only job is to determine which of those their language actually uses. Children don't have to learn the difference between nouns, verbs, and prepositions; they only have to learn what the specific nouns, verbs, and prepositions of their language actually are. They don't have to learn what a direct object is; they only have to determine whether it comes after the verb (as in English) or before it (as in Japanese). All this knowledge and learning, of course, operates at an unconscious level, just as most adult speakers have very little explicit knowledge of the grammatical rules they follow every day.

The poverty of the stimulus remains a controversial hypothesis, and some linguists have argued that Chomsky (who is not a specialist in child language acquisition) underestimated how much information is in the speech that a young child typically hears. The heart of the issue is the question of how much a child has to learn in order to acquire a language. At the Chomskyan end of the spectrum are linguists who argue that most of what we know about language is innate, and it only takes a little bit of exposure to the surrounding language for a child to learn the rest. At the other end of the spectrum are linguists who argue that most of what we know about language is learned, not innate. Children hear a lot of language, the argument goes, and if the examples they hear contain enough information for them to figure out how to construct a question or where to put a prepositional phrase, then by Occam's razor there is no need to hypothesize that children are born already knowing these things.

In this chapter, we will focus on one very narrow question in this extremely complex field: what do parents do when their children make grammatical mistakes? All children make mistakes while learning their native language; for example, as discussed in section 5.2.1 above, a child who has learned the regular rule for past-tense verbs in English might say *eated* instead of *ate*. Some linguists have argued that parents don't reliably correct their children when they do this (*No, that's wrong* or *Say 'ate' instead*). If this is true, then the mystery is how the child ever figures out that *eated* was wrong. On the other hand, other linguists have argued that parents really do provide their children with this kind of correction, known as *negative evidence* (i.e., an explicit indication that a particular sentence is incorrect).

Another way to put the question is whether negative evidence is *necessary* for a child to learn language. Even if we find that some parents do consistently correct grammatical mistakes, we can't conclude that negative evidence is necessary for language acquisition unless we can show that *all* children have access to it. If some children learn to speak without being corrected, then it must be possible to manage without negative evidence. Thus, this issue has important implications for the question of what children have to hear in order to learn language.

5.3.1 The classic study of caregiver feedback: Brown and Hanlon (1970)

The classic study of negative evidence is Brown and Hanlon (1970). This was the first paper to investigate whether parents correct their children's ungrammatical utterances, and for over a decade it was the *only* such study. The data analyzed in this paper comes from a large set of transcripts of mother-child interaction involving three children, known as 'Adam', 'Eve', and 'Sarah'. The children were recorded in their homes one or more times each week over a period of several years. The transcripts from this project became the first corpus of child language; they were digitized in the 1980s as CHILDES (the CHIld Language Data Exchange System), which now includes data from many other studies and is freely available online for research.

Brown and Hanlon analyzed parents' responses to four specific grammatical constructions: yes-no questions, *wh*-questions, tags (*This is a ball, <u>isn't it?</u>*), and negative sentences. These are constructions that the syntactic theory of the time predicted to be complex – sensibly so, since young children often take a while to master them fully. Brown and Hanlon wanted to know how children come to learn which of their productions are grammatical and which are ungrammatical; they conducted two analyses examining whether parents respond differently to grammatical and ungrammatical utterances, thus possibly giving their children a hint as to which is which.

For their first analysis, Brown and Hanlon coded each of the children's productions of these four constructions as either 'primitive' (i.e., ungrammatical in the adult language) or 'well-formed'. They included data only from the later months of the project, when the children were old enough that they were actually attempting these constructions fairly often. Then they coded each adult response to these utterances as a 'sequitur' (an appropriate response that demonstrated understanding of what the child had said) or a 'non sequitur'

Table 5.1 *Proportions of parents' sequiturs and non sequiturs in response to children's primitive (P) and well-formed (WF) utterances, by grammatical construction. Roger Brown and Camille Hanlon, Derivational complexity and order of acquisition in child speech,* Cognition and the Development of Language, *J. R. Hayes, ed., 1970, Table 1.10. Reprinted by permission of John Wiley & Sons.*

	Yes-No		Wh		Tags		Negatives		Means		
	P	WF	P	WF	P	WF	P	WF	P	WF	
Sequiturs	.70	.83	.44	.45			.70	.31	.61	.53	Eve
Non Sequiturs	.18	.13	.37	.18			.20	.49	.25	.27	
Sequiturs	.48	.46	.45	.37	.54	.56	.00	.24	.31	.36	Adam
Non Sequiturs	.50	.43	.50	.52	.42	.44	.86	.52	.62	.49	
Sequiturs	.47	.52	.38	.52	.52	.36	.33	.41	.42	.45	Sarah
Non Sequiturs	.53	.47	.62	.43	.48	.57	.56	.51	.55	.50	
									.45	.45	Means
									.47	.42	

(a response or question that suggested the parent did *not* understand what the child had said, or no response at all).

Brown and Hanlon hypothesized that if the parent obviously fails to understand what the child has said, the child may conclude that he has made a mistake. If children really do get reliable feedback in this way, then sequiturs should tend to occur after well-formed utterances and non sequiturs should tend to occur after primitive utterances. Table 5.1 summarizes Brown and Hanlon's results, and it doesn't show the expected pattern. The overall means at the bottom right of the table show that non sequiturs were slightly more likely to occur after primitive than well-formed utterances, but the difference is extremely small and not statistically significant. In addition, there's a large amount of variation evident in the rest of the table: there is no consistent pattern either across parents or across construction types.

In a second analysis, Brown and Hanlon explored whether parents provide a more explicit kind of feedback. They found all of the parents' utterances from two stages of the project that were either explicit approvals (*That's right, Very good*) or explicit disapprovals (*That's wrong, No*). They also coded the child's utterance immediately before the (dis)approval as either correct or incorrect. If parents are explicitly correcting their children's language, then we should expect to find more approvals after well-formed utterances and more disapprovals after primitive ones. Table 5.2 summarizes the results. The expected pattern is simply not there; in fact, in all but one of the cases (Eve at Stage V), the difference goes in the wrong direction – parents were more likely to offer approval after mistakes!

Table 5.2 *Parents' approvals and disapprovals in response to children's correct and incorrect utterances. Roger Brown and Camille Hanlon, Derivational complexity and order of acquisition in child speech,* Cognition and the Development of Language, *J. R. Hayes, ed., 1970, Table 1.11. Reprinted by permission of John Wiley & Sons.*

Stage II

	Sarah			Adam			Eve	
	Correct	Incorrect		Correct	Incorrect		Correct	Incorrect
App.	4	9	App.	4	3	App.	6	19
Dis.	4	6	Dis.	2	0	Dis.	3	5

Stage V

	Sarah			Adam			Eve	
	Correct	Incorrect		Correct	Incorrect		Correct	Incorrect
App.	23	4	App.	13	6	App.	33	29
Dis.	12	2	Dis.	7	1	Dis.	12	15

Brown and Hanlon conclude that parents don't provide explicit correction when their children say something ungrammatical. In fact, their impression from the transcripts is that parents respond based on whether or not what the child says is true, not whether it is grammatical.

(2) Approval of truthful, ungrammatical utterances (Brown and Hanlon 1970, 49)

a. ADAM: Draw a boot paper.
MOTHER: That's right. Draw a boot on paper.

b. EVE: Mama isn't boy, he a girl.
MOTHER: That's right.

(3) Disapproval of untruthful, grammatical utterances (Brown and Hanlon 1970, 49)

a. ADAM: And Walt Disney comes on Tuesday.
MOTHER: No, he does not.

b. SARAH: There's the animal farmhouse.
MOTHER: No, that's a lighthouse.

Thus, Brown and Hanlon failed to find any evidence that parents give their children feedback when they make mistakes. For years, this paper was *the* definitive study of the question, and many linguists took the results to mean that children simply don't get negative evidence at all. If correct, this conclusion supports the Chomskyan theory that much of language is innate; to this day, many formal models of language acquisition are designed to work without negative evidence.

But this study is a small one, with only three children, and it's impossible to know how much these results tell us about what parents do in general. In addition, Brown and Hanlon considered only two kinds of feedback, and for one of them (explicit approval and disapproval), they found only a few examples. It's possible that parents provide feedback in other ways, or that we would see an effect in a larger dataset. Fortunately, researchers took up the question again in the 1980s, leading to a series of studies that probe parent-child interactions in further detail.

5.3.2 *Repetitions and expansions as feedback: Hirsh-Pasek et al. (1984)*

Hirsh-Pasek et al. (1984) were concerned that Brown and Hanlon's results were too limited to justify the conclusion that children get no negative feedback during language acquisition. In a new study, they addressed two issues: whether parents provide negative evidence in some form other than explicit approval or disapproval, and whether parental feedback depends on the child's age.

Hirsh-Pasek et al. studied 40 upper-middle-class mother-child pairs; the children ranged in age from two to five years old. The children were all enrolled in the same nursery school where the mothers served as teaching assistants on a rotating basis. For each pair, the researchers videotaped one half-hour interaction before school on a day when the mother worked as an assistant. These interactions were coded using a system very similar to that of Brown and Hanlon: children's utterances were coded as either well-formed or ill-formed, and mothers' responses were coded as approval or disapproval (or neither). In addition, mothers' responses were coded again for whether or not they repeated part of the child's immediately preceding utterance. The three coding categories were 'strict repetitions', 'loose repetitions', and 'non-repetitions'; an utterance was counted as a strict or loose repetition if it differed from what the child had just said in only a few specific ways.

(4) Differences between children's utterances and mothers' responses allowed in 'repetitions' (coding scheme of Hirsh-Pasek et al. 1984, 84)

a. Correction of an ill-formed utterance
People lives in Florida → *People live in Florida*

b. Interchange of *I* and *you*
I in school → *You're in school*

c. Addition of filler words
It fell in there → Yes, it fell in there
d. Interchange of content words and proforms
Where did you get them? → Where did you get these things?
e. Addition or deletion of modifiers
What do you do with a wooden block? → What do you do with a little wooden block?
f. Partial repetition
That's a mailbox → A mailbox
g. Repetition plus more material
Pat had a slide → Pat had a slide but I don't know what she did with the slide

Table 5.3 summarizes the results for explicit approval and disapproval, pooled across all children. Like Brown and Hanlon, Hirsh-Pasek et al. found no evidence that mothers tend to approve of grammatical utterances and disapprove of ungrammatical ones. If anything, the results go the wrong way (mothers approved of 84% of well-formed utterances and 86% of ill-formed ones), and at any rate the difference isn't even close to being statistically significant. Hirsh-Pasek et al. agree with Brown and Hanlon's impression that mothers give approval or disapproval in response to the truthfulness of the child's utterance, not its grammaticality.

But the repetitions tell a different story. As Table 5.4 shows, for most age groups, mothers were no more or less likely to repeat a well-formed utterance than an ill-formed one. But for the two-year-olds, mothers repeated 21% of their children's ill-formed utterances (42 out of 202) but only 12% of well-formed utterances, a statistically significant difference.

On the basis of these results, Hirsh-Pasek et al. conclude that mothers do in fact respond differently to their children depending on whether what the child has just said is grammatical or not: they are more likely to repeat ungrammatical utterances. Moreover, this effect appears to be limited to two-year olds; it wasn't found with older children. It's theoretically possible, then, that a child could use these differences to help zero in on the correct grammar: *If Mom repeats what I just said, maybe I made a mistake somewhere; if she moves on, I'm probably fine.*

But the simple existence of a difference doesn't guarantee that children actually use it; Hirsh-Pasek et al. themselves emphasize this point. For one thing, we certainly do *not* see a pattern whereby mothers always repeat ungrammatical utterances and never repeat grammatical ones; overall, they repeat less than a third of the time, but they tend to do so a little more often when the child has said something ungrammatical. Thus, the fact that Mom repeats what the child has just said isn't a terribly reliable indicator

Table 5.3 *Mothers' approval and disapproval in response to children's well-formed and ill-formed utterances. Kathy Hirsh-Pasek, Rebecca Treiman, and Maita Schneiderman, Brown & Hanlon revisited: Mothers' sensitivity to ungrammatical forms,* Journal of Child Language *1984, Table 2. Reprinted by permission of Cambridge University Press.*

	Approval	Disapproval
Well-formed	147	29
Ill-formed	38	6

Table 5.4 *Mothers' repetitions and non-repetitions of children's well-formed and ill-formed utterances, broken down by age. Kathy Hirsh-Pasek, Rebecca Treiman, and Maita Schneiderman, Brown & Hanlon revisited: Mothers' sensitivity to ungrammatical forms,* Journal of Child Language *1984, Table 3. Reprinted by permission of Cambridge University Press.*

	Repeated	Not repeated	
Two-year-olds			
Well-formed	42	307	$\chi^2(1) = 6.93$
Ill-formed	42	160	$P < 0.01$
Three-year-olds			
Well-formed	45	219	$\chi^2(1) = 0.40$
Ill-formed	10	66	n.s.
Four-year-olds			
Well-formed	30	261	$\chi^2(1) = 0.0001$
Ill-formed	6	57	n.s.
Five-year-olds			
Well-formed	32	462	$\chi^2(1) = 1.36$
Ill-formed	6	44	n.s.

of whether the child's utterance was grammatical or not. Another consideration is the fact that Hirsh-Pasek et al.'s results average over forty different mothers; we don't know whether *all* the mothers exhibited this difference, or whether only some did. If we're looking for feedback that is *necessary* for language learning, then something that only some mothers do can't be it.

Finally, we might ask whether the researchers' definition of what counts as a 'repetition' is the same as the child's: are these differences robust if we use other criteria? A related issue is *why* a repetition would signal to the child that something is wrong. Hirsh-Pasek et al. allowed for many minor changes in the utterances that they classified as repetitions; some of these were explicit corrections of the child's utterance, but others were not. Repetitions with corrections might draw the child's attention to the specific part of the utterance that was wrong, but only if the child can distinguish genuine corrections from other minor alterations. In other words, how does the child know that the parent who changed *lives* to *live* in example (4a) was correcting a mistake, but that the parent who added *little* in example (4e) was not?

This study, then, is valuable for two reasons. First, it replicates Brown and Hanlon's findings about explicit (dis)approval with a larger group of children. Second, it shows that parents may indeed respond differently to grammatical and ungrammatical utterances by children, albeit in subtler ways than previously imagined.

5.3.3 The immediate effect of feedback: Saxton (2000)

Even if parents do correct their children's mistakes, there's no guarantee that children actually listen. Several anecdotes along these lines have circulated among linguists for decades:

(5) A child's reluctance to imitate, quoted from Jean Berko Gleason in Cazden (1972, 92)

CHILD: My teacher holded the baby rabbits and we patted them.
MOTHER: Did you say your teacher held the baby rabbits?
CHILD: Yes.
MOTHER: What did you say she did?
CHILD: She holded the baby rabbits and we patted them.
MOTHER: Did you say she held them tightly?
CHILD: No, she holded them loosely.

(6) A child's resistance to correction, Braine (1971, 160–161)

CHILD: Want other one spoon, Daddy.
FATHER: You mean, you want THE OTHER SPOON.
CHILD: Yes, I want other one spoon, please, Daddy.
FATHER: Can you say 'the other spoon'?
CHILD: Other... one... spoon.
FATHER: Say... 'other'.
CHILD: Other.
FATHER: Spoon.

CHILD: Spoon.
FATHER: Other... spoon.
CHILD: Other... spoon. Now give me other one spoon?

Anecdotes like these are charming, but we need more systematic evidence if we want to learn whether parental feedback (if given at all) actually affects how children speak. This is the question addressed by Saxton (2000), who investigated whether children actually appear to be sensitive to the implicit feedback documented by Hirsh-Pasek et al. Saxton studied the CHILDES transcripts for one child (Eve) to see whether she was more likely to correct her own ungrammatical utterances after certain types of adult responses.

Saxton chose eleven types of errors to study and identified all of Eve's utterances that contained at least one error. Error categories included mistakes like incorrect forms of irregular verbs (*Where it goed?*), lack of plural *-s* on nouns (*I cut scissor*), and omission of the subject of the sentence (*Spill soup*). The adult response to each error was coded as belonging to one of five categories:

Negative evidence: The adult repeats and corrects the relevant part of the child's utterance.

CHILD: He was the *baddest* one.
ADULT: Yeah, he sounds like the *worst*.

Negative feedback: The adult indicates in a non-specific way that something was wrong with the child's utterance.

CHILD: I just *blowed* on your dinner for a little bit.
ADULT: On my dinner?

Adult move-on: The adult continues the conversation.

Positive input: The adult's response contains a correct example of the grammatical construction for which the child made a mistake, but doesn't use the child's exact words.

Non-error-contingent clarification question: The adult asks for clarification about something unrelated to the child's grammatical error.

Finally, Saxton coded the child's response to the adult's response with one of three categories: 'Use Correct' (the child uses a correct form of the grammatical construction for which she had just made a mistake), 'Persist-with-Error' (the child makes the same mistake again), and 'Child Move-On' (all other responses). If children are sensitive to negative evidence and negative feedback as a suggestion that their utterances may have been incorrect, then we should expect them to self-correct more often after these responses.

Table 5.5 summarizes the results. The first thing to notice is that the vast majority of Eve's responses were move-ons; in other words, most of the time,

Table 5.5 *Eve's self-corrections after adult responses. Adapted from Table 2 of Matthew Saxton, Negative evidence and negative feedback: Immediate effects on the grammaticality of child speech,* First Language *20, pp. 221–252, copyright 2000. Reprinted by permission of SAGE Publications.*

Adult response	Use correct		Persist-with-error		Child move-on	
Negative evidence	157	7.8%	344	17.2%	1505	75.0%
Negative feedback	69	6.6%	241	22.9%	744	70.6%
Adult move-ons	56	2.9%	453	23.4%	1424	73.7%
Positive input	629	6.5%	1506	15.6%	7495	77.8%

she wasn't just repeating herself (probably a good thing for her parents' sanity). Second, she was slightly more likely to correct herself after negative evidence (7.8% of the time) than after an adult move-on (2.9% of the time); Saxton reports that the difference is statistically significant at $p < 0.003$. Thus, these results suggest that Eve may in fact have been using adult responses to monitor her own speech: she was more likely to correct herself if she heard an adult model a correct form of what she had just said than if the adult simply moved on with the conversation.

Note, though, that Eve's overall rate of self-correction was fairly low, and that these results average over nine months, a period during which her language developed dramatically. Saxton hypothesized that adult feedback might be more important at some stages of development than others. A child who has only just begun to use a particular construction, for example, may not yet be able to handle feedback in a useful way. To test whether feedback had a larger effect in later stages, Saxton identified for each grammatical construction the age at which Eve began producing that construction with at least 50% accuracy, and analyzed only the subset of the data in which Eve's performance was 50% or better.

Table 5.6 compares the results of the two analyses. Compared to the averages across the entire 9-month period (left column), Eve was much more likely to self-correct in her later stages of development. Moreover, she was more likely to self-correct following negative evidence and negative feedback than following an adult move-on or positive input. Saxton concludes that parental feedback does indeed appear to affect children's speech, at least in the short term.

Returning to our larger question of whether children use parental feedback in learning language, Saxton's study provides us with a definite 'maybe'. On the one hand, Eve does appear to use language differently depending on her mother's responses of various types; she's more likely to correct her own

Table 5.6 *Eve's responses to adult responses over the entire 9-month observation period and from the point at which she had attained* 50% *accuracy. Adapted from Table 3 of Matthew Saxton, Negative evidence and negative feedback: Immediate effects on the grammaticality of child speech,* First Language *20, pp. 221–252, copyright 2000. Reprinted by permission of SAGE Publications.*

Adult response	All data		Data from 50% accuracy	
Negative evidence	7.8%	(157)	20.5%	(84)
Negative feedback	6.6%	(69)	17.4%	(40)
Adult move-ons	2.9%	(56)	7.1%	(32)
Positive input	6.5%	(629)	9.5%	(465)

mistakes after her mother says something that suggests her previous utterance may have been incorrect in some way. On the other hand, it's hard to know whether these short-term differences translate into long-term effects. Do these self-corrections really show that Eve has learned something, or is she merely repeating her mother's words without understanding the difference between her own previous utterance and her mother's corrected one? In addition, even if Eve does use her mother's feedback, can we conclude that all children do the same thing, or even that all children get similar kinds of feedback? There's a difference between concluding that some children are able to use negative evidence, and concluding that negative evidence is *necessary* in order to learn language.

5.3.4 *The short-term and long-term effect of feedback: Morgan et al. (1995)*

Morgan et al. (1995) conducted an analysis similar to Saxton's. Instead of analyzing a wide range of grammatical constructions for just one child, though, they examined just two constructions and included data from Adam, Eve, and Sarah. In addition, they explored both the short-term effects of parental feedback (whether the child immediately self-corrected) and the long-term effects (whether hearing more feedback for a particular construction encouraged the child to improve faster).

The two constructions analyzed by Morgan et al. were articles (*the*, *a*) and *wh*-questions. In English, certain types of nouns must be accompanied by an article (or, more precisely, by a *determiner*; see section 2.2.1 for details), but young children frequently omit them (e.g., *Mama isn't boy* instead of *Mama isn't a boy*). In *wh*-questions, Standard English requires the *wh*-word to be followed by a particular type of verb called an *auxiliary* that would ordinarily occur after the subject of the sentence; young children frequently fail to move the auxiliary, producing questions like *Why you didn't put the top on?* instead of *Why didn't you put the top on?*

Like previous researchers, Morgan et al. found that mothers were more likely to expand on the child's utterance (i.e., to repeat part or all of it, possibly adding new material) if it was ungrammatical, but more likely to move on if it was grammatical. These effects were significant both for articles and for *wh*-questions ($p < .01$ for each construction for each child). To assess the short-term effect of these maternal response types, they examined whether children were more likely to self-correct ungrammatical utterances after expansions versus move-ons. In contrast to Saxton's results, Morgan et al. found no evidence for a pattern like this; in fact, in several cases, they found that children were more likely to self-correct after move-ons! The results did not change when the researchers considered only repetitions of the same noun or only interactions from stages when the children had attained at least 50% accuracy in the relevant construction. In other words, the children didn't appear to be using parental feedback to correct their speech.

Morgan et al. also explored whether parental feedback appeared to have a long-term effect on children's speech. Although they failed to find an effect here too, these analyses are more difficult to interpret, and their statistical methods have been criticized by Bohannon et al. (1996).

At least for short-term effects, when compared with Saxton's findings, Morgan et al.'s results suggest the opposite conclusion: there is no evidence from this particular analysis that parental feedback has any effect on how children learn to speak. Of course, just as Saxton's results don't prove that all children respond to negative evidence, Morgan et al.'s don't prove that none do. Clearly, further research is necessary to determine whether, and to what extent, children's language is actually affected by their parents' implicit feedback.

5.3.5 General conclusions

These studies bear on several interlocking questions about how children learn language. To the first question, whether parents systematically and explicitly correct their children's grammatical mistakes, we can answer a resounding 'no'. This was the original finding of Brown and Hanlon, and to my knowledge every study of the issue since then has arrived at the same conclusion.

As we have seen, though, a related but more subtle question is whether parents do *anything* that could provide children with reliable information as to whether their utterances are correct or not. To this question we can give a qualified 'yes': several studies have found that parents are more likely, for example, to ask for clarification in response to an ungrammatical utterance, but to simply move on with the conversation in response to a grammatical one.

These questions are interesting and worth studying in their own right – but for many people, they're important because of their implications for language learning in general. For many linguists, the Big Question is the nature of humans' ability to use language: to what degree is language an innate ability, and to what degree is it learned? To discover the answer, we need to know something about what conditions are necessary in order for a child to learn language, and part of this is knowing what kind of feedback the language learner receives. The less evidence children have for the rules they're learning, the more evidence linguists have that children are drawing on innate knowledge in order to do what they do. By contrast, if we find that all the information necessary to learn a particular grammatical rule is present in the child's environment, there's no reason to assume that the relevant knowledge was present at birth.

But if we want to understand how first-language acquisition works in general, then these studies are only the beginning of the necessary research. Note that all these studies assume a very specific model of children's linguistic socialization: conversation happens between the child and an adult caretaker (almost always the mother); there are exactly two people involved in the conversation; the adult is focused on the child and frequently repeats or expands on the child's utterances. As we have seen, this is a typical pattern for many middle-class western families, but when we take a more global perspective we see that it's far from the only one. It's all well and good to discover that some middle-class parents tend to expand on their children's ungrammatical utterances; but before we conclude that this kind of feedback is necessary for language acquisition, we should remind ourselves that there are societies in which adults simply do not interact with children in this way. If we want to apply what we know about language acquisition to general questions of human cognition, then cross-linguistic and cross-cultural research is crucial.

For many parents, the most pressing question is 'What should I do to help my child learn language?' Linguists typically reply, 'Relax – you're doing fine.' It's certainly not necessary to give children explicit instruction or correct them when they make mistakes; one of the few points of agreement in the literature is that parents don't do this consistently anyway, and their kids are fine. Each child acquires language at a different rate, but overall, patterns of language acquisition appear to be remarkably stable even across cultures with very different child-rearing practices. Children, it seems, are born ready to learn language, and as long as they're surrounded by a community of language users, they will succeed.

5.4 Summary

- Many western adults believe that adults teach language to children, usually by speaking directly to them. But this belief is far from universal, and there are societies in which adults rarely speak directly to young children.
- Children around the world acquire language in similar ways, regardless of how adults interact with them. Explicit instruction is not necessary to learn a first language.
- Some research suggests that children whose parents talk to them more have more advanced linguistic skills. But we must be cautious in interpreting results like these, since they rely on imperfect measures of children's linguistic abilities and may be confounded by culture-specific assumptions.
- There is no evidence that parents generally correct their children's grammatical mistakes.
- Some parents tend to repeat or expand on their children's utterances, but it is unclear whether children actually use this kind of feedback to correct their own speech. Since there are societies in which this kind of interaction is rare, it is unlikely that repetitions and expansions are absolutely necessary for language acquisition.

For further reflection

(1) Interview a parent with young children from a country other than your own. How does the parent usually talk to his or her children? What kinds of experiences does the parent believe children need in order to learn language? In what ways are the parent's beliefs and practices related to children and language similar to your own beliefs (or those of your parents), and in what ways are they different?

(2) Go to the online CHILDES database (http://childes.psy.cmu.edu/) and navigate to the Providence database (`Browsable Database` → `Eng-NA` → `Providence`). Browse through some of the transcripts. Find one example of a parent offering explicit approval in response to something the child says, and one example of a parent offering explicit disapproval. As far as you can tell from the context, why do you think the parent responded with (dis)approval? Was the parent reacting to the child's grammatical correctness, the truth or falseness of the child's statement, whether the child was being polite, or something else?

Important: Although parts of CHILDES are freely available online, the database is intended for researchers. If you have problems or questions, please contact your instructor, not the people who maintain CHILDES.

(3) Other studies of parental feedback include Penner (1987), Bohannon and Stanowicz (1988), and Farrar (1992). Read one of these papers and compare it to the studies discussed in this chapter. How were children's and adults' responses coded? What did the researchers find? Are you convinced by the results?

Further reading

Lust (2006) is an introductory-level textbook on child language acquisition. Lieven (1994) is a useful summary of some cross-cultural differences in how children are spoken to, and what these differences imply for theories of language acquisition.

Gleitman and Newport (1995) summarizes the major arguments that language is innate. Goldin-Meadow and Mylander (1990) is a review of research on homesign systems of deaf children of hearing parents. Derek Bickerton is the leading proponent of the view that creolization is driven entirely by children; Bickerton (1983) is an accessible summary of his views. The authoritative reference work on SLI is Leonard (2014).

The results of the Hart and Risley study are reported in Hart and Risley (1995); a highly condensed summary of the same material can be found in Hart and Risley (2003). For critiques, see Dudley-Marling and Lucas (2009), Miller and Sperry (2012), Michaels (2013), and Blum and Riley (2014). Hoff (2006) summarizes a large body of literature on the relationship between children's environment and their language development. Labov (1976) describes the ways in which standard language assessments are inappropriate for some children. Zentella (2005) discusses how the literacy practices of some communities are often not recognized by schools and other institutions, and Miller et al. (2005) review the literature on storytelling skills in working-class communities.

Following Hirsh-Pasek et al. (1984), a large number of studies have investigated whether parents respond differently to children's grammatical and ungrammatical utterances; examples include Penner (1987), Bohannon and Stanowicz (1988), Morgan and Travis (1989), Furrow et al. (1993), Post (1994), and Strapp (1999). Studies that explore whether these responses affect children's speech include Farrar (1992) and Chouinard and Clark (2003); the latter studies children learning French and English.

Bibliography

Bickerton, Derek. Creole languages. *Scientific American*, 249(8):116–122, 1983.

Blum, Susan D., and Kathleen C. Riley. Selling the language gap. *Anthropology News*, August 7 2014.

Bohannon, John Neil, III, Robert J. Padgett, Keith E. Nelson, and Melvin Mark. Useful evidence on negative evidence. *Developmental Psychology*, 32(3):551–555, 1996.

Bohannon, John Neil, III and Laura Stanowicz. The issue of negative evidence: Adult responses to children's language errors. *Developmental Psychology*, 24(5):684–689, 1988.

Braine, Martin D. S. On two types of models of the internalization of grammars. In Dan I. Slobin, editor, *The Ontogenesis of Grammar: A Theoretical Symposium*, pages 153–186. Academic Press, New York, NY, 1971.

Brown, Roger, and Camille Hanlon. Derivational complexity and order of acquisition in child speech. In J. R. Hayes, editor, *Cognition and the Development of Language*, chapter 1, pages 11–53. Wiley, New York, NY, 1970.

Cazden, Courtney B. *Child Language and Education.* Holt, Rinehart and Winston, New York, NY, 1972.

Cho, Grace E., and Peggy J. Miller. Personal storytelling: Working-class and middle-class mothers in comparative perspective. In Marcia Farr, editor, *Ethnolinguistic Chicago: Language and Literacy in the City's Neighborhoods*, chapter 4, pages 79–101. Lawrence Erlbaum Associates, Mahwah, NJ, 2003.

Chouinard, Michelle M., and Eve V. Clark. Adult reformulations of child errors as negative evidence. *Journal of Child Language*, 30(3):637–669, 2003.

Dudley-Marling, Curt, and Krista Lucas. Pathologizing the language and culture of poor children. *Language Arts*, 86(5):362–370, 2009.

Farrar, Michael Jeffrey. Negative evidence and grammatical morpheme acquisition. *Developmental Psychology*, 28(1):90–98, 1992.

Furrow, David, Constance Baillie, Jennifer McLaren, and Chris Moore. Differential responding to two- and three-year-olds' utterances: The roles of grammaticality and ambiguity. *Journal of Child Language*, 20(2):363–375, 1993.

Gleitman, Lila R., and Elissa L. Newport. The invention of language by children: Environmental and biological influences on the acquisition of language. In Lila R. Gleitman and Mark Liberman, editors, *An Invitation to Cognitive Science: Language*, volume 1, chapter 1, pages 1–24. The MIT Press, Cambridge, MA, 2nd edition, 1995.

Goldin-Meadow, Susan, and Carolyn Mylander. Beyond the input given: The child's role in the acquisition of language. *Language*, 66(2):323–355, 1990.

Green, Lisa J., *African American English: A Linguistic Introduction.* Cambridge University Press, Cambridge, 2002.

Hart, Betty, and Todd R. Risley. *Meaningful Differences in the Everyday Experience of Young American Children.* Paul H. Brookes Publishing Company, Baltimore, MD, 1995.

Hart, Betty, and Todd R. Risley. The early catastrophe. *Education Review*, 17(1):110–118, 2003.

Heath, Shirley Brice. *Ways with Words: Language, Life, and Work in Communities and Classrooms.* Cambridge University Press, Cambridge, 1983.

Hirsh-Pasek, Kathy, Rebecca Treiman, and Maita Schneiderman. Brown & Hanlon revisited: Mothers' sensitivity to ungrammatical forms. *Journal of Child Language*, 11(1):81–88, 1984.

Hoff, Erika. How social contexts support and shape language development. *Developmental Review*, 26(1):55–88, 2006.

Labov, William. Systematically misleading data from test questions. *The Urban Review*, 9(3):146–169, 1976.

Leonard, Laurence B. *Children with Specific Language Impairment*. Language, Speech, and Communication. The MIT Press, Cambridge, MA, 2nd edition, 2014.

Lieven, Elena V. M. Crosslinguistic and crosscultural aspects of language addressed to children. In Clare Gallaway and Brian J. Richards, editors, *Input and Interaction in Language Acquisition*, chapter 3, pages 56–73. Cambridge University Press, Cambridge, 1994.

Lust, Barbara C. *Child Language: Acquisition and Growth*. Cambridge Textbooks in Linguistics. Cambridge University Press, Cambridge, 2006.

Michaels, Sarah. Déjà vu all over again: What's wrong with Hart & Risley and a "linguistic deficit" framework in early childhood education? *LEARNing Landscapes*, 7(1):23–41, 2013. Available at http://www.learninglandscapes.ca/images /documents/ll-no13/michaels.pdf.

Miller, Peggy J., Grace E. Cho, and Jeana R. Bracey. Working-class children's experience through the prism of personal storytelling. *Human Development*, 48(3):115–135, 2005.

Miller, Peggy J., and Douglas E. Sperry. Déjà vu: The continuing misrecognition of low-income children's verbal abilities. In Susan T. Fiske and Hazel Rose Markus, editors, *Facing Social Class: How Societal Rank Influences Interaction*, chapter 6, pages 109–130. Russell Sage Foundation, New York, NY, 2012.

Morgan, James L., and Lisa L. Travis. Limits on negative information in language input. *Journal of Child Language*, 16(3):531–552, 1989.

Morgan, James L., Katherine M. Bonamo, and Lisa L. Travis. Negative evidence on negative evidence. *Developmental Psychology*, 31(2):180–197, 1995.

Ochs, Elinor. Talking to children in Western Samoa. *Language in Society*, 11(1):77–104, 1982.

Ochs, Elinor, and Bambi B. Schieffelin. Language acquisition and socialization: Three developmental stories and their implications. In Richard A. Shweder and Robert A. LeVine, editors, *Culture Theory: Essays on Mind, Self, and Emotion*, chapter 11, pages 276–319. Cambridge University Press, Cambridge, 1984.

Penner, Sharon G. Parental responses to grammatical and ungrammatical child utterances. *Child Development*, 58(2):376–384, 1987.

Post, Kathryn Nolan. Negative evidence in the language learning environment of laterborns in a rural Florida community. In Jeffrey L. Sokolov and Catherine E. Snow, editors, *Handbook of Research in Language Development Using CHILDES*, pages 132–173. Routledge, New York, NY, 1994.

Saxton, Matthew. Negative evidence and negative feedback: Immediate effects on the grammaticality of child speech. *First Language*, 20:221–252, 2000.

Singleton, Jenny L., and Elissa L. Newport. When learners surpass their models: The acquisition of American Sign Language from inconsistent input. *Cognitive Psychology*, 49(4):370–407, 2004.

Strapp, Chehalis M. Mothers', fathers', and siblings' responses to children's language errors: Comparing sources of negative evidence. *Journal of Child Language*, 26(2):373–391, 1999.

Wiley, Angela R., Amanda J. Rose, Lisa K. Burger, and Peggy J. Miller. Constructing autonomous selves through narrative practices: A comparative study of working-class and middle-class families. *Child Development*, 69(3):833–847, 1998.

Zentella, Ana Celia. Premises, promises, and pitfalls of language socialization research in Latino families and communities. In Ana Celia Zentella, editor, *Building on Strength: Language and Literacy in Latino Families and Communities*, Language and Literacy, chapter 1, pages 13–30. Teachers College Press, New York, NY, 2005.

6 'Adults can't learn a new language'

Every human being learns at least one native language as an ordinary part of growing up. Exceptions are rare – severe abuse, for example, or physical or mental disorders that interfere with ordinary first-language acquisition. Not only that, but the process of learning a first language is remarkably uniform across individuals and communities: children typically go through similar stages in a similar order, although the exact timing of those stages is different for every child. And the outcome is always the same: every adult is a fluent, competent speaker of his or her native language.

But learning a second language is a very different thing. As discussed in Chapter 7, people vary widely in whether they speak multiple languages; and if so, how those languages are learned, and why. In some communities, it's ordinary and expected that people will continue to learn new languages into adulthood; in others, learning a second language is a rare accomplishment. And the outcome is anything but uniform: some people eventually learn a second language so well that they're almost indistinguishable from native speakers, while others have a strong accent even after decades of experience.

Second-language learning, then, leaves us with two mysteries: Why isn't it as successful as learning a first language? And why is it so much easier for some people than for others? In this chapter, we will explore these two related questions; our case study will focus on whether there is a 'critical period' for second-language learning – a restricted age range outside of which it's simply impossible to learn a new language as well as a native speaker. To put it differently: if you start learning a new language at 40, are you doomed to failure? Or, if you don't succeed, are you just not trying hard enough?

6.1 Age and second-language acquisition

6.1.1 The critical period hypothesis

The most obvious difference between first- and second-language acquisition is age. Your first language, of course, is the one (or perhaps more than one) that you learn as an infant and very young child. By definition, though, a second language is one that you learn *after* you already have a first language; we can't meaningfully talk about second-language acquisition until a person is old enough to already have a first language. And so, by necessity, second-language learners are older than first-language learners.

Many people believe that it's precisely this age difference that makes first- and second-language acquisition different things. The idea, essentially, is that all humans are capable of learning a language natively while they're young. But at some point in the aging process, maturational changes (probably in the brain) take this ability away; if you start learning a language after this point, you will never be as fluent as a native speaker, because the language-learning abilities you had as a child are simply gone.

Among linguists, this idea is known as the *critical period hypothesis*. The name comes from phenomena in the animal kingdom that seem to involve age limits: some baby birds, for example, will become attached to an appropriate moving object (usually a parent) while they are young and follow it around, but only if they're exposed to the object within a specific time frame. A lot of the debate surrounding the critical period hypothesis has to do with whether age-related differences in second-language acquisition, if there are any, work the same way as critical periods elsewhere in the animal kingdom. Does the ability to learn a second language drop off sharply after a certain age, or is there a more gradual decline? After the critical period, are people uniformly unable to achieve native-speaker fluency in a second language, or are there a few exceptional individuals who can do this? In this chapter, we will use *critical period hypothesis* as a general term for the idea that age matters in some way for second-language acquisition, regardless of the specific kind of effect it has.

6.1.2 The critical period and first-language acquisition

Lenneberg (1967) was one of the first to propose that there is a critical period for language learning. Although the critical period hypothesis is now closely associated with second-language acquisition, Lenneberg's original argument actually focused on learning a *first* language. That is, if a person doesn't learn any language at all during childhood, will that person be able to learn a language later in life? Lenneberg's evidence was necessarily indirect, and parts of his argument were based on ideas that we now know are probably false (for example, claims about how the brain develops). But some of his arguments suggest that there may be something crucial about early childhood for learning language.

One piece of evidence comes from some of the very sad cases of people who weren't exposed to a language as children, usually due to extreme abuse or neglect. Lenneberg argued that children who are discovered young eventually go on to acquire language normally, but not children who are discovered later (after puberty, for example). One of the most famous examples of this situation is 'Genie', a girl who was discovered at the age of 13 after over 10 years of near-total isolation. Genie was discovered not long after scholars such as Lenneberg and Noam Chomsky had begun publishing claims about the biological nature of language, so her case was of intense interest to linguists. She eventually learned to say a few words but never came close to acquiring a full language; therefore, some linguists argue that the example of Genie supports the critical period hypothesis: because she was too old when she started learning language, she was never able to do so successfully.

Genie's story is consistent with the critical period hypothesis, of course, but it isn't conclusive proof. Studying people like Genie is difficult because it's impossible to distinguish between the effects of not being exposed to language from everything else in her history. Did Genie fail to learn language simply because she never heard it, for example, or did the abuse make her incapable of learning language? Is it possible that she already had language problems at birth? (It seems that one of the reasons Genie's father neglected her is that he believed she was mentally retarded, although of course today we can't know whether he was right.)

Somewhat less ambiguous evidence comes from deaf children. A deaf child of signing parents, of course, learns a sign language as a native language in the ordinary way. (See Chapter 3 for discussion of how signed and spoken languages appear to be fundamentally the same thing, except that the former are visual and the latter are auditory.) But 90% of deaf children have hearing parents, and many of these parents don't sign (or don't do so while their children are very young). The result is that some deaf children grow up with the same care and support most children get, with one exception – the deaf children aren't exposed to language.[1]

Deaf children in this situation typically learn to sign from their deaf peers; their age when this first happens varies widely – anywhere from the preschool years to young adulthood. Sign language researchers have consistently found that the earlier a person starts to sign, the better that person's signing will be. Even adults with decades of signing experience may still have an imperfect mastery of the language if they didn't learn to sign as children. Thus, the evidence from sign language is consistent with (although not conclusive proof of)

[1] Many deaf children of hearing parents are exposed to some sort of spoken language, especially if they have some residual hearing or if they become deaf in early childhood, after they have already begun to acquire spoken language. But they don't get anything like the input that a hearing child receives, and the input that they do get may come in a formal setting at an older age anyway. (Something similar is true of children who receive cochlear implants, which require intensive training to use and don't work well for everyone.) Children who are profoundly and prelingually deaf are rarely able to master spoken language.

the idea that there is a critical period for first-language acquisition: if you don't learn *some* language as a child, you will never achieve native competence in *any* language.

One other phenomenon that might shed light on the issue is the question of whether a person's language can change during his or her lifetime. If language can't be learned after childhood, then it seems logical that language shouldn't change later in life – in other words, the way you talk as a teenager is the way you will talk as a 90-year-old. You may learn new words as you grow older, but your basic grammatical system will not change. Some research suggests that minor changes are actually possible within a person's lifetime; for example, Harrington et al. (2000) studied Queen Elizabeth II of England's Christmas radio broadcasts and found that her pronunciation of vowel sounds changed between the 1950s and the 1980s: as time went on, her speech became more similar to that of younger speakers in southern England. Sankoff and Blondeau (2007) studied speakers of Montreal French for several decades, during a period when the pronunciation of the *r* sound in the language was changing rapidly. Most of the speakers they recorded were consistent throughout their lifetimes: this means that the *r* sound was changing mostly because older speakers with the old pronunciation were being replaced by younger speakers with the new pronunciation. But a few speakers actually changed their own pronunciation: they used the old *r* sound at the beginning of the study, but eventually shifted to the new *r*.

It's hard to know exactly how to interpret examples like these, but they give us tantalizing hints about the degree to which language is truly 'fixed' during childhood. On the one hand, these are relatively minor changes – subtle shifts in pronunciation, not a major restructuring of the entire grammar of the language. This, combined with the fact that most of Sankoff and Blondeau's subjects did *not* change their pronunciation after adolescence, suggests that something like the critical period hypothesis is on the right track. But the fact that some individuals *do* show changes in their language over their lifetimes tells us that language may not be completely fixed during childhood after all; it's still malleable to at least some degree, although just how much it is able to change is still an open question.

Not all linguists accept these kinds of arguments for or against a first-language critical period, and at any rate the questions of whether a critical period exists for first- and second-language acquisition are logically independent. (For example, maybe learning a first language in childhood gives you a foundation that allows you to learn more languages later in life – but if you don't learn any language in childhood, the door is closed forever.) But the evidence is suggestive, and so it's worth investigating whether there is any reason to think that there might be a critical period for learning second languages too.

6.1.3 *The critical period and second-language acquisition*

In many ways, our everyday experience suggests that children are better at learning a second language than adults are. Many immigrant families, for example, find that the adults struggle with the language of their new country, while the children pick it up from their schoolmates very quickly. A critical period could explain these differences: the children become native-like speakers because they started learning during the crucial window; the adults started after the window was closed, so their mastery of the new language will always be limited.

But our anecdotal impressions may not be accurate; it's true that many adults struggle with a second language, but it's also true that many adults become competent and fluent speakers of a language they first learned late in life. In addition, even if children really are better on average at learning a second language than adults are, that fact by itself doesn't prove that there is a critical period for second-language acquisition: children and adults are different in many ways, and it could be that adults have trouble with new languages for some reason other than just their age. In the next section, we'll look at several studies that have attempted to determine whether age alone affects how well someone is able to learn a second language.

A couple of points are in order before we begin. First, most modern research on the critical period hypothesis makes a distinction between how fast a person can learn a second language and the person's *ultimate attainment* – that is, how fluent the person eventually becomes. As it turns out, adults are often faster than children in the earliest stages of learning a second language, and older children are faster than younger children; some of the research on this phenomenon is reviewed in Krashen et al. (1982a). But the advantage for older learners disappears quickly – within a few months, usually less than a year. In other words, adults start well but plateau quickly; children may start more slowly, but they continue to improve in a way that adults often don't.

The critical period hypothesis also does *not* claim that children can learn a new language just by hearing a few words in that language; some minimum level of exposure is necessary. Passive media input (e.g., television) won't make a child bilingual, and even regular classroom instruction isn't enough if it's isolated from what children do the rest of the day. Some type of sustained immersion appears to be necessary, regardless of age.

The last point to keep in mind is that many researchers are interested not just in whether there *exists* a relationship between age and ultimate attainment, but also in the particular *shape* of that relationship. Some of this interest is related to the debate over whether certain age-related effects really count as a true 'critical period' (in its more general sense) or not. For example, everyone agrees that if all people who start learning a second language before some age

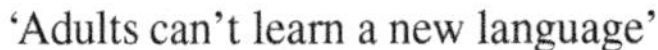

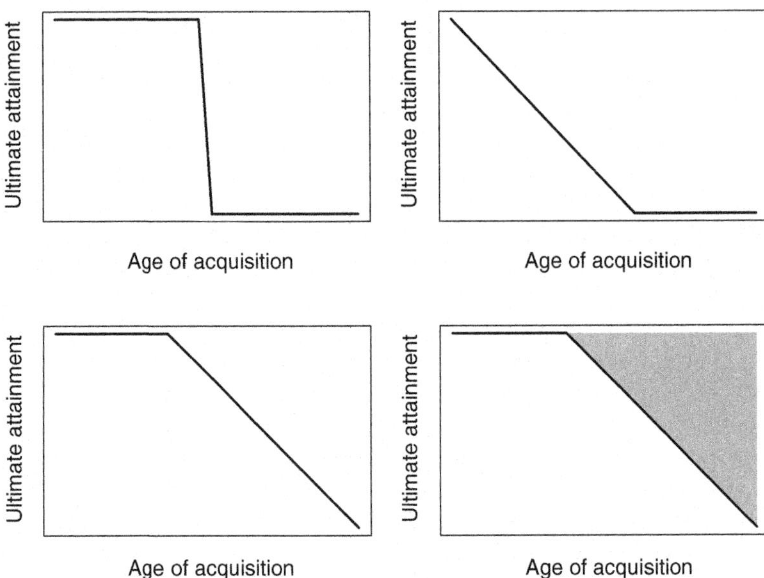

Figure 6.1 Examples of possible relationships between the age at which a person begins acquiring a second language and the person's ultimate fluency in that language.

(e.g., puberty) go on to become native speakers, but no one who starts after that age ever becomes fully fluent, then we would have clear evidence that there's a critical period for second-language learning; this is the scenario illustrated in the top left graph of Figure 6.1. But there are many other possibilities, and not everyone agrees on what kinds of relationships between age and ultimate attainment would count as a critical period. For example, maybe a person's fluency declines gradually with increasing age, but after a certain age ultimate fluency is uniformly poor (top right). Alternatively, maybe young learners do uniformly well, but ultimate attainment declines gradually with age after a certain point (bottom left). Or perhaps ultimate attainment declines uniformly with age of acquisition, and there is no obvious cutoff of any type.

Not only does the shape of the curve matter, but we might see different amounts of variation at different ages. The bottom right graph of Figure 6.1 shows one possibility. In this scenario, all young learners of a second language go on to become native speakers. After a certain age, ultimate attainment decreases, but not for everyone – some older learners struggle, while others do extremely well. In other words, in this scenario, starting young guarantees that a person will master a second language thoroughly; later in life, individuals can have very different outcomes.

As noted above, in this chapter we're using the term *critical period hypothesis* very loosely, as a general term for the idea that age by itself – not other differences among individuals that are correlated with age – affects how well a person will eventually learn a second language. Under this definition, all of the examples in Figure 6.1 would count as evidence for the critical period hypothesis. Thus, our primary interest in the studies discussed in the next section is whether they show *any* relationship between age and ultimate attainment, after controlling for possible confounding factors. But we should keep in mind that different researchers have different views of what the critical period hypothesis is (or should be), and many have a more specific interest in what *kind* of effect (if any) age has on fluency.

6.2 Case study: Are children more successful at learning a second language than adults?

6.2.1 Grammaticality judgments by Chinese and Korean speakers: Johnson and Newport (1989)

Johnson and Newport (1989) was one of the first large-scale studies of the critical period hypothesis, and it is the most well-known. The participants were 46 native speakers of Chinese and Korean who had immigrated to the United States at various ages; all of them had been learning English for at least five years and had been living in the United States for at least three. An additional group of 23 native English speakers was included for comparison. During the experiment, the subjects listened to a series of tape-recorded English sentences; for each sentence, they marked on a piece of paper whether they thought the sentence was grammatical or ungrammatical. The sentences were designed to test subjects' mastery of a variety of grammatical constructions in English, such as past-tense verbs and question formation.

As illustrated in Figure 6.2, there was a strong relationship between a subject's age of arrival in the United States and his or her performance on the test. The graph on the left shows the results for subjects who immigrated between the ages of 3 and 15; here, the youngest group performed just as well on the test as native speakers of English, and test scores declined gradually with increasing age of arrival. (The relationship between age and test score was significant at $p < .01$.) Subjects who arrived at 16 or later, shown in the graph on the right, performed more poorly in general (note that the y-axes for the two graphs are on different scales); also, within this group, there was no statistically significant relationship between age of arrival and test score ($p > .05$). In other words, after the age of 15, there was no benefit to starting a new language earlier or later.

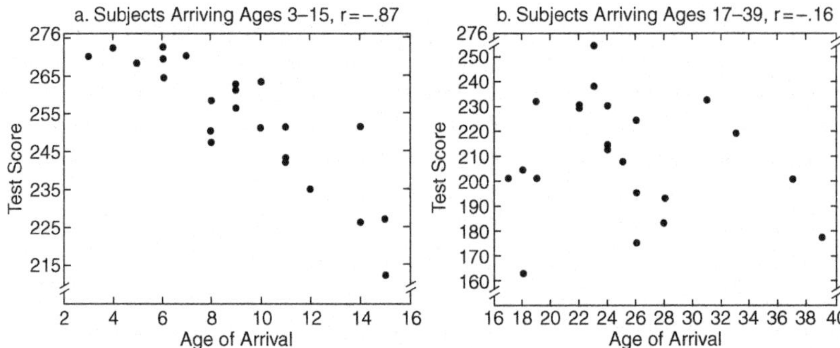

Figure 6.2 Relationship between age of arrival in the United States of Chinese and Korean immigrants and performance on an oral test of English syntax. Reprinted from *Cognitive Psychology*, 21, Jacqueline S. Johnson and Elissa L. Newport, Critical period effects in second language learning: The influence of maturational state on the acquisition of English as a second language, 60–99, copyright 1989, Figure 2, with permission from Elsevier.

To test whether they had really discovered an effect of age, Johnson and Newport checked several possible confounding variables. First, they found that there was no relationship between a subject's test score and the length of time he or she had been living in the United States ($p > .05$); in other words, their findings were not simply due to the fact that the subjects who had immigrated earlier had also been living in the United States longer, and therefore had more practice speaking English. Similarly, having taken English classes before immigration didn't improve the test scores of the late learners.

Johnson and Newport also asked the subjects several questions about their attitudes related to English – how motivated they were to learn it, how self-conscious they felt while learning it, and how strongly they identified with American culture. Not surprisingly, they found that attitudinal variables like these were related both to test scores *and* to age of arrival in the United States: subjects who identified more strongly with American culture, for example, tended to have higher scores and also tended to have immigrated at younger ages. However, Johnson and Newport found that even after they controlled statistically for variables like these, there was still a significant effect of age of arrival. In other words, younger immigrants weren't more fluent just because they were also more motivated to learn English; their age still mattered even after motivation was factored out. In fact, Johnson and Newport argued that age of acquisition was more important than any of the attitudinal variables they measured.

Based on these results, Johnson and Newport concluded that they had indeed found evidence for the critical period hypothesis. Before puberty (or thereabouts), younger is better: the youngest arrivals learned English just as well as native speakers, and performance gradually declined with age. After puberty, almost no one scored as well on the test as native speakers, but otherwise age didn't seem to matter – that is, immigrants who had arrived at 20 did no better, on average, than immigrants who had arrived at 30. There was much more variation among the older arrivals than there was among the younger arrivals.

Johnson and Newport managed to factor out several possible confounding variables in their study, and for this reason many linguists find their results highly convincing. But, of course, the experiment isn't perfect. One weakness is that the authors tested a relatively uniform group of subjects. To be convinced of the critical period hypothesis, we would want to see these results replicated with speakers of other languages, and with people from different demographic groups (all the subjects were students or faculty at an American university). In addition, although the researchers tested several possible confounds (such as motivation), there may well be other differences between older and younger arrivals that they couldn't control for. One final weakness of the study is that the test assessed one very narrow aspect of English competence: how accurately subjects could identify grammatical vs. ungrammatical English sentences that were presented orally. Other ways of testing fluency in a second language could yield very different results; in fact, in a follow-up study, Johnson (1992) found that subjects did better on a written version of the same test. Her findings suggest that the critical period, if it's real, may have different effects on different aspects of language: older arrivals are clearly at a disadvantage in oral language processing, but they are much more similar to younger learners on a written test.

6.2.2 Accent: Flege et al. (1995)

Johnson and Newport's study tested learners' mastery of English morphology and syntax: their ability to use the correct word order in sentences, and to use the appropriate inflectional suffixes on nouns and verbs. Flege et al. (1995) investigated another aspect of language learners' speech – their 'foreign accent'. Flege et al.'s subjects were 240 Italian immigrants to Canada, all of whom had been living there for at least 15 years, plus 24 native English speakers for comparison. The subjects read a list of English sentences, and then another group of native English speakers rated the recordings on how strong they thought the speaker's accent was.

Figure 6.3 shows the relationship between age of arrival and accentedness rating; each of the raters is plotted with a separate line. (The group of native speakers is shown with an arrival age of 0.) There is a clear trend: people

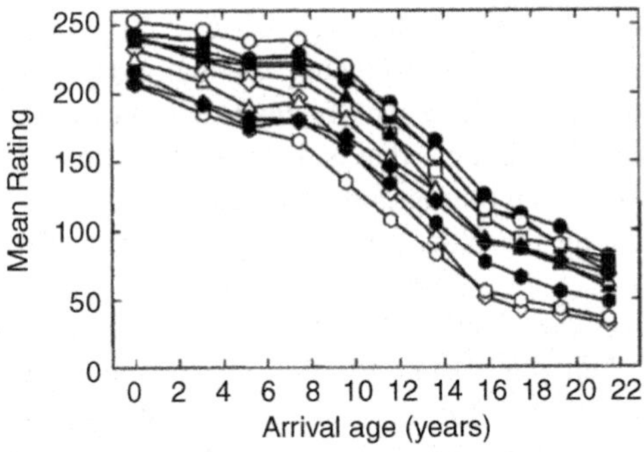

Figure 6.3 Foreign accent ratings by ten native English speakers for Italian immigrants who arrived in Canada at various ages. Native speakers are given an arrival age of 0. Reprinted with permission from James Emil Flege, Murray J. Munro, and Ian R. A. MacKay, Factors affecting strength of perceived foreign accent in a second language, *Journal of the Acoustical Society of America* 97(5):3125–3134. Copyright 1995, Acoustical Society of America.

who were older when they arrived in Canada were perceived to have stronger foreign accents; the relationship was statistically significant at $p < .01$. Flege et al. further concluded that there was no evidence for a steep decline at any particular age: they found that a straight line was just as good a fit for the data, statistically speaking, as a curved line with a sharp drop-off. Thus, their results suggest that age does matter for second-language acquisition, but there's no clear cutoff point that determines whether someone will have a foreign accent or not.

Like Johnson and Newport, Flege et al. tested for possible confounds such as how much the subjects used English vs. Italian and how motivated they were to learn English. Not surprisingly, factors like these were related to foreign accent too; people who used English more had weaker accents, for example. But there was a significant effect of age of acquisition even after controlling for these other variables, and in fact age of acquisition had a stronger effect on accent than any of the other factors Flege et al. tested.

Flege et al. concluded that age really does matter in the pronunciation of a second language: the older you are when you start learning the language, the stronger your accent will probably be. But they rejected the idea that age of acquisition has the kind of 'cutoff' assumed by many formulations of the critical period hypothesis; they found no evidence that foreign accent increases sharply at a particular age. (Some of the raters even detected differences between the native English speakers and the immigrants who had arrived as young as three years old!) Instead, they found a more gradual decline.

6.2.3 *The effect of aptitude: DeKeyser (2000)*

DeKeyser (2000) offers a different perspective on the critical period hypothesis. In several ways, DeKeyser's study was a replication of Johnson and Newport's, but with a different population: Hungarian immigrants (a total of 57) who had been living in the United States for at least 10 years. These subjects also seem to have been more diverse than Johnson and Newport's in terms of socioeconomic status and educational background.

The basic method was the same: subjects listened to recordings of English sentences and wrote down whether they thought those sentences were grammatical or ungrammatical. As shown in Figure 6.4, DeKeyser found a clear effect of subjects' age when they arrived in the United States; younger arrivals scored better. For all the subjects taken together, the relationship between age of arrival and test score was statistically significant ($p < .001$); interestingly, though, the relationship between age and score was *not* significant for just the group that had arrived before the age of 16, nor for just the group that had arrived after the age of 16. From this pattern, DeKeyser concluded that there is a clear drop-off around puberty: people who start to learn a second language before age 16 or so will do well, no matter what their precise age is; similarly, people who start after the age of 16 will do more poorly, regardless of whether they start at 20 or 40. Furthermore, there was no relationship between

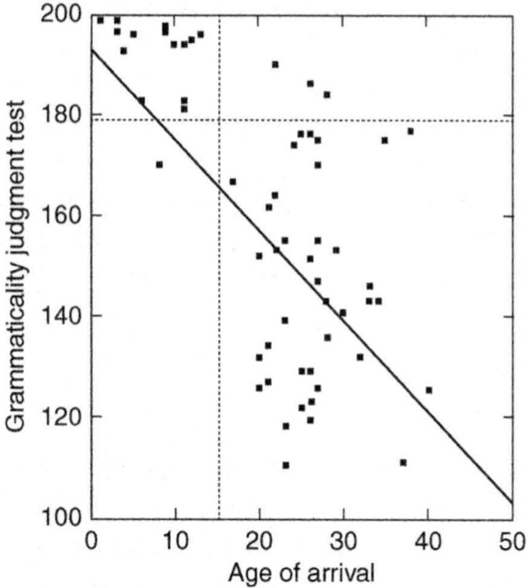

Figure 6.4 Relationship between score on a test of English syntax and age of arrival in the United States for Hungarian immigrants. Robert M. DeKeyser, The robustness of critical period effects in second language acquisition, *Studies in Second Language Acquisition* 22(4):2000, 499–533, Figure 1.

test scores and how old subjects were at the time of testing or how long they had been living in the United States.

DeKeyser not only asked subjects to take the English grammaticality test, he also gave them a standardized test of language-learning aptitude (in Hungarian). The idea behind this procedure was that if something like the critical period hypothesis is true, then a person who starts to learn a second language during the critical period is doing something fundamentally different from a person who starts after the critical period is over. Specifically, DeKeyser hypothesized that language learning during the critical period involves innate language-learning mechanisms that are universal to all humans (just like the mechanisms involved in first-language acquisition), but that language learning after the critical period is different, and some people are better at it than others. In support of this idea, DeKeyser found a statistically significant relationship between aptitude and English test score among subjects who had arrived after the age of 16 ($p < .05$): people with higher aptitude had better scores. But there was no relationship between aptitude and English test score among subjects who had arrived before 16.

DeKeyser's results are consistent with the hypothesis that learning a second language is different before puberty vs. after puberty. The results for the aptitude test are particularly striking; they suggest that anyone can learn a second language in childhood, but only some people have the necessary skills as adults. But one weakness of DeKeyser's study, which is true of several other tests of the critical period hypothesis, is that he had a small number of subjects who had started learning their second language during the putative critical period: only 15 of his 57 subjects were early arrivals. This means that experimental power is a serious problem in interpreting DeKeyser's results, especially since one of his crucial findings was a significant effect of aptitude among older arrivals but not among younger arrivals. Were test scores for the younger arrivals unrelated to aptitude because aptitude truly didn't matter for this group, or because the group was too small for the relationship to be seen?

6.2.4 Self-ratings in census data: Hakuta et al. (2003)

Hakuta et al. (2003) used a very different type of data to assess the critical period hypothesis: United States census records. They studied speakers of Spanish and Chinese in several states where detailed data for specific language groups was available from the 1990 census, and included only respondents who had been living in the United States for at least 10 years. This method provided a far larger number of respondents than any experimental study could hope to test: over 300,000 Chinese speakers and over 2 million Spanish speakers.

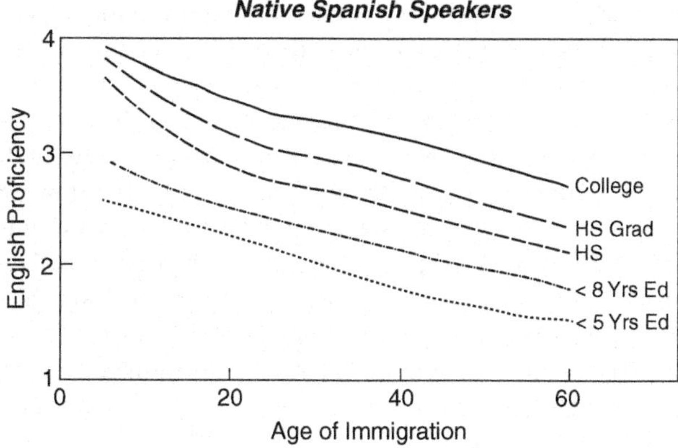

Figure 6.5 Smoothed curves representing English proficiency vs. age of arrival for Spanish speakers by level of education. Kenji Hakuta, Ellen Bialystok, and Edward Wiley, Critical evidence: A test of the critical-period hypothesis for second-language acquisition, *Psychological Science* 14(1), pp. 31–38, Figure 3, copyright 2003. Reprinted by permission of SAGE Publications.

Hakuta et al. calculated respondents' age of arrival in the United States based on the year they reported they had immigrated and their current reported age; they also calculated respondents' length of residence in the United States. One question on the census form asked respondents to assess their own ability to speak English: 'not at all', 'not well', 'well', 'very well', and 'speak only English'.

The curves in Figure 6.5 sketch the general relationship between age of immigration and English proficiency for the Spanish speakers; each curve represents a group with a different level of education. Hakuta et al. did find a clear effect of age, one that was independent of education or length of residence in the United States: people who had immigrated at older ages were less fluent in English ($p < .0001$). However, they did *not* find the kind of sharp drop-off around puberty suggested by some previous studies; fitting straight lines to the fluency-age relationship was statistically just as good as fitting curved lines, or a series of straight lines with a break around puberty. Thus, Hakuta et al. concluded that age does indeed matter in second-language acquisition, but that the effect of age doesn't take the form of a classical critical period: instead of a clear cutoff at a particular age, there's a gradual decline in ultimate fluency as a person's age increases.

The greatest strength of this study is the huge number of people in the dataset; thus, these results suggest that maybe the apparent cutoffs that previous studies found at puberty were just artefacts of their small sample sizes.

The obvious drawback of the study is the fact that the authors had no way to independently verify how fluent the respondents were in English. Not only that, but the question on the census form wasn't ideally worded: the response 'speak only English' was interpreted in this study as the highest level of English proficiency, but of course it could be that some respondents spoke English poorly but chose (or were required) to speak only English anyway. (However, Hakuta et al. report some evidence from other studies that responses to this question are, overall, a reasonably good proxy for English fluency.) Finally, Hakuta et al. were unable to calculate precise values for respondents' age, age at immigration, and so on, since the data was reported in blocks (e.g., 20–24 years, 25–29 years, and so on). But Wiley et al. (2005) performed a similar analysis on a subset of the census data for which exact values were available and got similar results.

6.2.5 *General conclusions*

Overall, studies of the critical period hypothesis present a mixed picture. On the one hand, it seems fairly clear that there's a real effect of age: the younger you are when you start to learn a second language, the more fluent you'll eventually become. But researchers differ on whether there's a certain age that marks the end of a person's ability to learn a new language to native proficiency; some studies have found a sharp decline at some age (often around puberty, because this is where researchers tend to look), but others find a more gradual decline throughout the lifespan. It seems fairly safe to conclude that age probably matters, but it's much less certain that the language-learning window ends abruptly.

All of the studies we have seen here attempted to control for other factors that are inevitably confounded with age, such as the length of time the person has been exposed to the language or how motivated the person is. But no study can control for everything, and critics of the critical period hypothesis have suggested many alternative interpretations of the age effect. We examine some of these factors in the next section.

6.3 Reasons for the age effect

Many researchers have argued that children are *not* better at learning a second language simply because they're young. Rather, there's something special about the behavior or environment of children that tends to make them better at this task than adults are. One idea, for example, is that children are less inhibited than adults; they aren't afraid of making mistakes, and so they are more willing to practice, experiment, and learn. Another suggestion is that children and adults face different social expectations: people are sympathetic with an adult who struggles with a second language, but less so with a child. It could even be that some adults have positive reasons for *not* wanting to become fully fluent in a new language; an adult immigrant, for example, might want to retain a foreign accent as a way of identifying with his or her native country.

There's a huge variety of hypotheses like these, and some are easier to test than others. The following sections review some of the major proposed explanations for the difference between children and adults other than just age.

6.3.1 Interference from a first language

Paradoxically, one possible reason so many adults struggle with a second language could be, not that their linguistic skills are deficient, but that they know their first language too well. Part of acquiring a second language is not just learning to follow new rules, but also learning *not* to follow the rules of your first language. Adults, by this reasoning, have a harder time than children because they've spent many more years using their first language: those rules are more firmly fixed in the adult than they are in the child.

In fact, there's good evidence that learning one language involves learning to ignore things that might be useful in a different language. Young infants, for example, are sometimes called 'universal listeners' because they can hear differences between very similar speech sounds that many adults can't. Young babies learning English can hear the difference between sounds like [k'] and [q'] (the former is similar to the *k* sound; the latter is produced slightly further back in the mouth) or [t] and [ʈ] (the latter is produced with the tongue curled slightly back). The [k']~[q'] contrast is important in Salishan languages (spoken in the Pacific northwest) and many others, and the [t]~[ʈ] contrast is important in languages such as Hindi; adult speakers of these languages, of course, can hear these differences. But the differences are *not* important in English, and adult speakers of English often have a very difficult time hearing them.

This seems to be a general phenomenon: babies can hear differences between sounds that their parents can't. In fact, Werker and Tees (1984) have shown that the change happens early, during the first year of life: they tested a group of infants learning English and found that their ability to distinguish between pairs like [q']~[k'] and [t]~[ʈ] disappeared somewhere between 6 and 12 months of age. The phenomenon is a puzzling one, because ordinarily we think of child development as a process in which infants learn new skills – but here, infants are actually *losing* abilities they used to have.

This pattern makes more sense if we think of it in terms of attention. A child learning English doesn't have to be able to hear the difference between [t] and [ʈ], but she does have to be able to distinguish between [v] and [w]; by ignoring the former differences, she can devote more attention to the latter. By contrast, a child learning Hindi doesn't have to distinguish between [v] and [w], but does have to distinguish between [t] and [ʈ]; this child will therefore benefit from the opposite strategy.

Selectively paying attention to just those differences that are important in your native language may be a good strategy for learning and speaking a first language, but it can obviously cause trouble when it comes to learning a second language. An adult English speaker has decades of experience ignoring the difference between [t] and [ʈ]; but if that person wants to learn Hindi, then suddenly those differences are very important. Maybe children do better at learning a second language because they've spent less time ignoring the differences that may turn out to be important in their new language: children need less 'retraining' than adults.

Something like this probably explains at least part of adults' difficulty in learning a second language, although linguists disagree about whether an explanation along these lines could account for *all* of the differences between children and adults. The question is very interesting for theoretical reasons if we want to understand in more detail how language learning works. But there's a sense in which the question is irrelevant for many practical purposes. If we want to know whether older language learners are likely to do as well as younger learners, then on some level it doesn't matter whether older learners struggle simply because they're adults, or because they're firmly entrenched in their first language. Either way, adults will have a harder time, and their needs will be different from those of children.

6.3.2 Children are more motivated than adults

Another idea is that children are more motivated to learn language than adults are. Children learn their native language so quickly, the argument goes, because otherwise they'll have no way to express their needs. Some researchers have even proposed that children are essentially *forced* to learn language in order to communicate with their caregivers, although there are reasons to be skeptical of this position:

> One would have to conclude from remarks like these that ordinary loving fathers and mothers routinely withhold comfort, food, and drink until their children master the crucial tool of language. Since even rudimentary command generally takes about a year to develop, it is a wonder that so many babies survive that awful first 12 months.
>
> Oyama (1982, 29)

When it comes to learning a second language, the idea is that children are more likely than adults to be thrown into a situation where they have no choice but to learn a new language – a new monolingual school, for example. Adults, by contrast, often have the resources to choose to interact at least some of the time with speakers of their native language, and so they have less reason to learn the new language thoroughly. Alternatively, maybe children are more sensitive to peer pressure than adults are, so they make a special effort to eliminate foreign features from their speech.

On the one hand, motivation is obviously very important; studies of second-language acquisition routinely find that the more motivated a person is to learn a new language, the more successful that person will be. But motivational differences don't seem to be enough to explain *all* of the differences between children and adults. And for the youngest and best learners – infants and toddlers – the hypothesis is essentially unfalsifiable, because we simply can't ask very young children questions like 'How much do you want to learn this language?' And even if we could, it's not clear how we would meaningfully compare their answers to those of adults.

By itself, the motivational hypothesis has the potential to blame second-language learners for their failures: if you haven't reached native-speaker fluency in your new language, that's because you just didn't try hard enough. But decades of research on second-language acquisition have made it clear that adult second-language learners face very real and difficult obstacles. Motivational differences may explain part of what's going on in second-language acquisition, but they cannot be the whole story.

6.3.3 You're doing it wrong

A final set of hypotheses can be grouped under the basic idea that adults are using ineffective methods to learn new languages; if they tried learning the way children do, they would have much more success. Ideas like these are especially popular among companies that sell language-learning products to adults, such as Rosetta Stone and Pimsleur. These businesses have an obvious financial incentive to de-emphasize the difference between adults and children: 'It's too late for you to master this language completely, but let's try anyway' is not a very convincing sales pitch.

But even more disinterested parties have suggested that adults' and children's experiences are not the same, and that this may affect how well they eventually learn a second language. Many researchers, for example, have pointed out that immigrants who arrive in a new country at different ages may have profoundly different experiences; the following patterns are common:

- Adults do much of their initial language learning in a classroom setting; children learn from peers in more natural social situations.
- Adults are taught the rules of the new language explicitly; children infer them implicitly.

- Adult native speakers may simplify their speech when talking to learners more than children do. Thus, child learners get more natural and complex input than adults.
- Children speak the new language more often, and in more situations, than adults do.
- Children get years of formal education in the new language; adults completed all their education in their first language.

Differences like these aren't trivial, and studies of the critical period hypothesis often attempt to control for them. Some studies have found that after accounting for things like the amount each person speaks the second language, the effects of age on ultimate fluency disappear; Flege et al. (1999) is one example. (Interestingly, this study found that age of acquisition had no effect on how well Korean immigrants learned the rules of English sentence structure, after variables such as amount of English use were controlled for, but that age of acquisition *did* affect the strength of their accent. This result suggests that age may have different effects on different aspects of language learning – in other words, maybe what we have are several distinct critical period*s*, not a single critical period.) Some other studies suggest that language use explains part of the age effect but not all of it. Unfortunately, some of these differences present us with a chicken-and-egg dilemma: does speaking the language more make you more fluent, or does becoming more fluent in the language encourage you to speak it more?

Thus, the status of these hypotheses is similar to that of the motivational hypothesis: how, and how much, you speak your second language obviously affects how fluent you will eventually become, but it's not clear that this is the whole story. Despite some companies' claims to the contrary, no one has discovered the magic bullet that will guarantee everyone the ability to learn a second language perfectly.

6.4 Summary

- Everyone learns a first language, but not everyone is able to master a second language to the same degree.
- Some linguists believe there is a *critical period* for language learning: a window of time in childhood during which it is possible to learn a second language with native-like fluency.
- A number of studies have shown that a person's ability to learn a second language declines with age. However, it is less clear whether there is a sharp decrease in this ability at a certain age, as proposed in many versions of the critical period hypothesis.

- There are many factors other than age that affect how well a person will be able to learn a second language. These factors probably explain some, but not all, of the age-related differences in second-language acquisition.

For further reflection

(1) There are many different factors that affect a person's experience in learning a second language, and how fluent the person ultimately becomes. Interview someone you know who has studied at least two languages beyond his or her native language, either formally or informally. In what ways were this person's language-learning experiences different, and how did those differences affect the person's success in learning each of those languages?

(2) Many commercial language-learning companies (e.g., Rosetta Stone and Pimsleur) make grandiose claims that they have discovered the secret of second-language acquisition and that their products can therefore help anyone learn a new language quickly or easily. Choose one such company and examine its claims about how second-language acquisition works – based on what you have learned in this chapter, are those claims true?

(3) Other studies of the critical period hypothesis include Bialystok and Miller (1999), Birdsong and Molis (2001), and Abrahamsson and Hyltenstam (2009). Read one of these studies and evaluate it. What kind of relationship between fluency and age of acquisition do the authors propose as a true 'critical period'? What kind of evidence for or against this relationship did the authors find? Do you find the authors' conclusions convincing? Why or why not?

Further reading

Ellis (1997) is a brief and accessible overview of second-language acquisition.

Mayberry and Eichen (1991) is an example of a study that provides evidence for a critical-period effect for first-language acquisition; a more general overview of this area can be found in Gleitman and Newport (1995). For second-language acquisition, relatively accessible reviews of the critical period hypothesis include DeKeyser and Larson-Hall (2005) (for) and Birdsong (2005) (against).

Genie's story is told in Curtiss (1977) and in a NOVA documentary (NOVA 1994).

DeWaard (2013) is an accessible evaluation of the Rosetta Stone language-learning software. Nielson (2011) attempted to study Rosetta Stone's effectiveness, but so many people dropped out of the experiment that she was unable to learn much about whether the product actually works.

There are many experimental studies of the critical period hypothesis; a few examples include Patkowski (1980), Bialystok and Miller (1999), Birdsong and Molis (2001), Abrahamsson and Hyltenstam (2009), and DeKeyser et al. (2010).

Bibliography

Abrahamsson, Niclas, and Kenneth Hyltenstam. Age of onset and nativelikeness in a second language: Listener perception versus linguistic scrutiny. *Language Learning*, 59(2):249–306, 2009.

Bialystok, Ellen, and Barry Miller. The problem of age in second-language acquisition: Influences from language, structure, and task. *Bilingualism: Language and Cognition*, 2(2):127–145, 1999.

Birdsong, David. Interpreting age effects in second language acquisition. In Kroll and de Groot (2005), chapter 6, pages 109–127.

Birdsong, David, and Michelle Molis. On the evidence for maturational constraints in second-language acquisition. *Journal of Memory and Language*, 44(2):235–249, 2001.

Curtiss, Susan. *Genie: A Psycholinguistic Study of a Modern-Day 'Wild Child'*. Perspectives in Neurolinguistics and Psycholinguistics. Academic Press, Boston, MA, 1977.

DeKeyser, Robert M. The robustness of critical period effects in second language acquisition. *Studies in Second Language Acquisition*, 22(4):499–533, 2000.

DeKeyser, Robert, Iris Alfi-Shabtay, and Dorit Ravid. Cross-linguistic evidence for the nature of age effects in second language acquisition. *Applied Psycholinguistics*, 31(3):413–438, 2010.

DeKeyser, Robert, and Jenifer Larson-Hall. What does the critical period really mean? In Kroll and de Groot (2005), chapter 5, pages 88–108.

DeWaard, Lisa. Is *Rosetta Stone* a viable option for second-language learning? *ADFL Bulletin*, 42(2):61–72, 2013.

Ellis, Rod. *Second Language Acquisition*. Oxford Introductions to Language Study. Oxford University Press, Oxford, 1997.

Flege, James Emil, Murray J. Munro, and Ian R. A. MacKay. Factors affecting strength of perceived foreign accent in a second language. *Journal of the Acoustical Society of America*, 97(5):3125–3134, 1995.

Flege, James Emil, Grace H. Yeni-Komshian, and Serena Liu. Age constraints on second-language acquisition. *Journal of Memory and Language*, 41(1):78–104, 1999.

Gleitman, Lila R., and Elissa L. Newport. The invention of language by children: Environmental and biological influences on the acquisition of language. In Lila R. Gleitman and Mark Liberman, editors, *An Invitation to Cognitive Science: Language*, volume 1, chapter 1, pages 1–24. The MIT Press, Cambridge, MA, 2nd edition, 1995.

Hakuta, Kenji, Ellen Bialystok, and Edward Wiley. Critical evidence: A test of the critical-period hypothesis for second-language acquisition. *Psychological Science*, 14(1):31–38, 2003.

Harrington, Jonathan, Sallyanne Palethorpe, and Catherine I. Watson. Does the Queen speak the Queen's English? *Nature*, 408(6815):927–928, 2000.

Johnson, Jacqueline S. Critical period effects in second language acquisition: The effect of written versus auditory materials on the assessment of grammatical competence. *Language Learning*, 42(2):217–248, 1992.

Johnson, Jacqueline S., and Elissa L. Newport. Critical period effects in second language learning: The influence of maturational state on the acquisition of English as a second language. *Cognitive Psychology*, 21(1):60–99, 1989.

Krashen, Stephen D., Michael H. Long, and Robin C. Scarcella. Age, rate, and eventual attainment in second language acquisition. In Krashen et al. (1982b), chapter 13, pages 161–172.

Krashen, Stephen D., Robin C. Scarcella, and Michael H. Long, editors. *Child-Adult Differences in Second Language Acquisition*. Issues in Second Language Research. Newbury House Publishers, Inc., Rowley, MA, 1982b.

Kroll, Judith F., and Annette M. B. de Groot, editors. *Handbook of Bilingualism: Psycholinguistic Approaches*. Oxford University Press, Oxford, 2005.

Lenneberg, Eric H. *Biological Foundations of Language*. Wiley, New York, NY, 1967.

Mayberry, Rachel I., and Ellen B. Eichen. The long-lasting advantage of learning sign language in childhood: Another look at the critical period for language acquisition. *Journal of Memory and Language*, 30(4):486–512, 1991.

Nielson, Katharine B. Self-study with language learning software in the workplace: What happens? *Language Learning & Technology*, 15(3):110–129, 2011. Available at http://llt.msu.edu/issues/october2011/nielson.pdf.

NOVA. Secret of the wild child, 1994.

Oyama, Susan. A sensitive period for the acquisition of a nonnative phonological system. In Krashen et al. (1982b), chapter 3, pages 20–38.

Patkowski, Mark S. The sensitive period for the acquisition of syntax in a second language. *Language Learning*, 30(2):449–471, 1980.

Sankoff, Gillian, and Hélène Blondeau. Language change across the lifespan: /r/ in Montreal French. *Language*, 83(3):560–588, 2007.

Werker, Janet F., and Richard C. Tees. Cross-language speech perception: Evidence for perceptual reorganization during the first year of life. *Infant Behavior and Development*, 7(1):49–63, 1984.

Wiley, Edward W., Ellen Bialystok, and Kenji Hakuta. New approaches to using census data to test the critical-period hypothesis for second-language acquisition. *Psychological Science*, 16(4):341–343, 2005.

7 'Being bilingual makes you smarter (or dumber)'

In many parts of the world, bilingualism or multilingualism is just a fact of life: if many languages coexist in the same area, then learning additional languages is an ordinary part of growing up. But there are other places in the world – for example, many areas of the United States and Canada – where a single language is so dominant that many people don't have the need, or even the opportunity, to learn more than one language.

Since bilingualism isn't a necessity in these places, it has naturally become a matter of choice. Individuals choose whether to learn and use an additional language; parents who speak a minority language choose whether to raise their children bilingual; schools choose whether to offer bilingual education or foreign-language immersion programs. And with these choices, the obvious question is, 'What's the *best* choice? Is bilingualism good or bad?'

Put that way, the question is obviously too simplistic. The first part of this chapter makes this point more thoroughly, illustrating just how varied 'bilingualism' is: there are many different types of bilingualism, at both the individual and social levels. It's just not possible to answer the question of what bilingualism is like 'in general'; the best we can do is talk about specific *ways* of being bilingual.

But there's also a long tradition of linguistic and psychological research that essentially *does* try to answer the question of whether bilingualism is good or bad. Specifically, there's a large body of research that explores whether bilingualism – especially in children – helps or harms a person's intelligence. One of the most fascinating things about this research tradition is that the consensus of the field changed dramatically during the twentieth century: early researchers were convinced that bilingualism was harmful, but most researchers today believe it's beneficial. In our case study at the end of this chapter, we'll take a closer look at these studies: what caused this reversal, and what (as far as we can tell) is the real effect of bilingualism?

7.1 What does it mean to be bilingual?

If we describe a person as *bilingual*, we mean the person speaks two different languages. Similarly, a *multilingual* person speaks several languages. The idea is simple – deceptively so. Consider the following scenarios:

A. A child has a mother whose native language is French and a father whose native language is German. She hears both languages from birth, generally speaking one language with each parent, and receives formal education in both French and German. As an adult, she uses both languages regularly.

B. A Vietnamese family immigrates to Canada. The parents, who had some formal instruction in English before arriving, use English in the workplace and Vietnamese at home. Their son first encounters English in his new junior high school; although he becomes a fluent speaker of English, he considers Vietnamese to be his first language. Their elementary-school-aged daughter also becomes fluent in English; as an adult, she can understand Vietnamese but doesn't speak it fluently.

C. A young man grows up in Paraguay, where both Spanish and Guaraní are widely spoken. He speaks Spanish in school and other official contexts, and Guaraní with his family and friends.

D. A child lives in a Kom-speaking community in Cameroon. When she starts school, the language of instruction is English.

E. An American student studies Japanese in high school, but there are few or no native Japanese speakers in his community to talk to. In college, he spends one semester studying abroad in Tokyo; after returning home, he has little opportunity to use the language.

F. A historian who studies ancient Rome knows enough Latin to read source documents related to her research, but she doesn't speak or write the language.

All the people in these scenarios have at least some knowledge of more than one language, but they differ in the types of knowledge they have. The girl in Scenario A is an example of a *balanced bilingual*: she speaks both languages equally well and in similar contexts. But, as the other examples suggest, many bilingual people are *unbalanced*. Roughly speaking, there are at least two ways a person's two languages might differ: the person might be more proficient in one language than the other, or the person might use the two languages in different contexts. When we consider the variation that exists along both of these dimensions, we see that there are many ways to be bilingual.

7.1.1 *Unequal proficiency in two languages*

Probably the most obvious example of unbalanced bilingualism is someone who learns a second language as an adult and never achieves native-speaker fluency. There is, of course, a huge range of variation here: some people reach near-native proficiency in their second language; others become competent speakers but are clearly more comfortable in their first language; others, like the student in Scenario E and the scholar in Scenario F, have such a temporary or narrow competence that reasonable people might disagree about whether they count as bilingual at all. (See Chapter 6 for more on the relationship between age and second-language acquisition.)

Even people raised with two languages from birth may have a 'stronger' and a 'weaker' language – for example, if the person spends more time speaking and hearing one language than the other. In fact, some researchers have argued that there's essentially no such thing as a balanced bilingual – that all bilinguals use their languages differently. At the very least, we can say that balanced bilinguals are in the minority.

It's also possible for a person's first language to eventually become the 'weaker' one. The parents in Scenario B will probably always be stronger in Vietnamese than in English; because they immigrated as a family, they never stopped speaking Vietnamese. Their use of the language will be further supported if they know other Vietnamese immigrants in their area, or if they maintain ties with relatives in Vietnam. But the situation might be very different for a young man who immigrates to a place where there are *no* speakers of his native language. If he has no opportunity to use his native language for several decades, he may well come to feel that his second language is stronger than his native one.

The daughter in Scenario B is a special case of someone whose first language eventually becomes the weaker one. In an important sense, her acquisition of Vietnamese is incomplete because she essentially stopped learning it while she was very young, before she reached full adult competence. Linguists have begun using the term *heritage language* for this kind of situation: a *heritage speaker* is someone whose acquisition of his or her first language was interrupted at an early age, or someone whose first language is not his or her dominant one. One way for this to happen is if the language isn't spoken in the wider community – for example, if the family moves to an area where their native language isn't spoken, or if a majority language overwhelms an endangered minority language. Heritage speakers often have excellent pronunciation; they may have very little 'foreign accent', and in any case they usually sound more native-like than adults who start learning the language from scratch. But their control of the grammar of the language is less good, and they may have a limited vocabulary. Thus, a heritage speaker isn't the same as a native speaker of the language, but she's also not the same as someone who starts studying the language as an adult.

7.1.2 *Using two languages in different contexts*

The scenarios above also illustrate how different languages can play different roles in a person's daily life. Unlike the girl in Scenario A, many bilinguals use their languages in different contexts and for different purposes. A person might use one language in school or at work and another language at home; a person might use one language only with particular family members, or only in religious contexts, or only with government officials.

Sometimes an entire community assigns specific functions to two or more languages. In the situation known as *diglossia*, the community uses at least two languages; one is associated with 'low' (L) functions and one with 'high' (H) functions. The 'low' language is the native language of almost everyone; it's spoken in the home and among friends as the language of intimacy and solidarity. The 'high' language is for official contexts, and some people may not encounter it at all until they start school. This language marks formal situations and may be the only language that is written. The classic cases of diglossia involve two languages that are very similar to each other, usually so closely related that they're called dialects of the same language (although they may not be mutually intelligible). In Switzerland, for example, Swiss German is the L variety and Standard German is the H variety; in the Arabic-speaking world, Standard Arabic is H while the local dialect is L. But it's also possible to have diglossia with two completely unrelated languages; a famous example is Paraguay, where the majority of the population speaks both Spanish (H) and Guaraní (L).

If a bilingual person uses her two languages in different contexts, it can be very difficult to evaluate how 'balanced' her two languages are in the first place. Someone who speaks one language at home and another language at work, for example, probably has different vocabularies in the two languages because she uses them to talk about different things. She may be perfectly fluent in both languages but feel odd about using them in the 'wrong' contexts. Indeed, we might ask whether it's even meaningful to talk about balance between the two languages, since they fulfill such different functions. It's important to keep these common situations in mind when we look at research on bilingualism, which often assumes that people use both (or all) of their languages in equivalent ways. Researchers may ask subjects, for example, how often they speak each of their languages, or they may administer equivalent vocabulary tests in each language and compare the subjects' scores. This is an understandable method – it's much easier to quantify how much a person uses one language versus another than it is to quantify the kinds of situations where a person uses them – but it means that we should be cautious in interpreting the results.

7.2 Bilingualism on a larger scale

For most of this chapter, we'll be talking about bilingualism at the individual level – in other words, a single person who uses two or more languages. But, obviously, bilingual people don't exist in a vacuum. There are many reasons to be bilingual; the social context of bilingualism affects how, and how often, each language is used. In this section, we will briefly survey the wide range of ways in which a society as a whole can be characterized as bilingual, and what this means for individuals.

7.2.1 Bilingual societies of monolingual individuals

One way to have a bilingual society is to have two groups of people, each associated with one language, where relatively few individuals actually speak both. Some famous examples of this situation are countries where language differences have been a source of conflict – French and English in Quebec, and Flemish and French in Belgium. And even the individual bilingualism that does exist may be asymmetrical. In Belgium, for example, people who live in Flemish-speaking Flanders are actually fairly likely to speak French, because they see the language as useful and globally prestigious. People from French-speaking Wallonia, on the other hand, don't see any use for Flemish outside Flanders and are reluctant to learn it.

Sometimes a region is officially bilingual, as enshrined in government policy, but nearly monolingual in practice. In the Republic of Ireland, both Irish and English have official status; both languages are required on road signs, in official government documents, and so on. However, only a small proportion of the population speaks Irish as a native language.[1] In fact, one of the goals of giving official status to Irish, in addition to affirming Irish dignity, was to help reverse the severe drop in the number of native Irish speakers that began in the late 1800s – although how well this has actually worked, if at all, is hotly debated.

7.2.2 Bilingual societies of bilingual individuals

These examples show that some bilingual areas are heavily populated with people who are actually monolingual. But there are also places where individual

[1] McCloskey (2008) describes how there's also a growing community of second-language speakers of Irish, although the variety that they speak and have passed along to their children is different in important ways from the Irish spoken in traditional Irish-speaking areas.

bilingualism, and even multilingualism, is the norm. Diglossia, of course, is one example: most of the population speaks two varieties, each serving a distinct social purpose.

There are also parts of the world that are so linguistically diverse that multilingualism is just a fact of life. In many parts of Africa and India, for example, it's common for a person to speak a local language at home; another, such as Yoruba or Hindi, at the regional level; and a colonial language, such as English or French, in higher education or business. From moment to moment, speakers have to choose which language is the appropriate one for that context. Naturally, this partly depends on what language(s) the people in the situation have in common; the whole point of a regional language is to let people communicate with each other even if they speak different local languages. But there are also conventions that look a lot like diglossia, such that some languages tend to be used in the public sphere and others in more intimate settings. Choosing a regional or national language over the local one can be a way for the speaker to demonstrate that the situation is a formal one.

A spectacular example of widespread individual multilingualism is the Vaupés region of the Amazon, a sparsely populated area the size of New England that straddles the border between Colombia and Brazil. This small region is home to more than 20 languages; some are related to each other (for example, some of the languages are about as similar as Spanish and Italian), but others are from completely different language families. Even though the area is linguistically diverse, the groups that live there share a large number of cultural traditions. One practice shared by most groups is that speakers of the same language are considered close relatives – essentially, brothers and sisters. This means that a man can't marry a woman with the same native language, because that would be incest. And so, when she marries, a woman moves to her new husband's community and inevitably brings with her a different language. The couple's children are socially identified with their 'father language', but of course they learn to speak the mother's language as well, and possibly languages spoken by other in-marrying women in the community (and their children). The result, not surprisingly, is massive multilingualism.

One of the most interesting things about this system is the egalitarian way the languages of the region are viewed. Residents of the Vaupés insist that none of the languages are better than any of the others (although they may have opinions about dialectal differences *within* languages), and they place a high value on learning to speak each language 'properly', without mixing in words from other languages. This attitude in a multilingual situation is far from universal; in diglossic settings, for example, the H variety is often (though not always) seen as better and more proper than the L variety. Alternatively, when two languages are associated with opposing social groups, language differences may be a source of conflict because they come to symbolize social differences. What the situation in the Amazon shows is that although language differences *can* be associated with social divides and antagonisms, they don't *have* to be.

7.3 Case study: Does being bilingual make you smarter?

If the examples we've seen make anything clear, it's that bilingualism is not just one thing – it can look very different across individuals and across societies. Not only do people speak different languages with varying degrees of competence, but they're inevitably embedded in a larger social context that has a profound impact on how they use those languages. This means that it's dangerous to study a specific group of bilingual people and draw conclusions about bilingualism in general. But we will forge ahead, partly because there's a large body of experimental literature that tries to do exactly that; as we examine these studies, we will keep in mind just how complex bilingualism really is on the ground. And, in fact, most researchers are careful to acknowledge that a single experiment is inherently limited, and that studying the full range of bilingualism is a massive endeavor.

The specific question we will investigate is whether bilingualism affects intelligence. In a nutshell, does being bilingual make you smarter? As we will see, the consensus of the field has changed dramatically: in the first half of the twentieth century, everyone agreed that bilingualism was a mental handicap that put a burden on children; today, people are equally convinced that being bilingual improves cognitive functioning in several ways. The question has been studied extensively because its implications are so important: for parents deciding whether to raise their children with one language or two, for educational systems dealing with bilingual students, and for governments adopting policies that promote (or discourage) bilingualism.

7.3.1 Early studies: Lewis (1959)

Hakuta (1985) describes how the early 1900s saw the convergence of two powerful forces in the United States: a new enthusiasm for intelligence testing among psychologists, and widespread worries about immigration. Many people believed that the latest immigrants from southern Europe – Italians, for example – were inferior to the previous generations of northern European immigrants. Armed with newly developed intelligence tests, psychologists set out to measure the mental abilities of various 'races'; a scientific assessment would determine whether those fears were true and help guide policy decisions.

Not surprisingly, researchers consistently found that newer groups of immigrants performed worse on these tests than those who had been in the country for a generation or two. Many people concluded that the tests confirmed what everyone had known all along: the Italians and Slavs were simply not as intelligent as the Swedes and Norwegians; the population of the United States was being diluted with people of inferior stock. Today, of course, it's easy to think of much more likely explanations for these early results: the older immigrants may have been more economically secure, with more formal schooling; they were more acculturated; they were assessed in less threatening settings (some immigrants were tested at Ellis Island; one study tested the intelligence of Japanese students in an internment camp during World War II!).

Another obvious confounding factor in these tests is language: the descendants of previous generations of immigrants were much more likely to be fluent or native speakers of English than the immigrants who were just arriving. Even at the time, a number of researchers investigated whether intelligence scores were subject to a 'language handicap' for people who took the test in an unfamiliar language. Unfortunately, it was difficult for many researchers to reckon with the possibility that intelligence tests, which offered psychology the dignity of being a quantitative science, could be flawed instruments. Instead of concluding that the standard tests were just not a fair measure of intelligence in people whose native language wasn't English, many researchers argued that being bilingual *itself* affected intelligence. Bilingualism, especially in children, was claimed to be a source of 'mental confusion' that slowed the mind. Researchers on both sides of the Atlantic began to explore the question directly, and study after study showed that bilingual children were simply not as intelligent as their monolingual counterparts.

Lewis (1959) is a typical example of this generation of studies. Lewis tested 375 10-year-old students in Wales; in addition to administering an intelligence test, he also had the students complete a questionnaire that asked how often they spoke Welsh and English in various contexts. Combining the questionnaire results with teachers' ratings of each student's proficiency in each language, Lewis divided the children into four groups:

Group 1: Children who always spoke Welsh with family members and almost always spoke it with friends.
Group 2: Children who often spoke Welsh in the home but sometimes spoke English as well.
Group 3: Children who spoke Welsh only occasionally.
Group 4: Children who spoke no Welsh at all, or spoke it only occasionally with friends.

The goal of this procedure was to establish an objective and sensitive measure of the *degree* to which children were bilingual, rather than simply classifying each one as either bilingual or monolingual. Since all the children were

Table 7.1 *Mean intelligence scores and standard deviations for each group. D. G. Lewis, Bilingualism and non-verbal intelligence: A further study of test results,* British Journal of Educational Psychology *1959. Reprinted by permission of John Wiley & Sons, Inc.*

Group	1	2	3	4
Mean	33.30	38.36	38.94	40.98
S.D.	16.37	15.95	16.26	17.69

exposed to English at school, Lewis interpreted Groups 1–4 as representing decreasing bilingualism as well as decreasing 'Welshness'.

The intelligence test was nonverbal, and Lewis gave the instructions in either English or Welsh, according to the student's preference. The results, shown in Table 7.1, indicate that students in the 'more bilingual' groups did in fact score lower on the test. Lewis reports the result of a statistical test confirming that not all four groups performed at the same level ($p < .05$), but the only comparison between individual groups that he reports is the difference between groups 1 and 4, which was significant at $p < .01$. This means that we don't know, for example, whether the small difference between Groups 2 and 3 is statistically significant. Lewis concludes that 'the bilingual child, having to make a choice between two languages... tends to be slightly slower at thinking than the monoglot' (Lewis 1959, 21).

Methodologically speaking, this study is commendable in several respects. Lewis made a serious effort to assess the degree to which his subjects actually spoke Welsh. He chose a nonverbal test of intelligence; many previous studies had come to the unsurprising conclusion that the language handicap of bilinguals is more apparent when they are given a verbal intelligence test, especially in their second language. In addition, he administered the test in Welsh for children who wanted it, so that children wouldn't perform poorly just because they didn't understand the instructions. He tested bilingual and monolingual children in the same regions and at the same schools, attempting to ensure that all children were from roughly equivalent social and economic backgrounds.

Despite Lewis's best efforts, though, this study has several fatal flaws. Most importantly, it's not clear that all the 'bilingual' children (especially in Group 1) were actually bilingual. It's notable, for example, that Group 1 was the only group for which teachers rated a substantial proportion of the students – 20 out of 93 – as having only a 'slight' knowledge of English. The students in Group 4 were clearly monolingual in English, but many of the students in Group 1 may have been essentially monolingual in Welsh. Thus, maybe the students in Group 1 scored poorly, not because they were bilingual, but because they didn't understand the language of their teachers and their education had suffered as a result.

In addition, although Lewis attempted to ensure that all the students came from largely equivalent backgrounds, it's difficult to be certain that he succeeded. (Lewis states that he collected data on the occupations of the students' parents, and that there were no differences among the four groups, but he doesn't provide any details on how this was done.) Given that English is a language associated with education, power, and global prestige, it may be that English-speaking families tended to have higher socioeconomic status, or tended to place a higher value on schoolwork and test-taking. As we have already observed, bilinguals don't exist in a vacuum.

This study is typical of research on bilingualism during the first half of the twentieth century: methodologically conscientious in some respects, aware of some potential confounding factors, but ultimately flawed in ways that make it unable to tell us anything about the general cognitive effects of bilingualism. The vast majority of studies from this period suffered from similar problems: they compared low-income bilinguals with middle-class monolinguals; they tested students in a language they didn't actually speak well, or weren't used to using in a school context; they didn't ensure that the students who were supposedly bilingual actually had a good command of both languages.

7.3.2 The turning point: Peal and Lambert (1962)

Despite these methodological flaws, the consensus by the early 1960s was that bilingualism is harmful. One study concluded that bilingualism is 'a hardship devoid of apparent advantage' (Yoshioka 1929, 479); another (Carrow 1957) reported the harmful effects of bilingualism in the pages of the *Journal of Speech and Hearing Disorders*, as though bilingualism were a disability.

The crucial turning point in our understanding of the cognitive effects of bilingualism was Peal and Lambert (1962), a study that Hakuta and Diaz (1985, 322) call 'the punctuation point in research'. Peal and Lambert were aware of the flaws in earlier experiments, and they wanted to conduct a more rigorous study that would isolate the effects of bilingualism from other social factors. Their subjects were 10-year-old French-speaking students in Montreal, some of whom also spoke English.

First, Peal and Lambert administered a series of language assessments to each child in both French and English. On the basis of students' scores, they selected two groups for further testing: one group with very low English scores (the French monolinguals) and one group with approximately equivalent English and French scores (the balanced bilinguals). Further, they analyzed the students' socioeconomic status and found that students in the bilingual group, on average, belonged to higher socioeconomic classes. To compensate for this, they analyzed only a subset of the bilingual students, those who were comparable in socioeconomic status to the monolinguals.

The students took a battery of intelligence tests, both verbal and nonverbal, all of which were administered in French. In keeping with previous research, Peal and Lambert expected to find that bilinguals would perform worse than monolinguals on the verbal intelligence tests, but that they would perform about the same on the nonverbal tests. To their surprise, the bilingual students actually performed at least as well as the monolinguals on every test, and *better* on many of them. Faced with data that contradicted the results of the earlier flawed experiments, Peal and Lambert concluded that the consensus of the field was wrong and that bilingualism actually offers a cognitive benefit.

Earlier studies were so flawed that it's hard to avoid the conclusion that they tell us very little about bilingualism, as opposed to the effects of social and economic factors on intelligence test scores. Because it used appropriate controls, Peal and Lambert's study is much more reliable than almost anything that came before it. But before we conclude that these new results prove that bilingualism has a general cognitive benefit, it's important to consider the fact that Peal and Lambert's study, just like previous ones, was conducted in a particular social context. Perhaps one of the most striking differences between it and previous research is the nature of the populations studied. Most of the previous research compared children who were bilingual to children who were monolingual in a prestige language: English as opposed to Welsh in Wales, or as opposed to Spanish in the United States. By contrast, Peal and Lambert's monolinguals spoke the *non-prestige* language of the community: they were French speakers in a region where power was disproportionately concentrated in the hands of English speakers. In other words, bilinguals in previous studies spoke an additional language with low prestige, whereas the French-English bilinguals in Montreal spoke an additional language with high prestige. It's possible, then, that the French-English bilinguals were privileged in other ways, even after controlling for socioeconomic status.

Although it wasn't perfect, Peal and Lambert's paper was such a clear improvement over previous work that it set a new standard for conducting research on bilingualism, and it changed the field very quickly. Whereas earlier studies had largely focused on poor children, many of whom had an incomplete command of one of their languages, most experiments conducted after Peal and Lambert's paper turned their attention to middle-class balanced bilinguals. As the experimental methods changed, so did the results: suddenly, study after study was finding a cognitive advantage for bilingual children. The next few studies we will examine focus on some of the specific ways in which bilingualism has been claimed to be beneficial.

7.3.3 Metalinguistic awareness: Bialystok et al. (2000)

Most of the early studies on bilingualism relied on a very general concept of intelligence. But human cognition is extraordinarily complex, and modern research is more likely to focus on specific effects that bilingualism might have. (Peal and Lambert themselves took a step in this direction; they suggested that bilingual children were particularly likely to do well on tasks that required 'cognitive flexibility'.)

Metalinguistic awareness is a term that refers, generally, to the ability to think and talk about language itself. Since children raised bilingually are exposed to two different linguistic systems from an early age, it's plausible that they might differ from monolingual children in their ability to reflect on language in a more explicit way. In addition to being an interesting topic in its own right, the question of whether bilingualism affects metalinguistic awareness has important practical implications for learning to read, which requires certain metalinguistic abilities.

Bialystok et al. (2000) studied a total of 121 4- and 5-year-old preschoolers; half lived in Canada and half in Israel. Within each group, half of the preschoolers were bilingual in Hebrew and English and half were monolingual. (The Canadian monolinguals spoke English; the Israeli monolinguals spoke Hebrew.) All the children were from middle-class backgrounds. Bialystok et al. didn't restrict their subjects to perfectly balanced bilinguals, but they ensured that all the bilinguals were competent in both languages and had at least one parent who spoke the non-dominant language of the community (Hebrew in Canada, English in Israel). All the children in the study had early literacy skills, as established by a screening test: they could write their names, recite the alphabet, identify printed letters, and so on. (The bilingual children could do this for both English and Hebrew.) However, none of the children could read independently.

One of the tests Bialystok et al. used was the word-size problem, in which the child was presented with two words and asked which one was longer. The experimenter always said both words out loud; the child sometimes saw the printed words as well. In every pair of words, one was short (one syllable) and the other was long (at least three syllables). In some cases (*congruent* pairs), the shorter word referred to an object that is smaller than the object referred to by the longer word in real life (e.g., *dinosaur* and *nut*); in other cases (*incongruent* pairs), the shorter word referred to a *larger* object (e.g., *butterfly* and *man*). The crucial question here is how well the child performs on incongruent pairs: can the child ignore the meanings of the words and focus on their linguistic form?

Table 7.2 shows the results for the incongruent pairs; not surprisingly, the task was a hard one, and none of the 4-year-olds performed significantly above

Table 7.2 *Means and standard deviations of the scores of monolingual and bilingual 4- and 5-year-olds on the incongruent pairs in the word-size task. Asterisks mark groups who performed significantly better than chance (0.50) at* $p < .01$. *Ellen Bialystok, Tali Shenfield, and Judith Codd, Languages, scripts, and the environment: Factors in developing concepts of print,* Developmental Psychology *36(1):66–76, 2000, Table 4. Adapted with permission of the American Psychological Association.*

		Language	
Age and group	*n*	English	Hebrew
		Canadian sample	
4-year-olds			
Monolingual	16	0.48 (0.20)	
Bilingual	15	0.59 (0.22)	0.48 (0.29)
5-year-olds			
Monolingual	15	0.55 (0.22)	
Bilingual	15	0.78 (0.23)*	0.70 (0.22)*
		Israeli sample	
4-year-olds			
Monolingual	13		0.42 (0.24)
Bilingual	14	0.50 (0.22)	0.62 (0.22)
5-year-olds			
Monolingual	22		0.57 (0.28)
Bilingual	21	0.72 (0.24)*	0.76 (0.21)*

chance. Among the 5-year-old monolinguals, the results were the same – but the 5-year-old *bilinguals* scored significantly better. We can construct a plausible explanation for why the bilinguals were better at these tests: because they have extensive experience dealing with two different labels for a single object, they are less likely than monolinguals to think that the name of a thing is inherently connected to the thing itself. In other words, since English-Hebrew bilinguals know that a particular winged insect could be called either *butterfly* or *parpar*, they are quicker to appreciate what linguists call the *arbitrariness of the sign*.

It's encouraging that the bilingual children performed better than their monolingual counterparts in *both* languages, and that this difference appeared in two different countries. This consistency suggests that we're dealing with a genuine effect of bilingualism, not an artefact of social or cultural differences. But although the results are promising, this study is certainly not the end of the story. For one thing, although many studies have found similar advantages in metalinguistic awareness for bilingual children, others have concluded that there is no benefit for bilingualism, or that it's limited to certain kinds of metalinguistic tasks, or that the benefit disappears as children get older. In another study (Bialystok et al. 2005), Bialystok and colleagues themselves found that the bilingual advantage was much less clear for English-Cantonese bilinguals' understanding of print, possibly because the two languages have writing systems based on fundamentally different principles.

In addition, this study should not inspire ambitious parents to run out and enroll their children in bilingual preschools just to give them an academic edge (although early language immersion can be a valuable experience for other reasons). By themselves, these results don't tell us whether the bilingual advantage in metalinguistic awareness leads to other differences later in life. Does this extra metalinguistic ability allow bilinguals to start reading earlier than monolinguals, or do the monolinguals catch up so quickly that the difference has no practical effect?

7.3.4 Executive control: Kovács and Mehler (2009)

It's not terribly surprising if bilinguals and monolinguals differ in their language-related abilities – after all, it's precisely their *linguistic* experience that makes them different. But Peal and Lambert's study found that bilinguals performed better on *nonverbal* intelligence tests as well as verbal ones. Subsequent research has suggested that there may be differences between bilinguals and monolinguals even in domains that aren't obviously related to language.

Kovács and Mehler (2009) is a particularly remarkable study of bilingualism because the children studied were only 7 months old. For these infants, who cannot yet speak, 'bilingual' means 'exposed to two languages from birth'. Kovács and Mehler were interested in *executive control*: the ability to plan, to focus one's attention, and to switch between tasks.

The researchers conducted three different experiments, each with 40 infants, 20 of whom were being raised in monolingual Italian-speaking homes and 20 of whom were being raised in a home where both Italian and some other language were spoken. During the first half of the experiment (the 'pre-switch' phase), the infant would hear a nonsense word and then see a colorful puppet on one side of a video screen. The puppet was always on the same side of the screen, and the infants eventually learned that when they heard a nonsense word, they would soon see the puppet. Since the colorful puppet was more interesting than the blank screen, the infants started looking toward the correct side of the screen in anticipation even before the puppet appeared. The left half of Figure 7.1 shows that infants did more looking toward the correct side of the screen as time went on.

During the second half of the experiment (the 'post-switch' phase), the puppet always appeared on the opposite side of the screen. This was challenging

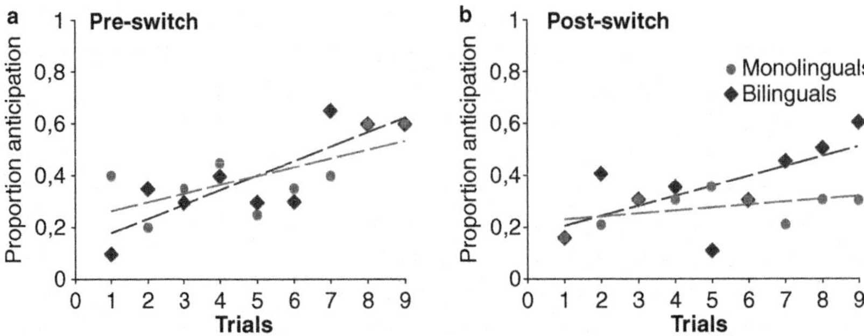

Figure 7.1 Proportion correct anticipatory looks in the pre- and post-switch phases of Experiment 1. Ágnes Melinda Kovács and Jacques Mehler, Cognitive gains in 7-month-old bilingual infants, *Proceedings of the National Academy of Sciences* 106(16):6556–6560, 2009, Figure 2.

because the infants had to 'unlearn' what they had just learned and start looking the other way. As shown in the right half of Figure 7.1, the bilingual infants eventually learned to look at the opposite side of the screen, but the monolinguals didn't. Kovács and Mehler conclude that only the bilingual infants had enough executive control to overcome what they had learned in the pre-switch phase and do something different in the post-switch phase.

Why should this be? After all, the relationship of language to executive control is much less obvious than its relationship to more specifically linguistic abilities. One suggestion is based on the finding that bilinguals never turn either language off; it appears that both languages are always active in the brain. If bilinguals are constantly having to focus their attention on one language and suppress the other, then maybe they are getting lots of extra practice with the very attentional skills involved in executive control.

7.3.5 Older adults: Kavé et al. (2008)

Much of the research on bilingualism and intelligence – including all the studies we have seen here – involves young children. We will conclude with one example of research on bilingualism in older adults.

Kavé et al. (2008) reviewed data from a long-term study of aging in Israel. The participants were between the ages of 75 and 94 in 1989, when the first interviews took place; two follow-up interviews were conducted over the next 12 years with participants who were still living and could be located. Among the data that the researchers collected was information about what languages the participants spoke and the results of a standard test of cognitive function. Kavé et al. were interested in whether participants who spoke

Table 7.3 *Means and standard deviations of scores on cognitive screening tests by number of languages spoken for three 'waves' of interviews. Lower scores are better. Gitit Kavé, Nitza Eyal, Aviva Shorek, and Jiska Cohen-Mansfield, Multilingualism and cognitive state in the oldest old,* Psychology and Aging *23(1):2008, 70–78, adapted from Table 2.*

	Wave 1		Wave 2		Wave 3	
Language group	*M*	*SD*	*M*	*SD*	*M*	*SD*
Bilingual	10.0	8.2	11.7	7.7	12.7	8.8
Trilingual	7.0	6.4	8.6	6.6	11.8	7.8
Multilingual	5.4	5.7	6.1	6.1	6.1	5.6

more languages – who had experienced a lifetime of bilingualism – had better cognitive functioning in old age.

Kavé et al. examined the 814 participants who spoke Hebrew and classified them as monolingual, bilingual, trilingual, or multilingual. Unfortunately, one major difficulty for the study was the fact that almost none of the participants were genuinely monolingual; they had been born during a time when almost no children learned Hebrew as their only native language, even in Israel. The 'monolingual' subjects in this study were those who reported that their native language was the one in which they were most fluent; 'bilingual' subjects were those who reported that they were most fluent in a language other than their native one. In this study, then, the comparison is not between those who know two languages and those who know only one, but between those who have learned a second language more or less thoroughly.

Table 7.3 summarizes the results for participants who were at least bilingual. Within each 'wave' of interviews, there's a clear trend: participants who spoke more languages had better scores on the cognitive screening test. Kavé et al. found a statistically significant benefit for speaking more languages ($p < .01$), even after they controlled for age, gender, place of birth, education, and age at immigration to Isarel. They conclude that lifelong bilingualism has a significant benefit in old age.

Of all the studies we have seen so far, this one provides the clearest evidence of a long-term practical benefit of bilingualism. Other researchers have found further evidence that bilingualism improves cognitive functioning in older adults, and that it may even delay the onset of Alzheimer's (see Baum and Titone 2014 for a review). Perhaps the most difficult problem with these promising findings is the question of which way causation goes. Does being bilingual protect against cognitive decline, or are people with better cognitive abilities both more likely to become bilingual early in life and less likely to experience cognitive decline later on?

7.3.6 General conclusions

The consensus in the middle of the twentieth century was that bilingualism harms a person's intelligence, but the studies on which the consensus was based were severely flawed. We have seen evidence from modern, better-designed studies that bilingualism actually appears to have a wide range of cognitive *benefits*, from obviously language-related tasks to more general areas such as executive control. Although we now have substantial evidence that bilingualism is beneficial in many ways, an appropriate degree of caution is still needed. For one thing, it's unclear whether some of the differences between bilinguals and monolinguals are large enough, or last long enough, to make a meaningful difference in people's day-to-day lives. Bilingual children may understand some basic principles of writing sooner than monolingual children, for example, but do they actually learn to read earlier?

Many of the researchers who study bilingualism, particularly in children, are interested in the interlocking questions of how bilingualism works in the brain and how it interacts with other general cognitive abilities. For this reason, many studies have a very narrow focus: Do bilinguals have an advantage on some types of executive control tasks but not others? What happens if we make the task harder in this way, or in that way? These studies also tend to focus on balanced bilinguals, on the assumption that we're more likely to see the effect of bilingualism (if it exists) in a balanced bilingual than in someone with limited knowledge of a second language. All this means that even though we now know much more about bilingualism than we used to, it's premature to declare 'Being bilingual makes you smarter!' and expect our statement to apply equally to a bilingual child of immigrants, an adult in a diglossic society, and a high-school student taking her first semester of French.

It's also not true that bilinguals are superior to monolinguals in every way; research on bilingualism has found a few areas in which bilinguals consistently perform just a little bit *worse* than monolinguals. Most notably, a bilingual child will typically have a slightly smaller vocabulary in each language early on than a child monolingual in that language; bilinguals are also slightly slower at retrieving words (for example, when naming pictures) than monolinguals. The situation is not nearly as dire as people used to think, but there clearly are times when it's appropriate to speak of a monolingual advantage.

Where does all this leave us? First of all, we now know that childhood bilingualism is *not* harmful, and in several domains it even appears to be beneficial. This finding has important practical consequences. Several decades ago, parents who spoke different languages (or parents who had immigrated to a new country) were warned against raising their children bilingually, for fear that the children would be confused and delayed. We can now reassure parents that they will not harm their children by raising them with two languages. In addition, the more we know about these issues, the more informed we will be when making policy decisions that encourage or discourage bilingualism. There are obviously many other considerations that go into deciding, for example, whether a school should offer bilingual education for children of immigrants, or immersion in a foreign language for monolingual children; but it's helpful to know that bilingualism *per se* doesn't damage a child's intelligence, and that it may even be beneficial in domains like executive control and metalinguistic ability.

On the other hand, we must remember that bilingualism is extremely complex; despite the progress we have made, there is a great deal that we still don't know. Bilingualism is not a magic bullet; enrolling your child in a French immersion preschool may well be a valuable experience that introduces her to a new language and culture, but it doesn't guarantee her admission to Harvard. Hakuta (1985) argues that asking 'How does bilingualism affect intelligence?' is the wrong question to begin with:

> The fundamental question is misguided, for it entails two key simplifying assumptions. The first assumption is that the effect of bilingualism – indeed, the human mind – can be reduced to a single dimension (ranging from "good" to "bad"), and that the treatment (bilingualism) moves the individual child's standing up or down the dimension. The second assumption is that choosing whether the child is to be raised bilingually or not is like choosing a brand of diaper, that it is relatively free of the social circumstances surrounding the choice.
>
> Hakuta (1985, 43–44)

Perhaps the safest thing to say is that there are many positive reasons to learn a second language: it may allow someone to communicate with more people, to explore new cultures, to enjoy that language's literature, to pursue new business opportunities, to appreciate his ethnic or religious heritage. People who want to learn a second language, or who want to raise their children with two languages, have no reason to fear that they are sacrificing their or their children's intellectual abilities by doing so.

7.4 Summary

- Some bilingual people speak both languages about equally well; many others are more fluent in one language than the other.
- Many or most people who speak multiple languages tend to use those languages in different contexts. When an entire community uses two languages, one for formal situations and the other for informal ones, the situation is called *diglossia*.

- During the first half of the twentieth century, it was widely believed that bilingualism lowered children's intelligence. However, the studies that supported this conclusion were severely flawed.
- Recent research on bilingualism strongly supports the claim that being bilingual has cognitive benefits in a range of domains, including metalinguistic ability and executive control.

For further reflection

(1) Interview someone you know who uses two or more languages on a daily basis. What purposes does this person use each language for? What circumstances or choices led to this person becoming bilingual? How does this person feel about being bilingual – positive, negative, or indifferent?

(2) Read Rodriguez (1980) and Abbady (2013), two accounts of children growing up in a multilingual environment. How was the children's choice of language affected by the larger social context in which they were living? What values did the children and their parents attach to the various languages in the environment, and to the importance of being monolingual or bilingual? What conclusions do you draw from these two stories about the social context of language use?

(3) Other studies of the cognitive effects of bilingualism include Ben-Zeev (1977) (metalinguistic ability), Carlson and Meltzoff (2008) (executive control), and Goetz (2003) (theory of mind). Read and evaluate one of these papers. What do the authors conclude? Are you convinced by the results? Why or why not? What are the limitations of the study?

Further reading

An accessible overview to bilingualism is Grosjean (2010); Grosjean (1984), although older, is similarly accessible and emphasizes the social and political dimensions of bilingualism. Grosjean and Li (2013) is a more detailed introduction to what we know about the psycholinguistics of bilingualism.

Heritage languages are reviewed in Polinsky and Kagan (2007) and Benmamoun et al. (2010). The classic paper on diglossia is Ferguson (1959); Rubin (1968) describes the situation in Paraguay, and Choi (2005) provides a more recent perspective. Summaries of multilingualism in the Amazon include Sorensen (1967) and Jackson (1983); Stenzel (2005) has more recent observations.

The literature on bilingualism and intelligence is quite large. Hakuta (1985) provides an excellent and accessible overview of twentieth-century research and its social context. More technical reviews of post-1962 research include Bialystok (2001) and Bialystok et al. (2009); Adesope et al. (2010) is a meta-analysis of relevant studies.

Bibliography

Abbady, Tal. No English! *The New York Times*, June 29 2013. Available at http://opinionator.blogs.nytimes.com/2013/06/29/no-english/?_php=true&_type=blogs&_r=0.

Adesope, Olusola O., Tracy Lavin, Terri Thompson, and Charles Ungerleider. A systematic overview and meta-analysis of the cognitive correlates of bilingualism. *Review of Educational Research*, 80(2):207–245, 2010.

Baum, Shari, and Debra Titone. Moving toward a neuroplasticity view of bilingualism, executive control, and aging. *Applied Psycholinguistics*, 35(5):857–894, 2014.

Ben-Zeev, Sandra. The influence of bilingualism on cognitive strategy and cognitive development. *Child Development*, 48(3):1009–1018, 1977.

Benmamoun, Elabbas, Silvina Montrul, and Maria Polinsky. White paper: Prolegomena to heritage linguistics. Available at http://scholar.harvard.edu/mpolinsky/publications/white-paper-prolegomena-heritage-linguistics, 2010.

Bialystok, Ellen. *Bilingualism in Development: Language, Literacy, and Cognition*. Cambridge University Press, Cambridge, 2001.

Bialystok, Ellen, Tali Shenfield, and Judith Codd. Languages, scripts, and the environment: Factors in developing concepts of print. *Developmental Psychology*, 36(1):66–76, 2000.

Bialystok, Ellen, Gigi Luk, and Ernest Kwan. Bilingualism, biliteracy, and learning to read: Interactions among languages and writing systems. *Scientific Studies of Reading*, 9(1):43–61, 2005.

Bialystok, Ellen, Fergus I. M. Craik, David W. Green, and Tamar H. Gollan. Bilingual minds. *Psychological Science in the Public Interest*, 10(3):89–129, 2009.

Carlson, Stephanie M., and Andrew N. Meltzoff. Bilingual experience and executive functioning in young children. *Developmental Science*, 11(2):282–298, 2008.

Carrow, Mary Arthur. Linguistic functioning of bilingual and monolingual children. *Journal of Speech and Hearing Disorders*, 22(3):371–380, 1957.

Choi, Jinny K. Bilingualism in Paraguay: Forty years after Rubin's study. *Journal of Multilingual and Multicultural Development*, 26(3):233–248, 2005.

Ferguson, Charles A. Diglossia. *Word*, 15:325–340, 1959.

Goetz, Peggy J. The effects of bilingualism on theory of mind development. *Bilingualism: Language and Cognition*, 6(1):1–15, 2003.

Grosjean, François. *Life with Two Languages: An Introduction to Bilingualism*. Harvard University Press, Cambridge, MA, 1984.

Grosjean, François. *Bilingual: Life and Reality*. Harvard University Press, Cambridge, MA, 2010.

Grosjean, François, and Ping Li, editors. *The Psycholinguistics of Bilingualism*. Wiley-Blackwell, Oxford, 2013.

Hakuta, Kenji. *Mirror of Language – The Debate on Bilingualism*, chapter 2: Bilingualism and intelligence, pages 14–44. Basic Books, Inc., New York, NY, 1985.

Hakuta, Kenji, and Rafael M. Diaz. The relationship between degree of bilingualism and cognitive ability: A critical discussion and some new longitudinal data. In Keith E. Nelson, editor, *Children's Language*, volume 5, chapter 10, pages 319–344. Lawrence Erlbaum Associates, New York, NY, 1985.

Jackson, Jean E. *The Fish People: Linguistic Exogamy and Tukanoan Identity in Northwest Amazonia*, chapter 9: The role of language and speech in Tukanoan identity, pages 164–178. Number 39 in Cambridge Studies in Social Anthropology. Cambridge University Press, Cambridge, 1983.

Kavé, Gitit, Nitza Eyal, Aviva Shorek, and Jiska Cohen-Mansfield. Multilingualism and cognitive state in the oldest old. *Psychology and Aging*, 23(1):70–78, 2008.

Kovács, Ágnes Melinda, and Jacques Mehler. Cognitive gains in 7-month-old bilingual infants. *Proceedings of the National Academy of Sciences*, 106(16):6556–6560, 2009. Available at http://www.pnas.org/content/106/16/6556.full.

Lewis, D. G. Bilingualism and non-verbal intelligence: A further study of test results. *British Journal of Educational Psychology*, 29(1):17–22, 1959.

McCloskey, James. Irish as a world language. In Brian Ó Conchubhair, editor, *Why Irish? Irish Language and Literature in Academia*, pages 71–89. Arlen House, Galway, 2008.

Peal, Elizabeth, and Wallace E. Lambert. The relation of bilingualism to intelligence. *Psychological Monographs: General and Applied*, 76(27):1–23, 1962.

Polinsky, Maria, and Olga Kagan. Heritage languages: In the 'wild' and in the classroom. *Language and Linguistics Compass*, 1(5):368–395, 2007.

Rodriguez, Richard, An education in language. In Christopher Ricks and Leonard Michaels, editors, *The State of the Language*, pages 129–139. University of Chicago Press, Chicago, IL, 1980.

Rubin, Joan. *National Bilingualism in Paraguay*. Number 60 in Janua Linguarum: Studia Memoriae Nicolai van Wijk Dedicata. Mouton, The Hague, 1968.

Sorensen, Arthur P., Jr. Multilingualism in the Northwest Amazon. *American Anthropologist*, 69(6):670–684, 1967.

Stenzel, Kristine. Multilingualism in the Northwest Amazon, revisited. In *Memorias del Congreso de Idiomas Indígenas de Latinoamérica*, volume II, Austin, TX, 2005. Center for Indigenous Languages of Latin America.

Yoshioka, Joseph G. A study of bilingualism. *Journal of Genetic Psychology*, 36(3):473–479, 1929.

Part III

Language in use

8 'Women talk more than men'

Language differences mark social differences in many different ways. Certain ways of speaking may be associated with a particular geographic region, socioeconomic class, ethnicity, or age. Since gender is such a socially important characteristic of a person, we shouldn't be surprised to find language differences along gender lines as well.

But as soon as we move beyond a general acknowledgment that men and women might speak differently, things become murky very quickly. Plenty of people have ideas about exactly *how* men and women use language differently; in the United States, for example, the following opinions are very common:

- Women talk more than men.
- Men are more direct; women are more polite.
- Women speak more correctly than men.
- Men speak more confidently than women.

For linguists, the first step is figuring out whether claims like these are actually true. And if a study does find that men and women speak differently in some way, we're left with a whole new set of questions. For example, suppose you conducted an experiment and found that women were more likely to say *um* than men. Does this mean that women are more insecure than men? Or that they're more thoughtful and take more time deciding what to say next? How much do the results depend on the design of the experiment? For example, was the data collected in a lab setting, or from a corpus of spontaneous conversation? If it was a lab setting, could the task have biased the results? Were the subjects discussing a topic that men might traditionally be expected to know more about? Were subjects giving monologues, conversing in pairs, or talking in small groups? Were they talking with others of the same sex or the opposite sex?

As we will see, factors like these have a huge effect on how men and women speak. It turns out that there are very few statements of the form 'Women are X-er than men' (or vice versa) that are generally true, with the obvious exception of 'Men tend to have lower voices than women'.[1] Usually, the best we can do is say 'Women tend to be X-er than men *in such-and-such a situation*'.

Before we turn to two specific case studies – whether women talk more than men in general, and whether women are more likely to use tag questions – we will survey observations about men's and women's language from a variety of settings. Beliefs about differences between men and women, and actual differences in men's and women's speech, vary surprisingly in different circumstances – a fact that underscores the importance of understanding the social context in which language is used before we make broad generalizations.

8.1 Western commentary on language and gender

Many people today believe that women tend to have better verbal skills than men – girls learn to talk sooner than boys, women perform better on tests of verbal ability, and so on. There's some research to support this idea, although the differences (if real) are very small: there's much more variation among individual men and women than there is between the two groups.

Historically, though, the belief that women's language is superior to that of men is something of an anomaly. A medieval English song collected in Salisbury (2002, 247–249) praises women effusively, with many glowing descriptions of their speech: women keep secrets, never gossip, and aren't prone to talking too much; they are pleasant company. But every stanza ends with the line *Cuius contrarium verum est* – Latin for 'of which the opposite is true'. The joke is that the song appears to praise women, but a person who knows Latin (at the time, almost exclusively men) would realize that the song is actually highly insulting.

8.1.1 Jespersen on women's language

Closer to our own era, we can see examples of early-twentieth-century views of women's language in the work of Otto Jespersen. One of the fathers of modern linguistics, Jespersen devoted one chapter of his classic book on language (Jespersen 1922) to gender differences. The title of the chapter – 'The woman' – suggests from the start that ordinary language use is defined by the way men speak; if women speak differently, they're deviating from the norm.

Many of Jespersen's specific comparisons suggest that women's language is deficient relative to men's. He says that women tend to use

[1] Even differences that are physiologically based aren't immune to social influences. Men typically have longer throats than women (because they tend to be taller), and this difference affects the acoustics of their vowels – but Johnson (2006) shows that some societies have larger male-female differences than others.

more 'refined' expressions, but goes on to address the 'danger of the language becoming languid and insipid if we are always to content ourselves with women's expressions ... vigour and vividness count for something' (p. 247). He claims that women have smaller vocabularies than men, although to his credit he considers (but ultimately rejects) the possibility that this could be the result of unequal educational opportunities. Jespersen goes so far as to recommend that a person who is just beginning to study a foreign language should read 'ladies' novels' because they will be easier to understand.

Even when Jespersen goes out of his way to compliment women for their unique linguistic abilities, it's hard to avoid the impression that women are being damned with faint praise:

> Woman is linguistically quicker than man: quicker to learn, quicker to hear, and quicker to answer. A man is slower: he hesitates, he chews the cud to make sure of the taste of words, and thereby comes to discover similarities with and differences from other words, both in sound and in sense, thus preparing himself for the appropriate use of the fittest noun or adjective.
>
> [W]omen much more often than men break off without finishing their sentences, because they start talking without having thought out what they are going to say....
>
> Jespersen (1922, 249, 250)

Jespersen paints a picture in which women's language is simple and superficial, while men's language is deep, complex, and thoughtful. His evidence is scant and unsystematic – in fact, many of his examples of 'women's speech' are taken from women's dialogue in plays and novels written by men! Clearly, we're seeing a summary of some common beliefs about women's language from Jespersen's time, not a scientific investigation.

8.1.2 Men Are from Mars, Women Are from Venus

The end of the twentieth century saw the rise of an alternative view of men's and women's language, one that is just as much a product of its time as Jespersen's views were a product of his. Books such as John Gray's *Men Are from Mars, Women Are from Venus* and Deborah Tannen's *You Just Don't Understand* argue that men and women have different ways of speaking – different 'languages' – that are equally good. When men and women talk to each other, the result is frequent miscommunication, and the solution is for each gender to learn the other's language. Gray's book famously frames gender differences with a parable of interspecies communication – he imagines that men and women come from different planets, and provides 'translations' of common Martian and Venusian expressions.

Many of Gray's specific observations sound a lot like Jespersen's; the difference is that Gray, much more than Jespersen, goes to great lengths to argue that women aren't deficient, just different. Jespersen claims, for example, that women overuse intensifiers: *awfully pretty*, *terribly nice*, *I'm so glad you've come*. Gray, too, states that women are prone to exaggeration and overgeneralization (*No one listens to me anymore*), but he argues that statements like these are really requests for understanding and support and aren't meant to be taken literally. Similarly, Gray claims that women don't think before speaking, but he puts this in a positive light:

> Women think out loud, sharing their process of inner discovery with an interested listener. Even today, a woman often discovers what she wants to say through the process of just talking. This process of just letting thoughts flow freely and expressing them out loud helps her to tap into her intuition. This process is perfectly normal and especially necessary sometimes.
>
> But men process information very differently. Before they talk or respond, they first silently "mull over" or think about what they have heard or experienced. Internally and silently they figure out the most correct or useful response. They first formulate it inside and then express it.
>
> Gray (1992, 67–68)

Both *Men Are from Mars, Women Are from Venus* and *You Just Don't Understand* were extraordinarily popular and spent years on bestseller lists. They offered a non-threatening and reassuringly egalitarian diagnosis of male-female relationship problems: both partners are acting in good faith, but they're speaking different languages. Neither language is 'better' than the other; they're just different, and the solution is easy: learn your partner's language.

8.1.3 Claimed gender differences: Empirical and social assessments

Are Gray and Tannen right that men and women differ in these ways? In some cases, the answer is clearly 'no'. Gray, for example, claims that women (but not men) say things like *oh*, *hmmm*, and *uh-huh* while the other person is speaking. This phenomenon is known as *backchanneling*; it's a way for the listener to indicate that he or she is paying attention. Backchanneling is *not* exclusive to women: some of the studies we will examine below collected data on backchanneling and found that men do it just as much as women (see sections 8.3.4 and 8.3.5).

On the other hand, one reason these books are so popular is that some people genuinely recognize themselves in these descriptions of men and women. It would be naïve to say that there's nothing there. Tannen, for example, sums up the two communication styles she identifies as 'report talk' (men) and 'rapport talk' (women). We will see below that there is indeed evidence that men, at least in some situations, are more likely to use language to accomplish tasks, while women are more likely to use language as a tool to maintain social relationships.

But to the extent that Gray and Tannen may have identified a genuine difference between (some) men and (some) women, what is the *cause* of that difference? One possibility, of course, is that we're dealing with an inherent sex-linked biological difference. Although we can't rule it out as a possibility, this hypothesis turns out to be very difficult to prove because it's so hard to control for social factors that might also lead to differences between women and men.[2] In addition, the striking cross-cultural variation in the supposed 'natural' behavior of men and women should make us suspicious of the conclusion that our own culture has happened to hit on an innate biological difference. If community A believes that women naturally behave one way, while community B believes that they are naturally the opposite, we can't avoid the conclusion that social expectations play a crucial role in what men and women actually do.

A second possible cause of gender differences is separate socialization; Tannen explicitly argues for this hypothesis. The basic idea is that girls play with girls, boys play with boys, and in the process they learn different ways of speaking – different languages – that persist into adulthood. According to this hypothesis, girls grow up in communities that place a high value on using language to maintain social relationships, while boys grow up in communities where language is a tool for getting tasks done. There is some research that lends partial support to this idea, but it's unlikely to be the whole story. It's not true, for example, that children play exclusively in single-sex groups; moreover, there are more similarities than differences between girls' and boys' interactions during play.

A third possible explanation appeals to differing social expectations of men and women, particularly as they relate to power. Men, for example, may be expected to take the lead in a group problem-solving task: contributing ideas, debating what to do, and formulating a solution. Women may be expected to take a more indirect (and possibly less valued) role: acknowledging others' contributions, facilitating compromise, and generally ensuring that the group works smoothly. According to this view, it's not that men and women have inherently different ways of speaking; rather, to the extent that they adopt conventional male and female roles (which

2 Biological explanations for sex differences have recently had a resurgence in popularity; examples include Sax (2005), Brizendine (2006), and Brizendine (2010). Unfortunately, much of this work appears to suffer from careless handling of the scientific evidence; for discussion, see Liberman (2006a) and links therein.

often involve a power difference), they use language in service of those roles.

These last two ideas roughly correspond to two models of gender and communication known as the *difference* model and the *dominance* model, respectively. Ultimately, it seems that neither model by itself is likely to give us a full understanding of the relationship between gender and language. The difference model falls short when it ignores the fact that both men and women are perfectly capable of using a variety of linguistic tools when the situation requires; the difference model may also minimize the role that social power undeniably plays in some situations. Critics have also noted that even though proponents argue that men's and women's ways of speaking are equally valid, they're more likely to advise women to accommodate to men's styles rather than vice versa. The dominance model, on the other hand, may be in danger of ascribing *all* typically 'female' communication strategies to power differences, rather than valuing those strategies on their own terms.

8.2 Language and gender in context: Ideals and behavior

One thing the difference and dominance models have in common is that they both emphasize the *context* in which language is used. The difference model invites us to consider how all-male and all-female groups may differ in their ideals regarding how language should be used and in the kind of behavior that's expected from group members. The dominance model focuses on how broader beliefs affect actual language use and how these things interact with status and power, especially in male-female interaction.

In this section, we will look at two common beliefs about men's and women's language – that women are more polite than men, and that they speak more correctly – as they relate to specific sociolinguistic contexts. The specific examples illustrate two larger themes: first, that beliefs about what men and women 'naturally' do vary widely across communities; and second, that men and women's actual behavior is influenced heavily by community ideals about language and expectations about men and women.

8.2.1 Polite men and aggressive women

In contemporary western contexts, women are widely seen as indirect and polite where men are direct and blunt. Women's indirectness is sometimes framed as a problem or deficiency – hence the abundant advice for women in the business world on how to negotiate, ask for what they want, and be assertive. Alternatively, this indirectness is also sometimes framed as an asset; one of the arguments for including more women in management positions is that they bring with them a more cooperative and collaborative style than their male peers. Either way, the belief that women are inherently more indirect than men is very strong.

For this reason, many people are surprised to learn that this belief isn't universal. As it turns out, different communities can have very different ideas about how men and women naturally behave.

Politeness in rural Madagascar

Keenan (1996) describes how indirectness and avoiding confrontation are highly prized in rural Madagascar. Direct questions, criticism, and any other behavior that might put another person on the spot are strongly tabooed. Indirectness is especially important in the formal speech mode known as *kabary*, which involves heavy use of allusions, proverbs, and other roundabout ways of making a point. *Kabary* involves elaborate self-deprecation on the part of the speaker and doesn't directly criticize others; when such criticism is necessary (for example, when a wrongdoing in the community needs to be discussed, or when another person's *kabary* is inadequate), the ability to do so in a subtle and non-confrontational way is the mark of a skilled speaker.

These highly valued ways of speaking and acting are associated with men: it's men who know how to act appropriately and maintain good social relationships. Men and women alike believe that only men are skilled enough for *kabary*; women are too direct and unsophisticated. Women are more likely to display anger and behave in other socially inappropriate ways.

Interestingly, there are situations where women's 'unskilled' behavior is useful. When someone in the community has behaved inappropriately, it's women who will publicly and directly criticize the person's actions. In the marketplace, women are the ones who bargain with customers. In a sense, women are called upon whenever it is socially necessary to be direct and aggressive – not because they are seen as having a skill set complementary to men's, but because they are seen as lacking the sophistication that prevents men from engaging in those kinds of activities.

The kros *in Papua New Guinea*

Madagascar isn't the only place where public displays of anger are associated with women. Kulick (1993) describes a specifically female speech genre in the village of Gapun in Papua New Guinea: the *kros*. During a *kros*, the speaker delivers a long, angry monologue from inside her house, directed at the person or persons who have wronged her. The following excerpt, translated from Tok Pisin, gives the flavor of a *kros*:

> You're a fucking rubbish man. You hear?! Your fucking prick is full of maggots. You're a big fucking semen prick. Stone balls!...

Fucking black prick! Fucking grandfather prick! You've built me a good house that I just fall down in, you get up and hit me on the arm with a piece of sugar cane! You fucking mother's cunt!

Kulick (1993, 522)

Only women deliver *kroses*; a married man who has been wronged will get his wife to deliver one for him. (This option is obviously unavailable to widowed and divorced men, who do occasionally give their own *kroses*.) Both men and women see the *kros* as an example of natural female behavior: women are 'disruptive, divisive, begrudging, antisocial, and emotionally excessive' (Kulick 1993, 512). With the possible exception of 'emotionally excessive', these characteristics are precisely the opposite of the ones westerners typically associate with women.

By this point, contemporary western ideas about women's superior verbal skills are starting to look anomalous. Obviously, societies vary in what they believe about women's speech: according to the medieval song discussed above, women are gossipy and unable to keep secrets; according to Jespersen, women are languid and insipid; according to rural Malagasy communities, women are unskilled and blunt. What all these beliefs have in common is not the specific characteristics that are attributed to women, but the idea that women are inferior to men. Where assertiveness and directness are highly valued, those behaviors are considered to be characteristic of men; where indirectness and self-effacement are highly valued, *those* behaviors are attributed to men.

This is not to say that men and women are exactly the same after all. It seems clear that Malagasy women really do engage in more public displays of anger than men, and that women in Jespersen's day really were more likely than men to use euphemisms when referring to bodily functions. Rather, these examples tell us that before we conclude that some difference between men and women in our own culture is a natural consequence of male and female biology, we need to seriously consider the role that social expectations play in shaping that behavior.

One final note: it's not entirely true that women are generally believed to have superior verbal skills, even in contemporary western contexts. One glaring exception is the fact that many speech patterns associated with young women are heavily stigmatized – consider the 'valley girl' stereotype. Another example is the phenomenon known as 'uptalk': rising intonation at the end of a sentence. The popular story about this pattern is that it shows that the speaker – almost always assumed to be a young woman – is uncertain, lacks self-confidence, and can't commit to anything. (A person who uses this pattern, of course, may have entirely different reasons for doing so: to signal that the conversation isn't over, for example, or to invite the listener to respond to what has just been said.) Thus, even in a context where women in the abstract are believed to have better verbal skills, the particular speech patterns associated with young women are often dismissed as annoying habits that are unworthy of a serious speaker.

8.2.2 The correctness of women's speech

Another common idea is that women speak more 'correctly' than men – or, as linguists would say, that women's speech is closer to the standard than men's speech. As it turns out, there's a great deal of truth to this idea: in many communities, men are more likely to use certain non-standard forms than women are (see Labov 1990 for a review of research in this area). However, the following two examples demonstrate that we can't just stop there and proclaim that women's speech is generally more standard than men's; as it turns out, gender interacts with community ideals and with social class in complex and interesting ways.

Covert prestige in Norwich

Sociolinguists have consistently found that individual people use language differently in different situations, and that this variation has social meaning. In one common pattern, there are two different versions of a sound, word, or other linguistic unit. One version is prestigious and associated with the standard dialect of the language; the other version is stigmatized and associated with a non-standard dialect. Although some members of the community are more likely to use one version than the other, most people use both, and their choice depends on the situation.

In many dialects of English, the verbal suffix *-ing* (*walking*, *talking*, *reading*) shows this kind of variation. The prestige variant of this suffix is pronounced [-iŋ], where [ŋ] is the *ng* sound in *singer*. The non-prestige variant is pronounced [-ən], where [ə] is the short vowel in the second syllable of words like *bacon* and *woman*. Using the non-prestige variant is often referred to as '*g*-dropping', but this is inaccurate: neither variant actually contains a [g]. (Compare the [g] in *finger* to the lack of [g] in *singer*; the prestige pronunciation of *-ing* is like *singer*, not *finger*, for most people.) Practically everyone uses both pronunciations of *-ing*; people tend to use [-iŋ] more often in formal contexts and [-ən] in informal contexts.

Trudgill (1983) found many examples of this pattern in a study of sociolinguistic variation in the city of Norwich. Consistent with previous research, he identified three factors that affected how likely a person was to use the prestige or non-prestige variant:

1. Middle-class speakers were more likely to use the prestige variant than lower-class speakers.
2. People were more likely to use the prestige variant in more formal contexts.
3. Women were more likely to use the prestige variant than men.

In addition to recording people's speech and counting how often they used each variant in different contexts, Trudgill explicitly asked his subjects how they spoke. Not surprisingly, he found that people weren't very good judges of their own speech; moreover, the ways in which people's self-evaluations were inaccurate tells us something about their attitudes toward the standard dialect. A sizeable number of women claimed that they were more likely to use the prestige variant than the non-prestige variant, even when this wasn't true. This *over-reporting* of their use of the prestige variant isn't terribly surprising; it suggests that many women aspired to speak 'correctly' (i.e., the standard dialect) and were a bit too optimistic about whether they were succeeding.

Among men, a different story emerged. A surprising number of men *under-reported* their use of the prestige variant: that is, they claimed that they were more likely to use the non-prestige variant, even when this wasn't true. (Some women under-reported as well, but men were far more likely to do so.) In other words, these men thought their speech was less 'correct' than it actually was. Trudgill suggests that there is a difference between the *overt prestige* of the standard dialect and the *covert prestige* of the local, non-standard dialect: even though most speakers claim that the standard is better, the behavior of the under-reporting men suggests that what they really value is the non-standard variety of the local community, perhaps because it's associated with 'toughness' and 'maleness'.

What we see here is a difference between men and women that involves attitudes as well as behavior. The standard dialect is valued by both men and women as the correct and proper way to speak. The non-standard dialect, by contrast, may hold subtly different social meanings for the two groups: men are more likely than women to assign a different kind of prestige to non-standard forms, one related to its role in maintaining solidarity in the local community.

Jocks and burnouts

Eckert (2011) found a different kind of interaction between gender and language ideals in a Detroit high school, where about half the students identified themselves as members of one of two salient social groups. *Jocks* were oriented toward the school and the world outside Detroit; they were typically middle-class and college-bound. *Burnouts* were typically working-class and were oriented toward the local community.

Students used a number of behaviors to mark themselves as either jocks or burnouts, and naturally one of these behaviors was their speech. Eckert analyzed three sounds that were in the process of changing; for each sound, there was a 'conservative' variant (the one associated with the standard dialect) and a 'progressive' variant (the one associated with the local community). Not surprisingly, the jocks tended to use the conservative variants, while the burnouts tended to use the progressive variants.

If women's speech is generally more standard than men's, then we would expect the most conservative speakers to be the jock girls; this is exactly what Eckert found. But the burnout girls had the most *progressive* speech: it was marked by local features even more than the speech of the burnout boys. In other words, we can't say that women are always more standard in their speech than men; the burnout girls in this high school had the most non-standard speech of any group.

Eckert suggests that girls in both groups needed to mark their identity using language. Boys could participate in a variety of activities to demonstrate their status as jocks or burnouts; for example, jock boys could run for student government or play sports. But fewer of these opportunities were available to girls in the 1980s (when the research was conducted), so they found it necessary to use language instead. Thus, the girls went even further than the boys in making sure that their speech showed which group they belonged to.

The larger lesson to be learned from this example is that it's inappropriate to treat gender separately from other social categories such as class. A person speaks, not just as a man or a woman, but as a particular *kind* of man or woman. Just as men and women don't differ in the same ways in Madagascar and the United States, they also may not differ in the same ways in separate local communities even in the same country.

8.3 Case study: Do women talk more than men?

One of the most popular current beliefs about language and gender is that women are more talkative than men. The idea appears periodically in popular science writing or in relationship advice, often accompanied by authoritative-sounding numbers: 'Women use an average of 20,000 words a day; men use only 7,000.' Liberman (2006b) documented as many examples as he could find of purported male and female words-per-day averages, and discovered two things. First, the numbers vary hugely: women are claimed to use anywhere from 7,000 to 50,000 words per day; men, from 2,000 to 25,000. Second, not a single author backs up his or her numbers with a reference to a scientific study of male and female speech patterns. The numbers appear to be plucked out of thin air, and some of them live on as zombie statistics, lumbering from one popular science book to the next.

Few researchers have actually tried to calculate daily word counts for men and women (although see section 8.3.6 below), but a huge number of studies have explored how much men and women talk in particular situations. We will survey a small sample of the enormous literature on this subject, examining how the behavior of both men and women is affected by the specific setting they're in.

8.3.1 Decision-making in small groups: Aries (1982)

Studies of gender and amount of talk can be divided roughly into two groups: those in which subjects were asked to accomplish a specific task (and had to talk in order to do so), and those in which subjects engaged in relatively unstructured conversations. We will begin with several examples of studies of the former type.

Aries (1982) tested college students in groups of 5 to 6. Each group was presented with a hypothetical ethical dilemma and had 40 minutes to arrive at a consensus on what should be done. Some of the groups were all-male or all-female; others were mixed-sex. Aries chose to study students at a competitive liberal arts college on the hypothesis that they would be less likely to exhibit gender stereotypes than the general population.

Table 8.1 shows three measures of subjects' verbal behavior. *Verbal Acts Initiated* is a count of how many times a subject spoke during the group discussion; Table 8.1 displays proportions of verbal acts initiated by men and women separately out of the total number of verbal acts in their group. For the single-sex groups, obviously, the proportions are at 1.0 because only men (or women) were present. But for the mixed-sex groups, an interesting difference emerges: women spoke more than men, contributing 55% of the total verbal acts (a difference that Aries reports as significant at $p < .02$). So far, the results support the idea that women tend to talk more than men.

However, further differences emerge when we examine specific types of verbal acts. Aries coded verbal acts into two categories: *Attempts Answers*, opinions or suggestions relevant to the task at hand; or *Reactions*, statements of agreement or disagreement with something someone else had said. Table 8.1 presents these types of verbal acts as proportions of the total verbal acts initiated for each gender in each group type; thus, in mixed-sex groups, 55% of men's contributions were coded as Attempts Answers. The proportions don't add up to 1.0 because some verbal acts didn't fall into either category.

The results show that in mixed-sex groups, men and women were engaging in different *kinds* of talk. When men spoke, they were more likely than women to offer an original contribution to the problem at hand; when women spoke, they were more likely than men to react to something someone else had said. (Aries reports that both of these differences were significant at

Table 8.1 *Proportions of total verbal acts initiated by act type, gender, and group type. Reproduced with permission of authors and publisher from: Aries, E. J. Verbal and nonverbal behavior in single-sex and mixed-sex groups: Are traditional sex roles changing?* Psychological Reports, *1982, 51, 127–134. © Psychological Reports 1982.*

		Single-sex Groups		Mixed-sex Groups	
Category		Male $n = 7$	Female $n = 6$	Male $n = 8$	Female $n = 8$
Verbal Acts Initiated	*M*	1.0	1.0	.45	.55
	SD	0.0	0.0	.07	.07
Attempts Answers	*M*	.47	.46	.55	.45
	SD	.08	.05	.05	.06
Reactions	*M*	.19	.25	.22	.30
	SD	.06	.07	.06	.02

$p < .02$.) We can characterize this difference by saying that men engaged in more task-oriented behavior than women, while women engaged in more social-emotional behavior (acknowledging others' contributions) than men. Interestingly, this difference appears to be much smaller or even absent in the single-sex groups, where men and women had similar rates of both types of verbal acts.

One notable feature of this study is how the overall amount of talk contributed by each gender was measured: a simple count of how many times each person spoke. Alternatively, we could measure the total amount of time each person spent talking, or how many words each person said. Neither measurement is clearly better than the other, but the fact that men and women in the mixed-sex groups engaged in different kinds of talk suggests that the two measurements might lead to different conclusions. Specifically, it seems likely that offering an opinion or suggestion would tend to involve more talking than reacting to someone else's statement; the latter could be no more than a simple *Yeah*. It's possible that the men in the mixed-sex groups actually spent *more* time talking than the women, even though they took fewer conversational 'turns'. We don't have the relevant data for this study, but a number of other experiments have found exactly that: when measured by number of conversational turns, women appear to talk more; when measured by total time speaking or number of words, men appear to talk more. (For an example, see section 8.3.4 below.) This effect complicates our conclusions in two ways: it further demonstrates that men and women appear to be engaging in different kinds of talk, and it forces us to specify exactly what we mean by 'talking a lot'.

8.3.2 Gender imbalance in small groups: Karpowitz et al. (2012)

If men and women behave differently depending on whether they're in single-sex or mixed-sex groups, we might also expect their behavior to be affected by the *composition* of mixed-sex groups. Does a man behave differently in a group composed mostly of other men, versus a group composed mostly of women?

Karpowitz et al. (2012) investigated this question in the context of democratic deliberation. They presented groups of five subjects each with four principles of income redistribution; examples included one rule by which no income was redistributed at all, and another by which just enough was redistributed so that everyone received at least some minimum amount. Each group was required to choose the principle they felt would be most just for society at large, and which would also be applied to group members' own income from work they did later in the experiment. (This work involved correcting misspelled words, although subjects didn't know the nature of the work when they voted – for all they knew, they might have been pulling weeds or playing the harmonica.) Karpowitz et al. systematically varied both the gender composition of the groups and the decision rule that they used in voting, either unanimous vote or majority rule. A total of 470 subjects participated in the experiment; they included both college students and non-student members of nearby communities.

Figure 8.1 shows the ratio of female-to-male speech in each condition, where amount of talk is measured by a person's talking time as a proportion of the entire group. Note that equal proportional participation by men and women would result in a ratio of 1.0. (Results are omitted for all-male and all-female groups, where such a ratio cannot be calculated.) Two major trends are obvious in Figure 8.1. The first is that regardless of the decision rule or the composition of the group, women almost always spent less time speaking than men. The only exception is in groups with four women who voted according to majority rule, where women on average spoke slightly more than men – but in this case, the difference between the ratio and 1.0 isn't statistically significant; therefore, the best we can say is that women and men in this condition spoke approximately the same amount. The second trend is that when the group required a unanimous vote, men spoke proportionally more when they were in the minority: the more women there were in the group, the more the remaining men talked.

Karpowitz et al., who were primarily interested in the implications of this study for democratic participation, observe that the mere presence of women in a group – even a lot of women – doesn't automatically ensure that women contribute equally to the discussion. (It would be interesting to study whether this effect remains the same in different contexts – for example, if the women

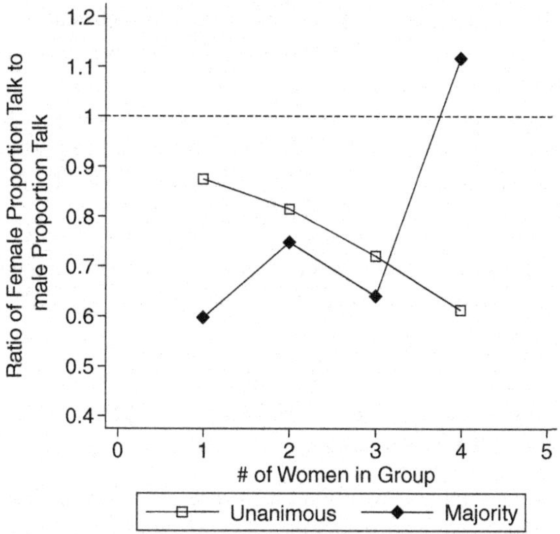

Note: A ratio of 1 means equality of speech participation.

Figure 8.1 Ratio of female to male speech participation by experimental condition. Christopher F. Karpowitz, Tali Mendelberg, and Lee Shaker, Gender inequality in deliberative participation, *American Political Science Review* 106(3):533–547, 2012, Figure 1.

are elected officials who represent constituents and not just themselves.) For our purposes, it's clear that this study provides no evidence for the supposed inherent talkativeness of women: it was the men who talked either the same amount or more in every case.

8.3.3 College classrooms: Sternglanz and Lyberger-Ficek (1977)

The group discussions examined in the previous two studies we have seen are somewhat artificial. Perhaps most saliently, the groups were composed of strangers: people who, for the most part, didn't know each other and were unlikely to meet again after the study was over. In the obvious everyday examples of groups that would be likely to engage in this kind of intense interaction – friends, co-workers, colleagues – group members know each other reasonably well, and this acquaintance is likely to affect how they behave.

One reason studies typically use artificially constructed groups of strangers is that this is much easier than going out and finding pre-existing groups that are willing to be observed, while simultaneously controlling for important demographic and situational variables. However, there is a substantial body of literature on one particular group interaction setting: the college classroom.

There's certainly no guarantee that fellow students are intimately acquainted, especially in large classes, but at the very least the class has become a familiar environment by the end of the term.

Sternglanz and Lyberger-Ficek (1977) observed one session each of 60 college classes. They were interested in whether men tended to participate more than women, and whether students' participation was affected by the gender of the teacher. The results revealed two gender-related patterns:

1. When a male teacher initiated an interaction with students, men were more likely to respond than women ($p < .002$). When a female teacher initiated an interaction, there was no difference.
2. Men initiated more interactions (e.g., raising their hands or asking questions) than women did ($p < .003$). The effect was stronger in classes taught by male teachers than in classes taught by female teachers.

A number of similar studies have found the same pattern: in classrooms, men tend to do more talking than women. One thing we can't learn from Sternglanz and Lyberger-Ficek's study is how big this difference was; the authors report tests of statistical significance but not, for example, the average number of times men and women raised their hands. But what we *can* be certain of is that this study provides no evidence that women are inherently more talkative than men.

8.3.4 Casual conversation: Frances (1979)

All the studies we have seen so far examined talk in formal situations: subjects were asked to answer a question, solve a problem, or participate in the relatively formal setting of a college classroom. But people obviously behave differently in formal and informal settings, and the stereotype of women's talkativeness is closely associated with informal settings: women chatting with friends or haranguing their spouses. Maybe the studies we've seen so far just haven't looked for talkative women in the right places.

With this in mind, we turn now to Frances (1979), a study in which the participants were strangers who were asked to do nothing more than get to know each other during a brief conversation. The participants were students at the University of Chicago, 22 men and 22 women each from the Law School and the School of Social Service Administration. Each participant was recorded in two conversations, one with someone of the same sex and another with someone of the opposite sex. Conversations were seven minutes long, but only the last five minutes were analyzed.

Table 8.2 summarizes the results for the number of conversational turns and the average duration of those turns, broken down by the gender of the speaker

Table 8.2 *Amount of talk by gender of speaker and gender of addressee. Average total talk time is calculated from number of talk turns and average duration of talk turns; this figure was not present in the original table, and Frances reports that the differences are not significant. Time is given in seconds. Adapted from Table II of Susan J. Frances, Sex differences in nonverbal behavior,* Sex Roles *5(4): 519–535, 1979. With kind permission from Springer Science and Business Media.*

				Univariate	
Variable	Sex of partner	Mean for males	Mean for females	*F*	*p* <
Number of talk turns	Male	10.66	14.30	9.07	.004
	Female	14.32	14.32		
Average duration of talk turns	Male	16.64	11.02	3.93	.051
	Female	12.80	11.42		
Total talk time	Male	177.38	157.59		
	Female	183.30	163.53		

and the gender of the addressee. The paper doesn't report the average total talk time, because it wasn't significantly affected by sex, but we can calculate this from the other two averages; those numbers are included in Table 8.2 as well. The statistical test reported in the table tests whether there was a significant interaction between the sex of the speaker and the sex of the listener.

Subjects took an average of about 14 talk turns each during a conversation, except in one type of pair: men talking to men, who took only about 11 turns. By this measure, then, it appears that the women talked more – or, more accurately, that the presence of at least one woman in the pair encouraged more talk overall. But the average duration of those conversational turns suggests the opposite conclusion: during a given turn, men talked longer than women. (The test reported here shows a marginally significant interaction between the sex of the two speakers; in a separate analysis of the speaker only, Frances reports that men took significantly longer turns than women.) In fact, men's longer turns seem to have been enough to overcome the fact that they took fewer of them: there's a trend toward men spending more total time talking than women, regardless of the gender of their partner (although the trend isn't significant).

It's difficult to know what to make of these results. Do we conclude that the women talked more, since they took (and heard) more conversational turns; or that the men talked more, since their turns lasted longer? At the very least, this study does not support popular ideas about the talkativeness of women; there's little evidence here that the women were a great deal more talkative than the men. In addition, as with Aries (1982), there's a suggestion that men and women may have been engaging in different kinds of talk: women took and heard more conversational turns, but those turns were shorter. Finally, these results drive home the importance of being thoughtful about how we measure overall talkativeness: in this case, measuring the number of conversational turns and measuring the average length of those turns lead to opposite conclusions.

One other thing to note about Frances' results is that she also collected a great deal of data on backchanneling: she measured brief backchannel utterances (*Yes* or *I agree*) as well as some related non-verbal behaviors such as nodding. There were no significant differences between men and women for any of these behaviors. Of course, it may well be that women are more likely to backchannel than men (or vice versa) in other contexts. But, clearly, Gray's claim in *Men Are from Mars, Women Are from Venus* that men don't backchannel at all is simply false.

Like most studies, this one is vulnerable to the criticism that its subjects aren't representative of the broader population. Not only were they all students at a prestigious university, but they were enrolled in programs of study (Law and Social Service Administration) that might be likely to attract talkative people. Maybe the men weren't out-talked by the women here because we're dealing with a group of unusually talkative men to begin with. Alternatively, since all the pairs were strangers, maybe the men wanted to impress their conversational partners and talked more in order to do so.

8.3.5 Gender and power in romantic relationships: Kollock et al. (1985)

Kollock et al. (1985) is a striking study of how men and women behave in conversation, for two reasons: first, because the authors studied couples in existing romantic relationships, and thus (perhaps) elicited more natural conversation than you would expect between strangers in a lab; and second, because they carefully controlled for the relative power held by each member of each couple. Another unique aspect of this study is that the researchers studied both opposite-sex and same-sex couples. The data for same-sex couples is extremely interesting but turns out to be a bit difficult to interpret, so for reasons of space we will restrict our attention here to opposite-sex couples.

The researchers recruited couples who were either married or living together. Each couple filled out a questionnaire that assessed, among other things, the relative power of each member of the couple. (The couples were asked, for example, who usually had more influence in deciding where to go on vacation.) On the basis of these results, three groups of five couples each were selected for further interviews: couples where power was shared equally, couples where the male was substantially more powerful, and couples where the female was substantially more powerful.

Table 8.3 *Mean talking time in seconds by gender and couple type; Table 1 of Kollock et al. (1985).*

	Males	Females	Group Mean
Balanced couples	292	286	289
Couples with male more powerful	385	330	358
Couples with female more powerful	465	373	419
Group Mean	381	330	

During part of the interview, the couples read a series of five stories that described a conflict in a romantic relationship. Each member of the couple read the story separately and wrote down which character he or she believed was more justified; the couples then compared their answers and had to decide *together* who was more justified. To encourage the couples to disagree, the researchers secretly gave each partner a slightly different version of the story, slanted to favor one of the characters over the other. The interviewer left the room during these discussions, which were tape-recorded for later analysis.

Mean talking times for all three types of couples are summarized in Table 8.3. Among the couples where power was shared equally (the 'balanced' couples), both partners talked approximately the same amount. If the man was more powerful, he also tended to talk more; this suggests that talkativeness may be related to power rather than (or in addition to) gender. However, the couples where the woman was more powerful reveal a surprising pattern: the women talked far less than the men; in fact, the men in these couples were the most talkative group of all.[3]

This study seems likely to have elicited pretty natural behavior – the participants were long-established couples, and the interviews happened in their homes. This non-laboratory data fails to support the idea that women are inherently more talkative than men, or that wives typically talk more than their husbands. The results also demonstrate that the power dynamics of the situation have an important effect on how much people talk. However, the effect is not a simple one such as 'the more powerful person talks the most'; clearly, there's a complex interaction between gender and power at work here. (Kollock et al. did find a simpler effect of power on some other types of behavior: the more powerful partner was more likely to interrupt, and there was a trend towards the less powerful partner doing more backchanneling.) Perhaps the

[3] Kollock et al. report that there was a near-significant overall trend ($p < .10$) for men to talk more; however, they don't report male-female comparisons separately for each couple type, so we don't know which of these differences, if any, are significant.

most important conclusion we can draw from this study is that power matters, and it's unwise to draw conclusions from any study about how men and women talk without considering how power dynamics may have come into play.

8.3.6 Behavior over an entire day: Mehl et al. (2007)

The problem with nearly every study on the talkativeness of men and women is that laboratory experiments are inevitably situation-specific: subjects are asked to perform a particular task in a strange environment, often in a limited amount of time. If a study fails to find that women talk more than men, it's always possible that the researchers just happened to choose one of the few situations in which women are unusually quiet. The best evidence that women are natural talkers would come from a variety of situations: talking to friends, chatting with cashiers, engaging significant others in conversation, and so on. If we wanted to design a perfect study of this hypothesis, we would find a whole bunch of men and women, record them unobtrusively for days at a time, and compare the number of words each group spoke.

As it turns out, Mehl et al. (2007) is very close to this ideal experiment. The researchers studied the everyday speech of six groups of college students, five in the United States and one in Mexico, between 1998 and 2004. Subjects wore a microphone connected to a small digital recorder that recorded 30-second snippets of their speech periodically throughout the day; subjects didn't know when the recorder was on or off. Each subject wore the recorder for several days, and afterwards had the opportunity to delete any recordings he or she wished to (although, as it turned out, they did this only rarely). Subjects reported that they believed they were mostly unaffected by the presence of the recorder, although there's always the possibility that they had unconsciously altered their behavior.

The researchers counted the number of words spoken in each recording and, assuming that subjects were awake for 17 hours a day, used their sample to estimate the total words spoken per day by each subject. Although these numbers are clearly approximate (and we might ask whether the 17-hour day is an accurate estimate for college students), the extrapolation seems relatively safe in this case because the speech samples were taken throughout the day. Thus, the figures represent subjects' speech (or lack thereof) in a wide range of situations – attending class, folding laundry, eating lunch, or whatever else they happened to be doing.

At the low end, some subjects were estimated to speak only a few thousand words per day; at the high end, a few talkative individuals managed nearly 50,000. (Both extremes included both men and women.) For both men and women, though, the average is around 16,000; more precisely, the average for women is 16,215 and the average for men is 15,669. At $p = .248$, this difference is not statistically significant. Moreover, even if the difference *were* significant, the difference *between* the two groups is dwarfed by the variation *within* each group. There's simply no evidence here for the claim that women talk more than men, or that women talk three times as much as men, or that men use only 7,000 words per day.

As close as this experiment is to the perfect study of how much men and women talk, it is not above reproach. Like many social science experiments, this one involves a relatively homogenous group of college students, who may not be representative of the broader population. Furthermore, it's possible that certain types of people were less likely to volunteer for this study in the first place; for example, maybe especially talkative women were reluctant to be recorded for fear that they would reveal sensitive personal information. The huge amount of variation among both men and women makes this scenario unlikely, and we would have to add a very large number of talkative women or taciturn men to the results in order to come up with anything like the differences that have been claimed in the popular press – but it's always possible that the subjects were to some degree self-selected. Imperfect though it may be, this study casts further serious doubt on the claim that women talk a lot more than men; it's the best study of the question to date, and it's certainly more trustworthy than the *zero* studies supporting the numbers cited in Liberman (2006b).

8.3.7 Perception and reality: Cutler and Scott (1990)

The idea that women talk three times as much as men is clearly a myth: it's thoroughly discredited by the experimental literature, and the numbers that are often cited to accompany this claim were apparently plucked out of thin air. So why do so many people believe it anyway?

The cynical answer is that people will believe anything they're told, especially by reputed experts in the popular press, but this doesn't seem to be the whole story. One reason these statistics have such staying power appears to be that many people already believe something like this, and are convinced that their own experience is full of talkative women and laconic men. When yet another story about chatty women makes the rounds in the media, one of the most common reactions is 'Why did we need a study to tell us that?'

In all likelihood, many people genuinely *do* see more talkative women and silent men in their daily lives – they simply don't notice talkative men and silent women, or else consider them exceptions to the rule. Cutler and Scott (1990) is a fascinating illustration of the ways in which our beliefs about the world affect the way we perceive it. In this study, subjects listened to four brief

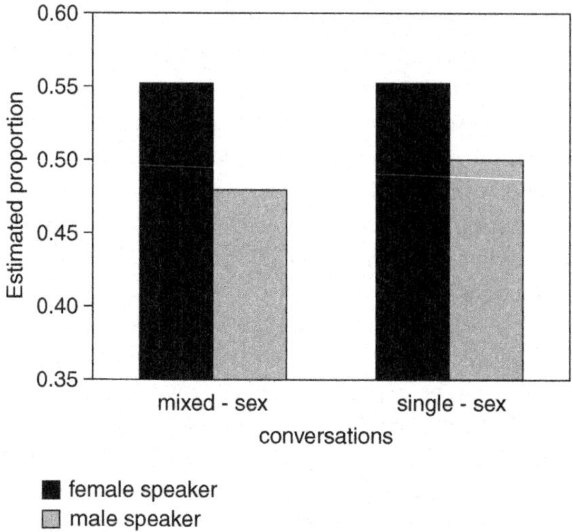

Figure 8.2 Average proportion of the conversation attributed to the first speaker, by gender of the first speaker and composition of the pair. Anne Cutler and Donia R. Scott, Speaker sex and perceived apportionment of talk, *Applied Psycholinguistics* 11(3):253–272, 1990, Figure 1.

dialogues and estimated what proportion of the total talking was done by each speaker.

As a matter of fact, three of the four dialogues had almost perfectly equal contributions from the two speakers, as measured by number of words; in the fourth, one participant spoke twice as much as the other. The dialogues were recorded by actors, and there were four versions of each: one in which the first speaker was female and the second speaker was male, one in which the first speaker was male and the second speaker was female, and two in which both speakers were of the same gender. Each subject heard only one version of each dialogue.

Figure 8.2 summarizes subjects' judgments about how much talk was contributed by the first speaker. For single-sex couples, subjects accurately estimated that both speakers contributed about 50% of the dialogue, regardless of whether the speakers were male or female. For mixed-sex couples, though, there is a striking difference: the first speaker was judged as contributing more than half of the conversation when the part was read by a woman, but as contributing less than half when the part was read by a man. In other words, when subjects heard a conversation between a man and a woman, they perceived the woman as talking more than she actually did.

The differences here aren't enormous – female speakers in mixed-sex pairs were estimated to contribute, on average, about 55% of the conversation – but the bias is clear. Our belief that women tend to talk more than men causes us to actually see more talkativeness in women, even when it's not there. It's easy to imagine other ways confirmation bias could reinforce popular opinion: a group of women chatting over drinks after work is a living demonstration of women's talkativeness, while a group of men doing the same thing is just normal social behavior.

8.3.8 General conclusions

There is not a shred of evidence that women use an average of 20,000 words a day while men use only 7,000 (or any of the other numbers that have been plugged into this formula). In fact, one consistent finding in the experimental literature has been that in many (but not all) situations, it's *men* who talk more. In the real world, gender is at best just one factor among many that affect language use; social expectations (some of which are related to gender), interpersonal dynamics and power relationships, and of course individual differences have a huge effect on how, and how much, people talk.

8.4 Case study: Do women use more tag questions than men?

In a now-famous book, *Language and Woman's Place*, Robin Lakoff argues that women's use of language is related to their subordinate place in society. She claims that women have been socialized to use language in a way that is polite, non-threatening, and submissive; this puts women in a double bind, because women who speak this way are viewed as uncertain and incompetent, while women who use 'masculine' language are labeled unfeminine and aggressive. Lakoff's conclusions were based on her personal impressions of language use among men and women she knew, and her work spawned a cottage industry of research on whether men and women really do differ in the ways that she claimed.

One of Lakoff's specific claims was that women are more likely to use a syntactic construction known as *tag questions*. A tag question appears at the end of a sentence and contains a pronoun plus *do*, *be*, *have*, or the modal verb of the main sentence; the tag is negative if the main sentence is positive, and vice versa. Lakoff argues that a tag question typically indicates that the speaker is uncertain about the statement, and that women tend to use tag questions in order to avoid expressing their opinions too directly.

(1) An 'uncertain' tag question, from Lakoff (1975, 16)
The way prices are rising is horrendous, <u>isn't it?</u>

Before we start counting tag questions in men's and women's speech, we should take a moment to consider the premise that tag questions express uncertainty. This is certainly a plausible function of tag questions; compared to the straightforward statement *The way prices are rising is horrendous*, the tag question in (1) seems to convey uncertainty or at least imply that the claim is open for discussion. On the other hand, when we look at a broad range of examples, it's easy to find tag questions that are anything but uncertain. Harris (1984), for example, studied questions of all kinds in the proceedings of magistrates' courts in Nottinghamshire County, where defendants are brought in for non-payment of fines or maintenance. Some of the tag questions uttered by the magistrates when questioning the defendants are downright aggressive:

(2) Non-tentative tag questions, quoted in Harris (1984, 10, 21)

a. Everybody else seems to have done something but you, don't they?
b. You'd better not argue with any foreman in the future, had you?
c. But you've shown no good will about that, have you?

Rather than conveying uncertainty about the main proposition, the tag questions in these examples essentially demand that the defendant agree with, or at least respond to, the magistrate's accusatory statement. It's inaccurate, then, to say that tag questions are always tentative.

Holmes (1982) studied tag questions in a large corpus of recorded speech from a variety of contexts – formal interviews in radio or television, classroom discussion, and casual conversation among friends. She argues that, considered from the point of view of their role in the larger discourse, there are two major types of tag questions. The first type, which she calls *modal* tags, provide information about the speaker's degree of conviction; basically, they express doubt or uncertainty.

(3) Modal tag questions, quoted in Holmes (1982, 51)

a. TEACHER: Is there a blackboard?
PUPIL: That could be a blackboard couldn't it?

b. A: It used to be – now what did it use to be called? The Estancia or something or other.
B: Used to be the Cantina didn't it?
A: No well well it's been various things.

By contrast, the tag questions that Holmes calls *affective* express something about the speaker's attitude toward the addressee. Holmes distinguishes among several subtypes of affective tags; *facilitative* tags, for example, are used to encourage the addressee to talk.

(4) Affective (facilitative) tag questions, quoted in Holmes (1982, 53–54)

a. HOSTESS: Ray had some bad luck didn't you Ray?
b. TEACHER: The hen's brown isn't she?
c. INTERVIEWER: It was because of the tension wasn't it?

Other tag questions are appended to relatively uncontroversial statements of opinion; Holmes argues that these tags establish solidarity between the speaker and the addressee by inviting the addressee to agree.

(5) Affective tags that express solidarity, quoted in Holmes (1982, 57–58)

a. These veggies are bloody good aren't they?
b. That's really strange isn't it?

These categories aren't intended to be exhaustive; for example, the magistrates' questions quoted above do not obviously fit into any of Holmes' categories. Nor are they mutually exclusive: Holmes notes that tag questions can be both modal and affective at the same time. The point is to emphasize that a single syntactic construction can have many different discourse functions; it's naïve to count tag questions and conclude, as a number of studies have done since Lakoff's work was published, that this is equivalent to measuring 'tentative language'.[4]

8.4.1 The social function of tag questions: Cameron et al. (1989)

Cameron et al. (1989) analyzed tag questions using Holmes' system of classification. They were interested in the relationship between gender and power, so they obtained data from two separate corpora: one set of conversations among middle-class adults, and one group of recordings from broadcast media in which there was a clear power difference between participants.

In the first corpus, a subset of the Survey of English Usage (SEU), Cameron et al. coded every tag question as either modal or affective and noted the gender of the speaker. Contrary to Lakoff's hypothesis, they found that men tended to use more tag questions of both types. Moreover, women and men used different kinds of tag questions: men were more likely than women to use modal tags. This latter pattern is particularly interesting because it suggests that men, not women, were more likely to use the kinds of tag questions that genuinely convey uncertainty.

The second corpus consisted of nine hours of recordings from a medical call-in radio show, televised classroom interaction, and a general television

[4] Lakoff's discussion of tag questions is very brief, but she does acknowledge that they have functions other than expressing uncertainty; she was certainly not suggesting that we can simply count tag questions as a proxy for tentativeness.

discussion program. In each setting, Cameron et al. distinguished between the 'powerful' conversational participants (doctor, teacher, presenter) and the 'powerless' participants (caller, student, guest). If tag questions mark uncertainty or tentativeness and therefore tend to be used by individuals in subordinate positions, we would expect the powerless participants in these conversations to use more tag questions.

But that's not what Cameron et al. found. Instead, the overwhelming majority of the tag questions in the corpus were spoken by the *powerful* participants; hardly any tag questions were used by the powerless participants, and those few that they did produce were all modal. (It's intriguing that the type of tag question favored by the powerless participants in these settings is the same as the type of tag question that emerged as characteristic of men in the SEU corpus.) Affective tags were used frequently and exclusively by the powerful participants. Moreover, in contrast to the SEU corpus, this dataset suggests that men and women use tag questions at approximately the same rate overall.

Where Lakoff suggested that overusing tag questions was related to the subordinate status of women, these results suggest that at least some tag questions are actually characteristic of people in positions of power. Facilitative tags may be the best illustration of why these two very different interpretations are both plausible: using a tag question to encourage you to speak could be an act of submission (I acknowledge that you have a better right to speak than I do) or just the opposite (I have the authority to give you permission to speak). It's the second dynamic that appears to play out in Cameron et al.'s real-world dataset.

These results are extremely suggestive, but we can't take them as the final word on the relationship between gender, power, and tag questions. One limitation of the second corpus is that it involves only 'friendly' power differentials – a very different dynamic from the one that Harris found in magistrates' courts, for example. It would be instructive to explore whether patterns of tag question use are different in a more confrontational setting. In addition, the power dynamic in television discussion shows is more complex than the simple powerful-powerless dichotomy. The powerful status of the television presenter is very clear if she's interviewing a local man who discovered the image of L. Ron Hubbard on his grilled cheese sandwich; it's much less clear if the interviewee is a high-ranking politician. Finally, Cameron et al. don't report any tests of statistical significance for their data, which means that we must treat these results with extreme caution.

What we can conclude for certain is that the meaning of tag questions, and how they're used by men and women, is anything but straightforward. Cameron et al. argue even more strongly than Holmes that tag questions, like any syntactic construction, have a variety of uses that are heavily influenced by the social context. Tag questions don't necessarily convey tentativeness – sometimes they convey just the opposite – and there is no evidence here that women are more likely to use tag questions anyway.

8.4.2 Group membership and solidarity: Reid et al. (2003)

Holmes argues that one function of tag questions is to maintain solidarity between the speaker and the addressee. What happens if that solidarity is disrupted? Reid et al. (2003) studied how men's and women's use of tag questions is affected by the degree to which they see themselves as part of the same group as their conversational partners.

Reid et al. asked 42 students at the University of Queensland, in pairs, to discuss a controversial topic for 10 minutes. The topics, such as 'Capital punishment should be instituted in Australia', had been determined by a screening questionnaire to be gender-neutral – that is, they found no differences between men and women in their position on the topics. Each pair consisted of one man and one woman; they were assigned a topic for which they had indicated opposite positions on the screening questionnaire. Before the discussion began, subjects received instructions that purported to tell them what the experiment was about. The researchers laid it on thick:

> We are comparing males and females in the way that they co-ordinate their discussions of different issues. In our previous research we have found that males and females differ quite sharply in the way that they approach issues such as (the topic of discussion). We can't give you any details, because we will be testing an explanation for these differences in today's study. What we can tell you, is that there is a very stable and consistent difference between males and females that has been found in several other studies. We will point these out to you after the discussion. We have separate databases for males and females, and at the end of today's study, we will enter your data into these databases for later comparison.

Half of the pairs received these instructions; the other half received instructions that were identical except that they substituted 'university and high-school students' for 'males and females'. Thus, pairs who were told that the study was about gender were made to feel that they were part of separate groups, while the pairs who were told that the study was about university and high-school students were made to feel that they were part of the same group.

Reid et al. were interested in 'tentative language' in general; in addition to tag questions, they counted 'hedges' (*probably*, *kinda*, etc.) and 'disclaimers' (*I think*, *seems to be*, etc.). Results for tag questions are not reported separately. We have already seen that it's dangerous, to say the least, to assume that tag questions are automatically tentative; Reid et al. state that they didn't count tag questions and other constructions that were used non-tentatively, but

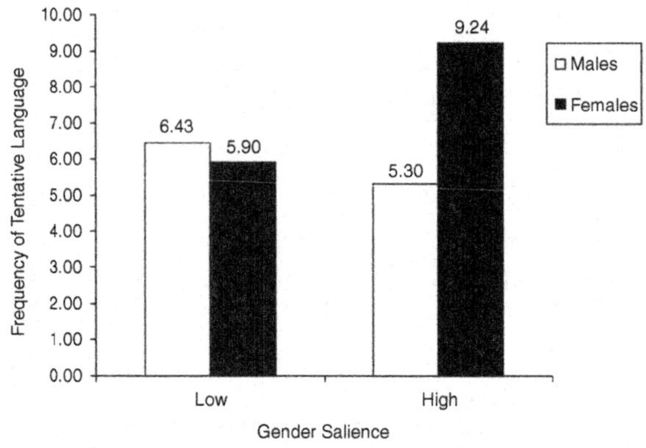

Figure 8.3 Frequency of 'tentative' language by gender and experimental condition. Scott A. Reid, Natasha Keerie, and Nicholas A. Palomares, Language, gender salience, and social influence, *Journal of Language and Social Psychology* 22(2), pp. 210–233, Figure 2, copyright 2003. Reprinted by permission of SAGE Publications.

unfortunately they provide no details on how they made these judgments. Thus, we should interpret these results with a great deal of caution.

These problems notwithstanding, Figure 8.3 reveals a striking difference between the two experimental conditions. In the low gender salience condition – where subjects were told that the experiment was about the difference between university and high-school students – there was no appreciable difference between men and women. But in the high gender salience condition, women used 'tentative' language much more, while men remained about the same.

We can't draw easy conclusions from this experiment about how men and women use tag questions; we don't know how much of the increase in women's tentative language involved tag questions as opposed to hedges or disclaimers. Nor can we be confident about men's and women's use of tentative language in general, given what we know about the dangers of using tag questions as an index of uncertainty. But these results strongly suggest that there is yet another layer of complexity to the contextual factors that affect language use: even something as simple as reminding the two participants in a conversation that they belong to two different genders can have a striking effect on their behavior.

8.4.3 Solving tasks as a group: McMillan et al. (1977)

In contrast to the largely dyadic interactions explored in the previous two studies, McMillan et al. (1977) investigated tag questions in a group setting. In this

Table 8.4 *Average number of tag questions per speaker by gender and composition of the group. Adapted from Table II of Julie R. McMillan, A. Kay Clifton, Diane McGrath, and Wanda S. Gale, Women's language: Uncertainty or interpersonal sensitivity and emotionality?,* Sex Roles *3(6): 545–559, 1977. With kind permission from Springer Science and Business Media.*

	Women	Men
Same-sex	2.64	1.83
Mixed	7.29	2.52

study, subjects solved a murder mystery in groups of 5 to 7; each member of the group received index cards with clues, which they had to share verbally (meaning that everyone in the group had to talk). The group sessions lasted 30 minutes.

As shown in Table 8.4, the women in this study tended to use more tag questions than the men; McMillan et al. report that not only was the overall difference between men and women significant, but that women used significantly more tag questions in mixed-sex groups than in same-sex groups ($p < .001$ for both comparisons). This pattern of results supports Lakoff's hypothesis that tag questions are used especially by women.

Interestingly, even though their results are consistent with Lakoff's hypothesis, McMillan et al. argue against the idea that tag questions (and other constructions mentioned by Lakoff, such as intensifiers and commands in question form) express women's uncertainty or tentativeness. Instead, they argue, these constructions are part of women's greater interpersonal sensitivity. On their view, using a tag question isn't a way of apologizing for expressing an opinion, but rather a way of showing active concern for other members of the group. They point out that men used slightly more tag questions in the presence of women (although the increase was not significant) and suggest that it's unlikely that the men were adopting a more subordinate position in mixed-sex groups.

Thus, even this set of results, which is more consistent with Lakoff's hypothesis than anything we have seen so far, is open to other interpretations. More generally, the complexity that we see associated with tag questions should make us cautious about trying to draw conclusions about people's thoughts or attitudes from low-level linguistic constructions or even individual words. Large linguistic datasets are becoming increasingly available, and researchers in many fields are eager to use them: journalists want to identify bias in the media; marketers want to monitor the mood of their customers on social media; historians want to study how social attitudes have changed over time; governments want to pinpoint potential criminal activity. Before we decide that a particular syntactic construction or a particular set of words reveals something about the thoughts and attitudes of the people who use it, we must be certain that it really is consistently associated with particular kinds of meanings. In the case of tag questions, we have a syntactic construction that simply has no straightforward connection to a single social meaning.

8.4.4 General conclusions

Lakoff's influential analysis of language and gender argued that women are more likely than men to use tag questions and other linguistic devices that indicate uncertainty. Subsequent studies have found some evidence that women are slightly more likely to use tag questions, although the difference (when there is one) is highly dependent on contextual factors. More importantly, however, detailed analysis has shown that tag questions have many uses and don't necessarily demonstrate tentativeness. In fact, there are situations where tag questions are characteristic of the more powerful individual. Overall, we should be extremely cautious when attempting to make simple connections between the linguistic form of an utterance and its social meaning.

8.5 Summary

- Many societies believe that men and women speak differently. Historically, men have typically been perceived as better speakers than women.
- Specific beliefs about how men and women are different vary from culture to culture. In modern western society, women are seen as more polite and indirect than men; in some other parts of the world, women are believed to be aggressive and unsophisticated.
- One popular current view is that men and women have different, but equally good, ways of speaking. Experimental work suggests that there are indeed some differences, but they are subtle and highly context-dependent. The reasons for these differences are still hotly debated.
- Women are frequently claimed to talk more than men. There is no experimental evidence to support this idea; the best studies show than men and women, on average, talk about the same amount.
- One scholar proposed the influential hypothesis that women use more tag questions than men and therefore are more tentative. There is evidence that

women use more tag questions in some situations, but tag questions have many functions other than expressing uncertainty.

For further reflection

(1) Interview two people you know who come from different countries; ask them whether they think men and women use language differently, and if so, for specific examples of these differences. In what ways are your interviewees' answers similar, and in what ways are they different? Which, if any, of the common beliefs about male-female differences discussed in this chapter were mentioned by your interviewees?

(2) Go to www.cambridge.org/kaplan and download the file 'Tag Questions', which contains excerpts from the Switchboard corpus with tag questions underlined. Read a sample of the conversations and identify one tag question with each of the following properties:

a. A modal tag question.
b. An affective tag question.
c. A tag question that is both modal and affective.
d. A tag question that shows uncertainty or tentativeness.
e. A tag question that does *not* show uncertainty or tentativeness.
f. A tag question that you are unsure how to interpret. Explain what kind of information you would need in order to understand it better (e.g., the intonation the speaker used).

To familiarize yourself with what is going on in these conversations, read Section 1, Section 8, and Attachment 2 of the Switchboard manual at the following url:

https://catalog.ldc.upenn.edu/docs/LDC97S62/swb1_manual.txt

(3) Other examples of research on language and gender include Hammen and Peplau (1978) and Brooks (1982) on amount of talk and Grob et al. (1997) on tag questions. Read and evaluate one of these papers. In addition to considering general questions of experimental methodology, think about the specific social context that the authors studied. In what ways might this context have interacted with gender to affect subjects' behavior?

Further reading

Cameron (2007) is a non-technical account of popular views on men and women and related linguistic research; this book emphasizes similarities between men and women. Eckert and McConnell-Ginet (2003) and Coates

(2004) are textbooks on language and gender; Coates and Pichler (2011) is a collection of important scholarly papers in the field. Cameron and Kulick (2003) is an accessible overview of research more generally on language, sexuality, and sexual identity.

The difference and dominance models discussed in section 8.1.3 are not the only way to understand gendered behavior. An alternative, known as the 'social constructionist' approach, considers how speakers use language to construct and maintain social identities, and emphasizes that gender and other social factors interact in ways that are highly context-specific. An example of this approach is Bucholtz (1998), a case study of 'nerd girls' in a Bay Area high school.

McLemore (1990) analyzes the functions of 'uptalk' in a Texas sorority.

The experimental literature on gender differences in language is enormous. Further examples of research on gender and amount of talk, at various levels of technicality, include Marlatt (1970) (interview setting), Hammen and Peplau (1978) and Martin and Craig (1983) (casual conversation among undergraduates), Martin et al. (1996) (casual conversation among elderly adults), Leet-Pellegrini (1980) (interaction between gender and expertise), and Boersma et al. (1981) and Brooks (1982) (college classrooms). James and Drakich (1993) present a highly accessible descriptive summary of a large number of studies on gender and amount of talk, arguing that the setting and task have an important effect on men's and women's behavior. Leaper and Ayres (2007) is a meta-analysis of gender and amount of talk, and Leaper and Robnett (2011) of gender and 'tentative language' (including tag questions). For a technical overview of gender differences in verbal ability, see Wallentin (2009).

Bibliography

Aries, Elizabeth Joan. Verbal and nonverbal behavior in single-sex and mixed-sex groups: Are traditional sex roles changing? *Psychological Reports*, 51(1):127–134, 1982.

Boersma, P. Dee, Debora Gay, Ruth A. Jones, Lynn Morrison, and Helen Remick. Sex differences in college student-teacher interactions: Fact or fantasy? *Sex Roles*, 7(8):775–784, 1981.

Brizendine, Louann. *The Female Brain*. Morgan Road Books, New York, NY, 2006.

Brizendine, Louann. *The Male Brain*. Broadway Books, New York, NY, 2010.

Brooks, Virginia R. Sex differences in student dominance behavior in female and male professors' classrooms. *Sex Roles*, 8(7):683–690, 1982.

Bucholtz, Mary. Geek the girl: Language, femininity, and female nerds. In Natasha Warner, Jocelyn Ahlers, Leela Bilmes, Monica Oliver, Suzanne Wertheim, and Melinda Chen, editors, *Gender and Belief Systems: Proceedings of the Fourth Berkeley Women and Language Conference*, pages 119–131, Berkeley, CA, 1998. Berkeley Women and Language Group.

Cameron, Deborah. *The Myth of Mars and Venus: Do Men and Women Really Speak Different Languages?* Oxford University Press, Oxford, 2007.

Cameron, Deborah, and Don Kulick. *Language and Sexuality*. Cambridge University Press, Cambridge, 2003.

Cameron, Deborah, Fiona McAlinden, and Kathy O'Leary. Lakoff in context: The social and linguistic functions of tag questions. In Jennifer Coates and Deborah Cameron, editors, *Women in Their Speech Communities: New Perspectives on Language and Sex*, chapter 7, pages 74–93. Routledge, London, 1989.

Coates, Jennifer. *Women, Men, and Language: A Sociolinguistic Account of Gender Differences in Language*. Studies in Language and Linguistics. Pearson Education, London, 3rd edition, 2004.

Coates, Jennifer, and Pia Pichler, editors. *Language and Gender: A Reader*. Wiley-Blackwell, Oxford, 2nd edition, 2011.

Cutler, Anne, and Donia R. Scott. Speaker sex and perceived apportionment of talk. *Applied Psycholinguistics*, 11(3):253–272, 1990.

Eckert, Penelope. Gender and sociolinguistic variation. In Coates and Pichler (2011), chapter 6, pages 57–66.

Eckert, Penelope, and Sally McConnell-Ginet. *Language and Gender*. Cambridge University Press, Cambridge, 2003.

Frances, Susan J. Sex differences in nonverbal behavior. *Sex Roles*, 5(4):519–535, 1979.

Gray, John. *Men Are from Mars, Women Are from Venus*. HarperCollins Publishers, New York, NY, 1992.

Grob, Lindsey M., Renee A. Meyers, and Renee Schuh. Powerful/powerless language use in group interactions: Sex differences or similarities? *Communication Quarterly*, 45(3):282–303, 1997.

Hammen, Constance L., and Letitia A. Peplau. Brief encounters: Impact of gender, sex-role attitudes, and partner's gender on interaction and cognition. *Sex Roles*, 4(1):75–90, 1978.

Harris, Sandra. Questions as a mode of control in magistrates' courts. *International Journal of the Sociology of Language*, 49:5–27, 1984.

Holmes, Janet. The functions of tag questions. *English Language Research Journal*, 3:40–65, 1982.

James, Deborah, and Janice Drakich. Understanding gender differences in amount of talk: A critical review of research. In Deborah Tannen, editor, *Gender and Conversational Interaction*, chapter 10, pages 281–312. Oxford University Press, Oxford, 1993.

Jespersen, Otto. *Language: Its Nature, Development, and Origin*, chapter XII: The woman, pages 237–254. George Allen & Unwin, London, 1922.

Johnson, Keith. Resonance in an exemplar-based lexicon: The emergence of social identity and phonology. *Journal of Phonetics*, 34(4):485–499, 2006.

Karpowitz, Christopher F., Tali Mendelberg, and Lee Shaker. Gender inequality in deliberative participation. *American Political Science Review*, 106(3):533–547, 2012.

Keenan, Elinor Ochs. Norm-makers, norm-breakers: Uses of speech by men and women in a Malagasy community. In Donald Brenneis and Ronald K. S. Macaulay, editors, *The Matrix of Language: Contemporary Linguistic Anthropology*, chapter 6, pages 99–115. WestviewPress, Boulder, CO, 1996.

Kollock, Peter, Philip Blumstein, and Pepper Schwartz. Sex and power in interaction: Conversational privileges and duties. *American Sociological Review*, 50(1):34–46, 1985.

Kulick, Don. Speaking as a woman: Structure and gender in domestic arguments in a New Guinea village. *Cultural Anthropology*, 8(4):510–541, 1993.

Labov, William. The intersection of sex and social class in the course of linguistic change. *Language Variation and Change*, 2(2):205–254, 1990.

Lakoff, Robin. *Language and Woman's Place*. Harper & Row, New York, NY, 1975.

Leaper, Campbell, and Melanie M. Ayres. A meta-analytic review of gender variations in adults' language use: Talkativeness, affiliative speech, and assertive speech. *Personality and Social Psychology Review*, 11(4):328–363, 2007.

Leaper, Campbell, and Rachael D. Robnett. Women are more likely than men to use tentative language, aren't they? A meta-analysis testing for gender differences and moderators. *Psychology of Women Quarterly*, 35(1):129–142, 2011.

Leet-Pellegrini, H. M. Conversational dominance as a function of gender and expertise. In Howard Giles, W. Peter Robinson, and Philip M. Smith, editors, *Language: Social Psychological Perspectives*, pages 97–104. Pergamon Press, Oxford, 1980.

Liberman, Mark. David Brooks, neuroendocrinologist. Language Log, September 17 2006a. Available at http://itre.cis.upenn.edu/~myl/languagelog/archives/003586 .html.

Liberman, Mark. Sex-linked lexical budgets. Language Log, August 6 2006b. Available at http://itre.cis.upenn.edu/~myl/languagelog/archives/003420.html.

Marlatt, G. Alan. A comparison of vicarious and direct reinforcement control of verbal behavior in an interview setting. *Journal of Personality and Social Psychology*, 16(4):695–703, 1970.

Martin, Judith N., and Robert T. Craig. Selected linguistic sex differences during initial social interactions of same-sex and mixed-sex student dyads. *The Western Journal of Speech Communication*, 47(1):16–28, 1983.

Martin, Mary, Priscilla Davis, and Jess Dancer. Conversations between older men and women: Turn-taking and topics. *Perceptual and Motor Skills*, 83(3f):1330, 1996.

McLemore, Cynthia. The interpretation of L*H in English. In Cynthia McLemore, editor, *Texas Linguistic Forum*, volume 32, pages 127–147, Austin, TX, 1990. University of Texas Department of Linguistics and the Center for Cognitive Science.

McMillan, Julie R., A. Kay Clifton, Diane McGrath, and Wanda S. Gale. Women's language: Uncertainty or interpersonal sensitivity and emotionality? *Sex Roles*, 3(6):545–559, 1977.

Mehl, Matthias R., Simine Vazire, Nairán Ramírez-Esparza, Richard B. Slatcher, and James W. Pennebaker. Are women really more talkative than men? *Science*, 317(5834):82, 2007.

Reid, Scott A., Natasha Keerie, and Nicholas A. Palomares. Language, gender salience, and social influence. *Journal of Language and Social Psychology*, 22(2):210–233, 2003.

Salisbury, Eve, editor. *The Trials and Joys of Marriage*. Medieval Institute Publications, Kalamazoo, MI, 2002.

Sax, Leonard. *Why Gender Matters: What Parents and Teachers Need to Know about the Emerging Science of Sex Differences*. Doubleday, New York, NY, 2005.

Sternglanz, Sarah Hall, and Shirley Lyberger-Ficek. Sex differences in student-teacher interactions in the college classroom. *Sex Roles*, 3(4):345–352, 1977.

Tannen, Deborah. *You Just Don't Understand: Women and Men in Conversation*. HarperCollins, New York, NY, 1990.

Trudgill, Peter. *On Dialect: Social and Geographical Perspectives*, chapter 10: Sex and covert prestige: Linguistic change in the urban dialect of Norwich, pages 169–185. Blackwell, Oxford, 1983.

Wallentin, Mikkel. Putative sex differences in verbal abilities and language cortex: A critical review. *Brain and Language*, 108(3):175–183, 2009.

9 'Texting makes you illiterate'

As social beings, humans are deeply invested in communicating with each other. As a result, we shouldn't be surprised that many technological developments are related to communication, and more specifically to language. Some language-related technologies are so old that we hardly think of them as technology at all – writing itself, for example. At the other end of the spectrum, we're highly sensitive to the newest technologies, such as various forms of electronic media.

When we use some technology to transmit language, its form isn't neutral: it shapes *how* we say things, and therefore also potentially *what* we say. It matters, for example, that writing (but not speech) is permanent, that it can be revised and edited, and that it carries only limited information about tone of voice. Telephone and radio transmit audio but not video; the listener has access to the voice but not to nonverbal cues. Telegrams used to be priced by the word, which encouraged senders to use as few words as possible in what became the classic 'telegraphic' style.

When a technology becomes widespread enough, it's theoretically possible that it could influence people's language even when they're not actively using the technology. In other words, a society might adopt a particular technology and find that its use of language in general changes as a result. In this chapter, we will explore popular worries along these lines related to technologies old and new. In a modern context, we'll focus particularly on text messaging, for three reasons: at the time of this writing, texting is a source of considerable public angst; many of the linguistic phenomena associated with text messages are actually characteristic of digital communication more generally; and there exists a body of scholarly literature on the topic. We will conclude with a look at several studies that investigate whether there's a connection between text messaging behavior and literacy skills.

9.1 Reactions to new and old technologies

Any new technology will be met with a mix of enthusiasm and trepidation. Baron (2009) describes how writing itself, which today we take for granted, was greeted with suspicion in many quarters: Plato, for example, worried that the written word was incapable of the kind of back-and-forth that characterized face-to-face communication, and that those who relied on writing would not properly exercise their memories. Clanchy (2013) documents medieval England's reliance on memory and living witnesses instead of written documents, especially in an age when it was extremely difficult to distinguish authentic from fake documents and most people were illiterate anyway. Technical means of writing, too, have evolved over time, and not every innovation is immediately embraced. The humble pencil is in fact a feat of engineering, and Petroski (1989, 178–179) notes that pencils with erasers attached were criticized by some who argued that students would have no motivation to avoid mistakes if they could correct them easily.

None of this means that we should embrace every new technology uncritically. Rather, it's useful to remind ourselves that both wild enthusiasm and abject fear are natural reactions to new and disruptive ways of communicating. The only sure way to discover the true effects of a particular technology, for good or for bad, is to go out and observe what happens when people actually use it.

9.1.1 The telegram

The electric telegraph was the first technology that let people transmit written messages quickly over long distances; it came into widespread use in the second half of the nineteenth century. Someone who wanted to send a telegram would write out the desired message, which was then transmitted via Morse code by a series of telegraph operators to its intended destination. Because telegraph companies charged by the word, users quickly learned to economize. Messages were phrased to be as short as possible; social formalities (use of titles, opening address as in a letter, and so on) were reduced or dropped entirely; function words (such as *the*, *a*, *be*) were omitted whenever possible. Entire industries developed codes so that common messages could be represented by a single word.

As a characteristic 'telegraphic style' became established, and as large numbers of people started using it regularly, concerns began to arise that language as a whole might be affected. O'Brien (1904), for example, worries that a person might be reluctant to send uncommon words by telegraph for fear that they would be misinterpreted somewhere along the line.

> He will not, for example, send the word "prevision," because somebody who handles the word on its journey would be almost sure to change it to the more familiar "provision." Whenever two words are thus closely alike, one in common use and the other rare, only

the former can with thorough safety be sent by telegraph. The wires are thus constantly shrinking the popular vocabulary....

O'Brien (1904, 468)

(See Liberman 2011 for more examples.) Naturally, not everyone agreed with this negative view of the telegraph; we can also find praise for the way the telegraph encouraged brevity and precision. An anonymous writer argued in 1848 that telegraphic language would improve literature:

Now the *desideratum* of the Telegraph – the great question most important to all who have any connection with it, is this – *How can the greatest amount of intelligence be communicated in the fewest words?* Is not this the very question which has been for centuries theoretically proposed by scholars as the ultimatum of language?... Every useless ornament, every added grace which is not the very extreme of simplicity, is but a troublesome encumbrance....

When a half column or more of every paper in the Union is filled with Telegraphic despatches; when these reports form a large part of the daily reading of thousands; when correspondence is hourly prepared and revised, throughout the whole extent of the United States, with a view to telegraphic transmission, is it too much to expect that this invention will have an influence upon American literature; and that that influence will be marked and permanent, and withal salutary?

'Influence' (1848, 411–412)

In retrospect, of course, we know that the telegraph was a herald neither of doom nor of utopia. (The essay just quoted, in fact, ends with such an over-the-top vision of the telegraphic future that one suspects it is a work of satire.) The telegraph is an especially instructive example because it's similar in several ways to the modern abomination of text messaging. Both encourage brevity – telegrams because each word represented an additional charge, text messages because each character requires a non-trivial amount of effort and space is limited. Indeed, many of O'Brien's fears wouldn't look out of place if we replaced the word 'telegram' with 'text message', especially when he refers to it as a 'new system of abbreviated writing' (467).

Today, of course, telegrams are no longer widespread; due to competition from more convenient forms of communication, many telegram services have stopped operating entirely. Given its similarity to the dreaded text messaging style, has the decline of the telegram led to general rejoicing and sighs of relief? Not at all. When Western Union sent its last telegram in 2006, there was an outpouring of nostalgia for a lost era and the distinctive style of telegrams.

Along the way, the telegram created a new and innovative form of communication, concise and heavily reliant on abbreviated phrases and punctuation in order to save cost. The best of them read like poetry.

Buncombe (2006)

Stories of famous telegrams are repeated as examples of ingenuity, including the probably apocryphal example of a writer who inquired about the sales of his latest book with the telegram *?* and received a *!* in reply.

Despite early worries, few people today would argue that the telegraph had a revolutionary effect on general language use – certainly not an impact on the scale feared by modern skeptics of text messaging. What is feared in one generation may be revered in the next.

9.1.2 Text messaging

Ya got trouble, right here in River City,
With a capital *T*, and that rhymes with *P*, and that stands for *Pool.*

'Ya Got Trouble', *The Music Man*

The modern technology most similar to the telegraph is text messaging: sending short messages of written text between mobile phones. In its earliest days, a number of factors conspired to encourage abbreviations in text messages:

- Text messages were limited to 160 characters; abbreviations allowed the user to fit more words into a single message.
- Many mobile phone plans charged by the text message, giving users an incentive to condense their conversations into as few messages as possible.
- Typing a text message was laborious and time-consuming; most letters, and all non-alphanumeric symbols, required several keystrokes. Phones' small screens made it hard to see more than a few words of the message at a time.

Many developments since the earliest days of text messaging have reduced the 'cost' of each character in a text message in terms of space, price, or labor: larger keyboards, predictive software, and so on. Nevertheless, abbreviation remains a device that is firmly associated with text messaging, and a person with a new phone and an unlimited texting plan may use abbreviations even when they're not strictly necessary.

As documented by Thurlow (2006), reactions to text messaging – at least in the popular media – are overwhelmingly negative and often practically apocalyptic in tone. Like Harold Hill, commentators warn that there's trouble in River City – with a capital *T*, and that rhymes with *P*, and that stands for *Phone*. 'Textese' is described as a new language of young people, one so riddled with shorthand that it's impossible for non-initiates to decipher. This new language has no intellectual or literary value; Sutherland (2002) describes it as 'bleak, bald, sad shorthand' and says that it 'masks dyslexia, poor spelling, and mental laziness'. Newspaper articles regularly feature teachers who are disturbed to see texting abbreviations showing up in their students' writing. If the trend continues unchecked, future generations will be unable to write properly or read more than a few sentences at a time.

Has text messaging doomed us all, or is it destined to leave hardly a trace on the broader language – or does the truth lie somewhere in between? There are at least two ways we can go about investigating this question. The first is to examine what text messaging actually looks like in practice. What exactly are these abbreviations that are the cause of so much concern? Are they qualitatively or quantitatively different from existing modes of abbreviation in speech or writing? Are they obviously reduced and inadequate representations of language, or is there reason to believe they might involve linguistic sophistication and creativity in their own right?

The second way to study the effects of text messaging is much more direct. If texting harms your language skills, then it should be possible to verify experimentally what is reported anecdotally: people who text more often, or use more abbreviations, should be worse readers and writers. After a survey of some of the linguistic features of text messages, we will turn to real-world studies of the connection between texting and literacy.

9.2 Text message abbreviations

Linguistically, text messaging practices offer a rich field of study. Researchers might ask questions about the linguistic organization of text messages at all levels: word choice, sentence structure, use of features from standard vs. non-standard dialects, similarity to speech vs. writing, discourse organization, and so on. Popular discussion of the language of text messaging, however, is overwhelmingly concentrated on abbreviations; this will be our focus here.

9.2.1 Types of abbreviations

When applied to text messaging, the term *abbreviation* actually covers a wide range of things. What these phenomena generally have in common is that the 'abbreviated' form is shorter (i.e., has fewer characters) than the same message would have if it were written in formal orthography. The following list is a general overview of abbreviatory techniques that are frequently associated with text messaging; it isn't the only way to classify these techniques, and of course not every texter uses abbreviations of every (or any!) type.

Abbreviations aren't unique to text messages; there are plenty of standardized abbreviations that are common even in formal writing, and style guides and dictionaries frequently include lists of common abbreviations and their uses. Even abbreviations that aren't currently accepted in formal contexts aren't necessarily exclusive to texting; many of these abbreviations originated elsewhere and are found in a much broader range of domains (digital or not). Chapter 3 of Crystal (2008) documents how many of the abbreviations that are associated with texting today are actually quite old. In this chapter, we will continue to refer to these abbreviations as *texting abbreviations* or *textisms*, keeping in mind that they're actually much more widespread. Much of our discussion would apply equally well to instant messaging or social networking sites, and is likely to remain relevant to future forms of digital communication as well.

Acronyms

One of the most-discussed methods of abbreviation found in text messages is the use of acronyms, of which the most famous is probably *LOL*, for *laughing out loud.*[1] Other well-known examples include *OMG* for *oh my god*, *IDK* for *I don't know*, and *TTYL* for *talk to you later*. Most or all of these acronyms are not exclusive to text messaging; they can be found in emails, online discussion boards, instant messaging, and so on. Acronyms are almost never written with periods and don't have to be capitalized, especially on mobile phones where entering all capital letters requires extra keystrokes.

Acronyms are an especially opaque type of abbreviation; unless the context makes it absolutely clear, it's virtually impossible to guess the meaning of a form like *IDK*. If you use an acronym that your reader doesn't happen to know, there's a good chance that you will be misunderstood. One argument against using acronyms, then, is that they put an undue burden on the reader and increase the odds of miscommunication.

But acronyms occur in formal writing too. Plenty of acronyms are so common that they require no explanation, particularly for names of institutions (*UN* for *United Nations*, *MIT* for *Massachusetts Institute of Technology*). Many standard English abbreviations come from phrases in other languages: *e.g.* for *exempli gratia* 'for example'; *Q.E.D.* for *quod erat demonstrandum* 'I have proven my point'; *R.S.V.P.* for *répondez s'il vous plaît* 'please tell me whether or not you will come to this event'. (The fact that these acronyms abbreviate Latin or French phrases makes them even more opaque than the standard texting examples.) Some English-based acronyms have become ordinary words (*laser* for *light amplification by the stimulated emission of radiation*, or *scuba* for *self-contained underwater breathing apparatus*) or are well on their way toward doing so (*asap* for *as soon as possible*, *awol* for *absent without leave*).

[1] Examples like these are also called *initialisms* or *alphabetisms*; some writers reserve each of these terms for a particular subtype of abbreviation. We will use the well-known word *acronym* here to cover a range of subtypes.

The argument against texting acronyms, then, can't just be that acronyms are ambiguous and should always be avoided. Nor can it be that texting acronyms aren't understood by all English speakers. When writing for a specialist audience, it's perfectly acceptable to use acronyms that are specific to the field; linguists, for example, expect each other – but not non-linguists – to understand *NP* (*noun phrase*), *PIE* (*Proto-Indo-European*), and *VOT* (*voice onset time*). The guiding principle, of course, is to know your audience: if there's a good chance that your readers don't know the acronym, then the best practice is to spell it out in full the first time you use it. This principle applies just as much in the digital world as it does in the analog world: if *IMHO* (*in my humble opinion*) is firmly established in a particular online discussion board, there is no sense in spelling it out (and doing so would probably be odd) – but you wouldn't use the acronym in an email to your great-grandmother who has just gotten her first computer. This principle applies not just to acronyms but to technical or specialist vocabulary in general.

Thus, there's no reason to characterize texting acronyms as 'assaults on the English language' (Deacon 2009). The real objection is that *these particular* acronyms happen not to have become generally accepted in formal contexts; there's nothing wrong with acronyms in general.

Names of letters and numbers

Perhaps the most salient texting abbreviation is the use of single letters and numbers to represent, not the ordinary sound of the letter or the quantity represented by the number, but the sound of the name of that character. Thus, *b* might represent the word *be*, *u* might stand for *you*, *2* for *to*, or *4* for *for*. Characters used in this way can stand alone or as part of a larger word: *2day* for *today*, *b4* for *before*. This type of abbreviation is especially noticeable because, unlike the use of acronyms, it is *not* a technique used in standard written English. Perhaps for this reason, these abbreviations are a favorite target of critics of text messaging, who frequently raise the specter of Hamlet texting *2B or not 2B*.

Although the principle of using a symbol to represent the sound of its name is not found in standard written English, it does appear in other writing systems. Hieroglyphic writing of ancient Egypt used this technique in ways that are remarkably similar to modern text-messaging practices. Example (1) illustrates how this works in English. By itself, the symbol *8* represents a particular quantity, which is also represented by the English word *eight*. In *gr8*, the *8* no longer has anything to do with number; it now represents only the sound of the word *eight*, which also happens to be the last part of the word *great*. Thus, in *gr8*, the letters *gr* are read with the sounds they represent (their ordinary use in written English), while *8* is read with the sound of the *word* it ordinarily represents.

(1) The rebus principle in English textisms

a. 8
'eight'

b. gr8
'great'

(2) The rebus principle in Egyptian hieroglyphs
(Mercer 1926, 6)

a. 𓁷
ḥr
'face'

b. 𓁷𓇌𓏏
ḥryt
'terror'

Example (2) shows a parallel example with hieroglyphs. The symbol 𓁷 in (2a) represents the word *ḥr* 'face'.[2] Example (2b) is a depiction of the word *ḥryt* 'terror'; here, the symbol 𓁷 represents not 'face' but the sound *ḥr*; the sound *y* is represented by 𓇌 and the sound *t* by 𓏏. The function of 𓁷 in example (2b) is exactly parallel to that of *8* in example (1b): it represents, not the idea usually associated with the symbol, but rather the sound of the word for that idea.

Abbreviations of this type also exist in a 'mixed' usage, both in hieroglyphic writing and in modern English texting. An alternative way of abbreviating the word *great*, shown in example (3b), is *gr8t*. The final *t* here is, strictly speaking, unnecessary; the word *eight* already ends in a *t* sound. We see a parallel example in (4). In (4a), the symbol 𓉐 represents the word *pr* 'house'. In (4b), 𓉐 represents the sound *pr*; however, the representation includes the additional symbol 𓂋, which also – redundantly – represents the *r* sound. The 𓏏, as before, represents the sound *t*, completing the word *prt* 'procession'. The 𓂻 is a special type of symbol known as a *determinative*: it indicates something about the meaning of the word it's attached to; here, the stylized image of walking legs is clearly consonant with the idea of human movement. Thus, like *gr8t* in (3b), the representation of 'procession' in (4b) is redundant; in both

[2] Although linguists have reconstructed the consonants of ancient Egyptian with a fairly high degree of certainty, much less is known about vowels, which in any case weren't represented in the writing system, as is typical for Semitic languages. Vowels are therefore usually omitted in representations of ancient Egyptian.

cases, extra characters (*t* and 𓂋, 𓏏) reinforce the intended reading of *8* and 𓉐 according to their sound, not their meaning.

(3) The rebus principle in English textisms: mixed use

a. 8
'eight'

b. gr8t
'great'

(4) The rebus principle in Egyptian hieroglyphs: mixed use
(Collier and Manley 1998, 154)

a. 𓉐
pr
'house'

b. 𓉐𓏏
𓂋𓂻
prt
'procession'

Despite the similarity between some types of hieroglyphic writing and some types of text message abbreviations, I have yet to hear a modern commentator decry hieroglyphs with the same fervor that is applied to texting. It's hard to avoid the impression that these abbreviations are condemned, not because they're inherently bad, but because they simply do not happen to be part of standard written English.

In fact, there's an argument to be made that abbreviations like these actually require a *higher* level of linguistic sophistication than the standard orthography. The writer has to be able to identify the part of a word that happens to sound like the name of a letter or number and isolate the letters associated with that sound, replacing them with the appropriate symbol. The reader must be aware of the new possibilities associated with each letter; in order to interpret an expression such as *cya soon* 'see ya soon', the reader has to figure out that *c* is supposed to be read as its name but *ya* is supposed to be pronounced according to the conventions of ordinary English spelling. Far from being a simplified or lazy form of writing, these abbreviations ask a great deal of both writer and reader.

Representation of speech

Another class of textisms alters the conventional spelling of the word in favor of a spelling that more closely reflects its pronunciation. Silent letters, which are abundant in English, are frequently dropped: *luv* for *love*, *nite* for *night*. Note that *nite* actually involves *adding* a silent *e*, in addition to dropping the *gh*. A writer who does this obviously knows that one of the functions of a final *e* in English is to indicate something about the quality of the preceding vowel; according to standard orthographic conventions, *nit* wouldn't have the intended pronunciation. Thus, even in the process of 'breaking' the rules, people who use these abbreviations actually demonstrate a thorough understanding of the general principles of English orthography.

Other alterations attempt to represent non-standard pronunciations. Some of these are extremely widespread, such as *wanna* and *gonna* for *want to* and *going to*, respectively; others represent a regional pronunciation, such as *anuva* for *another* in parts of Great Britain. As with other 'phonetic spellings', the writer has to understand how to use the resources of English spelling conventions to create an alternative representation of the word that the reader will be able to decode.

One interesting feature of both 'phonetic spellings' and examples like *2day* is the fact that their abbreviatory benefit is minimal: *luv* and *nite* are each just one character shorter than the standard spellings; *2* for *to* saves only one character, and *4* for *for* saves only two. A spelling like *wuz* for *was* saves no characters at all. These savings are far smaller than those of acronyms such as *LOL* or *TTYL*. Not only that, but on many phones entering a number requires extra keystrokes – either because the user has to open a separate menu or keyboard to access numeric characters, or because numbers are located at the end of the multipress cycle (e.g., the user presses the '2' key once for *a*, twice for *b*, three times for *c*, and four times for *2*). The fact that these abbreviations may not actually save very much time or space suggests that they are being employed as much for their sociolinguistic function as for their economic utility.

9.2.2 *How many abbreviations does the average text message contain?*

Popular accounts of texting typically give the impression that messages are so heavily abbreviated they're impossible for non-initiates to read. Written articles often include examples that are intended to show just how exotic and foreign this new form of communication is:

(5) An example of 'textese', Cabagnot (2000)
Mst f d tym dey usd ds knd f lng'ge 2 tlk 2 1 anthr nt 1ly n txt bt evn n wrtng ltrs 2.
'Most of the time they used this kind of language to talk to one another, not only in text, but even in writing letters, too.'

This example, which was constructed by the author of the article, does indeed look very different from standard written English. But do real text messages look like this, where every single word is abbreviated? A few studies have explored this question, and the answer is clearly 'no'.

- Thurlow and Brown (2003) asked 135 students at the University of Cardiff to transcribe five text messages they had sent the previous week. Across all the text messages they collected, 18.75% of words were abbreviated, an average of 3 per message.
- Lyddy et al. (2014) asked 139 Irish college students to transcribe up to 10 of their own text messages each: 24% of the words in these messages were abbreviated or used non-standard spelling; of these, a fifth just lacked capitalization.
- Ling and Baron (2007) collected texting diaries from 22 American college women. In the 191 texts that were transcribed, 3.2% of all words were abbreviated and only .005% were acronyms.
- Drouin and Driver (2014) asked 183 American college students to transcribe the last five text messages they had sent: 24% of words in these texts were coded as abbreviations; of these, nearly 40% were merely uncapitalized.
- Grace et al. (2014) obtained similar transcriptions from 150 Canadian and 86 Australian college students; under 20% of the words in these samples used textisms.
- Wood et al. (2011b) collected two weekends' worth of text messages from each of 119 British children between 8 and 12 years old. About 40% of the words in these messages were abbreviated; the rate of abbreviation varied by grade level.
- Wood et al. (2011a) lent mobile phones to 56 9- and 10-year-old British children and transcribed their text messages. Across the entire set of text messages, 15.6% of words were abbreviated. (See section 9.3.4 for more on this study.)

These figures suggest that abbreviations constitute a non-trivial proportion of many text messages, but more than half of texted words are fully written out: examples like (5) are *not* typical. There may well be individual texters who do this sort of thing, but the overall picture is not one in which text messages are uniformly dense and impenetrable.

9.3 Case study: Does text messaging hurt literacy skills?

The preceding discussion gives us serious reason to doubt that text messaging is destroying language and culture. Many of the abbreviations associated with text messages are no different in kind from abbreviations used in Standard English; none, not even the non-standard abbreviations, are unique to text messages. Some techniques, particularly the use of a letter or number to represent the sound of its name, actually require a degree of linguistic sophistication that could be helpful in developing literacy skills. And, at any rate, the available evidence suggests that abbreviations are used much less frequently than the popular press tells us.

We are left with two reasonable-sounding hypotheses about the actual effects of texting. On the one hand, stereotypical texting clearly involves an informal writing style, and it's logically possible that intensive exposure to this style could lead texters to forget some of the conventions of standard written English, or lack the necessary practice to follow them in formal writing. On the other hand, studies that have investigated this question systematically (as opposed to news articles on creeping textese in student work) regularly find that young people are aware of the informal nature of texting; the college students surveyed in Drouin (2011), for example, reported that they were more likely to use textisms with friends than with professors. Moreover, the argument that using abbreviations takes away from a person's exposure to the standard written language assumes that someone who is texting would otherwise be reading *War and Peace*. For some people, though, texting represents time that would otherwise not be spent reading or writing at all. In cases like these, text messaging could be beneficial simply by increasing a person's exposure to written language.

Given that there are plausible arguments on both sides, and in the face of the great diversity of texting practices, the only way to determine the truth of the matter is to go out and observe texting in the real world. As it turns out, there is now a sizeable body of literature on how text messaging affects students, particularly their literacy skills. We turn now to some of the studies that explore particular aspects of text messaging and how they are related to reading and writing standard English.

9.3.1 Brief exposure to textisms: Powell and Dixon (2011)

Powell and Dixon (2011) began with an observation established by previous research on spelling: when a person is exposed to an incorrect spelling of a word, that person is more likely to misspell the word later on. Since many textisms involve unconventional spellings, which are therefore incorrect in the context of standard written English, it's theoretically possible that texting abbreviations could have the same effect. Powell and Dixon designed an experiment to compare the effects of seeing a texting abbreviation versus seeing an ordinary misspelled word.

Table 9.1 *Pre- and post-test spelling scores by group and exposure type. D. Powell and M. Dixon, Does SMS text messaging help or harm adults' knowledge of standard spelling?,* Journal of Computer Assisted Learning *2011, Table 2. Reprinted by permission of John Wiley & Sons, Inc.*

Baseline condition	Exposure type	Testing occasion	
		Pre-exp (of 15)	Post-exp (of 15)
Textisms Group ($N = 44$)			
No exposure baseline ($N = 20$)	No exposure	12.55 (1.73)	12.70 (1.34)
	Exposure to textisms	12.50 (2.16)	13.10 (1.29)
Correct spelling baseline ($N = 24$)	Exposure to correct spellings	12.70 (1.33)	13.17 (1.76)
	Exposure to textisms	12.29 (1.90)	12.54 (1.82)
Misspellings Group ($N = 44$)			
No exposure baseline ($N = 18$)	No exposure	12.39 (1.69)	12.33 (1.91)
	Exposure to misspellings	11.61 (2.12)	11.22 (2.02)
Correct spelling baseline ($N = 26$)	Exposure to correct spellings	12.00 (1.60)	12.96 (1.22)
	Exposure to misspellings	12.62 (1.20)	12.15 (1.83)

The study involved 30 words (such as *accurate*), each of which has a common misspelling (*accurrate*) and is also susceptible to texting-style abbreviation (*aQr8*). The subjects, 94 British undergraduates, took a pre-test in which they spelled all 30 words. Subjects returned one week later and were divided into two groups: one group saw texting abbreviations on a computer screen for half of the words on the list, while the other group saw common misspellings for half of the words. Within each group, half of the subjects saw the correct spellings of the remaining words, while the other half didn't see the remaining words at all. Immediately afterwards, subjects took a post-test in which they spelled all 30 words again.

Table 9.1 summarizes the scores for students in each group, broken down further according to whether students saw a correct spelling of the word during the experimental phrase, an incorrect spelling, or no spelling of the word at all. Unsurprisingly, students' pre-test scores are all very similar, indicating that the groups all had roughly the same level of spelling ability to start with. What we want to know, of course, is whether scores went up or down in the post-test.

Within the Textisms Group, subjects performed significantly better on the post-test ($p < .01$); their improvement was not affected by how they had seen a given word during the exposure phase (not at all, as a textism, or with the correct spelling; $p = .38$[3]). This pattern suggests that subjects were not more likely to misspell a word simply because they had just seen an abbreviated version of it; in fact, their spelling of these words improved just as much as their spelling of words whose correct spelling they had just seen! These results provide no evidence that simply seeing a texting abbreviation makes someone a bad speller.

The results for the Misspellings Group tell a different story. Here, not surprisingly, subjects scored better on words when they were exposed to the correct spelling; however, when they were exposed to an incorrect spelling, they scored worse. (The difference between the effects of correct and incorrect spellings was significant at $p < .05$.) In other words, what we see here is a difference between textisms and ordinary misspellings: the latter interfered with subjects' ability to remember the standard spelling of a word, while textisms did not.

The obvious interpretation of these results is that texting abbreviations are something other than conventional misspellings: readers are affected by one but not the other. This is an argument that using text message abbreviations may not be harmful after all. However, it's important to treat these results with a healthy dose of caution, asking how well they represent real-world texting behavior. For one thing, subjects saw each incorrect spelling (whether a textism or not) only once during the exposure phase, and they took the post-test immediately afterwards. It's worth asking whether seeing a misspelling of any kind just once is the same is seeing it regularly over an extended period of time; in other words, could it be that texting abbreviations appear harmless here simply because subjects weren't exposed to them enough?

Another concern is the nature of the textisms used in the study. A few were common abbreviations (e.g., *2moro* for *tomorrow*) that are widely known. But many others were much less common and may have been unfamiliar to a substantial number of subjects (*mLOD* for *melody*, *LMNt* for *element*). The experimenter read each word out loud as it was shown during the exposure phase, so there is little worry that subjects simply didn't recognize what the abbreviations were supposed to stand for. However, there is still the very real possibility that subjects essentially ignored these examples because they were so unfamiliar, and that this is why the textisms had so little effect on post-test spelling scores. In addition, Powell and Dixon consistently used capitalization to indicate letters that were supposed to be pronounced with their letter name, not their ordinary sound; however, it isn't clear that their subjects used the same convention. The result is that the textisms used in the study are visually very different from the ordinary spellings of the words; perhaps this different

3 The authors do not provide a precise p-value for this effect, but it is possible to calculate one from the other statistics they report.

'look' allowed subjects to avoid interference between the abbreviated words and their conventional spellings.

Despite these misgivings, we can take these results as promising evidence that texting abbreviations aren't exactly the same as ordinary misspellings – clearly, the subjects in this experiment responded to the two very differently. This study suggests that texters are able to do exactly what they say they do: distinguish between the standard written language that is appropriate in formal contexts and the orthographic creativity that is appropriate elsewhere.

9.3.2 *Texting and literacy among schoolchildren: Kemp and Bushnell (2011)*

Powell and Dixon's study involved college students, but much of the popular anxiety about text messaging has to do with whether it harms the reading ability of younger students. To address this concern more directly, Kemp and Bushnell (2011) investigated the texting practices and literacy of 86 Australian fifth- and sixth-graders.

The students in this study completed two groups of tasks. The first was a series of standardized literacy tests of reading and spelling. The second involved reading and writing text messages on a phone provided by the experimenter. Each subject read two messages out loud from the phone, one in standard English and one in 'textese'; and translated two text messages provided by the experimenter by typing their translations into the phone, one from standard English into textese and one from textese into standard English. The text messages were deliberately designed to include a large number of words that could be abbreviated.

(6) Example of a text message from Kemp and Bushnell (2011, 26)

a. Conventional form:
Thanks for your great text message. Everyone forgives you and would like you to be here at basketball today.

b. Textese:
Thx 4 ur gr8 txt msg. Every1 4gives u and wood like u 2 b here at bsketbal 2day.

Kemp and Bushnell also asked students whether they used texting in their daily lives, and if so, whether they used the multi-press method (press the '2' key once for *a*, twice for *b*, and so on) or predictive software. For our purposes, the most interesting question is whether texters and non-texters had different scores on the literacy tests. As summarized in Table 9.2, all three groups of students (predictive texters, multi-press texters, and non-texters) had very similar scores. There's a trend for the non-texters to have slightly higher scores, but

Table 9.2 *Means and standard deviations of students' scores on three standardized literacy tests. N. Kemp and C. Bushnell, Children's text messaging: Abbreviations, input methods and links with literacy,* Journal of Computer Assisted Learning *2011, Table 2. Reprinted by permission of John Wiley & Sons, Inc.*

	Spelling	Reading	Non-word reading
Predictive texters (n = 45)	106.13 (8.17)	101.67 (7.76)	102.56 (9.31)
Multi-press texters (n = 29)	104.10 (17.87)	102.03 (12.72)	101.00 (11.15)
Non-texters (n = 12)	112.25 (18.20)	105.75 (12.03)	105.75 (12.03)
Overall	106.30 (13.76)	102.06 (10.28)	102.48 (10.33)

Kemp and Bushnell report that these differences are not statistically significant for any of the three tests.

This study provides us with no evidence that text messaging has any effect on a student's basic literacy skills, either for good or for bad. In addition, students' performance on the reading and writing tasks provides the tantalizing suggestion that using textisms actually involves linguistic *sophistication.* Kemp and Bushnell report that students with higher test scores also tended to be faster at reading and writing messages (both in standard English and in textese), and they were more accurate in interpreting the textese messages. These results suggest that using common text message abbreviations truly is a skill; if it were simply the product of laziness, we would expect the students with lower literacy scores to abbreviate more. Moreover, students produced very few abbreviations when translating messages into standard English: only 3% of all words were textisms, indicating that texters are fully capable of switching between formal and informal styles.

The most obvious weakness of this experiment is the fact that the texting task was artificial. Students did all of the reading and writing on an unfamiliar phone (although this is an improvement over previous studies in which students wrote text messages on paper), and of course translating a message into textese is very different from composing an original message on the fly. The textese messages composed by the researchers may also have been unrealistic, since they contained proportionally more abbreviations than the typical, real-world messages discussed in section 9.2.2. (I would also be interested to know how many 10-year-olds have ever wanted to tell a friend 'Thanks for your great text message.') The students may have recognized the artificial nature of the task and responded by using more textisms than they ordinarily would, especially since it was clear that the adults who administered the experiment *wanted* them to abbreviate. (Notably, the non-texters produced just as many abbreviations during the translation task as the texters.) Within the limits of the task, though, this study provides evidence that texting simply doesn't affect a person's overall literacy very much one way or the other.

9.3.3 Textisms and phonological knowledge: Plester et al. (2009)

As discussed above, many texting abbreviations challenge the writer or reader to reflect on the relationship between how a word is spelled and how it is pronounced. Plester et al. (2009) investigated whether a person's texting behavior is related to his or her ability to analyze the sounds of words, in addition to literacy skills and general cognitive abilities.

The subjects were 88 British sixth- and seventh-graders. To assess students' literacy and cognitive skills, Plester et al. administered a series of standardized tests, which measured vocabulary, spelling, reading, general cognitive ability, and phonological knowledge (i.e., ability to analyze the sounds of a word). Students also completed a questionnaire with demographic information and a summary of their texting habits. Finally, the students were given 10 real-world scenarios and asked to compose an appropriate text message (on paper) for each one; examples of these scenarios are given in (7).

(7) Examples of scenarios from Plester et al. (2009, 160–161)

a. It is Tuesday. You just got home from school, and you have so much homework to do that you don't think you will be able to go to the club you usually go to on Tuesday nights, but you know one of the others in the club will be coming by to pick you up. [You decide what kind of club: swimming, judo, tennis, music, scouts, guides, and the local youth club.]

b. You've just had a text from your Mum. She's in the middle of the supermarket and wants to know what you'd like for dinner. She's also forgotten to feed the dog and you know he's out of food.

Table 9.3 summarizes the relationships among the various measures taken by the researchers; some of these (such as the 'Composite cognitive score') are aggregates of several related tests. The number in each cell is the correlation coefficient (r) for the relevant two measures; a plus or an asterisk after that number indicates that the relationship is (at least marginally) statistically significant. Unsurprisingly, there are significant positive correlations among many of the ability scores: students with better phonological scores tended to have better spelling scores, students with higher cognitive scores tended to have higher reading scores, and so on.

The measure most directly relevant to our question is the age at which the student acquired his or her first phone, which is presumably a decent proxy

Table 9.3 *Correlation coefficients among demographic variables, texting behavior, and test scores;* '+': $p < .10$, '*': $p < .05$, '**': $p < .01$. *Beverly Plester, Clare Wood, and Puja Joshi, Exploring the relationship between children's knowledge of text message abbreviations and school literacy outcomes,* British Journal of Developmental Psychology *2009, Table 2, adapted. This material is reproduced with permission of John Wiley & Sons, Inc.*

	Age	Age of first phone	Composite cognitive score	Composite phonological score	BAS II spelling ability score	BAS II word reading ability score
Age						
Age of first phone	.366*					
Composite cognitive score	.038	−.136				
Composite phonological score	−.068	−.293**	.593**			
BAS II spelling ability score	−.166	−.212+ $p = .073$	.463**	.475**		
BAS II word reading ability score	−.139	.273*	.414**	.732**	.701**	
Ratio of textisms to total words in scenarios	.100	−.189	.016	.213+ $p = .076$	.135	.298*

for how long the student has been texting. Interestingly, age at first phone is *negatively* correlated with two of Plester et al.'s three literacy measures (phonological score and spelling ability score, but not word reading ability score). In other words, the students who received their first phone at a younger age (and therefore presumably had more experience with text messaging) had higher literacy scores on some of the tests. Here, then, we have evidence that not only does texting not cause any harm, but it might actually be beneficial.

Students' responses to the text messaging scenarios provide further support for this idea. To estimate the number of textisms different students were using, Plester et al. calculated the proportion of textisms in each message out of the total number of words in the message. Students' use of textisms was weakly correlated with phonological score and significantly correlated with reading ability: students with better phonological and reading ability tended to produce *more* textisms than students with weaker abilities in those areas. This pattern suggests a possible explanation for the relationship between students' literacy skills and the age at which they acquired their first phone: reading and writing textisms is a skilled and demanding task.

There are, of course, alternative explanations for this pattern of results. As in the previous study, it could be that students with better literacy abilities produced more textisms, not because this was their everyday behavior, but because they were skilled test-takers and recognized that the adult experimenters wanted them to do so. The relationship between literacy and students' age when they acquired their first phone could be mediated by socioeconomic status: maybe wealthier parents were both more likely to buy their children a phone at a younger age *and* better able to support their developing literacy skills (for example, by paying for tutors if necessary). This means that, as always, we should treat these results with an appropriate degree of caution: there's no reason yet to run out and buy a mobile phone for every child in hopes of raising literacy scores. At the very least, though, we can say pretty confidently that this study gives us one more reason not to panic that the rise of text messaging will bring about an apocalypse of illiteracy.

9.3.4 A randomized intervention: Wood et al. (2011a)

There are two major problems with all of the above studies. The first is that they rely on indirect means of assessing subjects' texting behavior. The ideal, of course, would be to assemble a large collection of real-world text messages and analyze those. But the practical obstacles to this approach are obvious: going into subjects' phones raises serious privacy concerns, especially for children; asking subjects to transcribe their own messages is tedious, and they probably won't keep it up for very long. There have nevertheless been some attempts to collect actual text messages, but unsurprisingly researchers have found this to be a difficult and frustrating approach.

The second problem with most studies of texting and literacy is that they're observational in nature: some people text and some don't, and researchers investigate whether these two groups are different in any way. The problem, of course, is that texters and non-texters are self-selected, and some of the same factors that affect whether or not a person chooses to text could also influence that person's literacy skills. In discussing the results of Plester et al. (2009), for example, we observed that a student's age when he or she acquires a first phone could be a proxy for how long the student has used text messaging, but it could also be related to the student's socioeconomic status, which in turn affects literacy. Alternatively, suppose we study another group of students and find that frequent texters have lower test scores. It could be that texting actually harms students; alternatively, it could be that people who consider high academic performance an important part of their identity are less likely to text (or less likely to admit how much they text) because this informal register isn't part of the image they want to project.

The perfect experiment to avoid some of these confounds would be a randomized intervention study: one where researchers take subjects without mobile phones, give phones to half of them, and observe whether the two groups have different literacy skills after some period of time. This approach wouldn't necessarily answer the question of whether different types of people choose to use textisms, but it would go a long way toward addressing other confounds such as socioeconomic status.

The logistical, financial, and ethical difficulties inherent in a study like this are obvious – but, amazingly, it's actually been tried. Wood et al. (2011a) studied 114 British schoolchildren between 9 and 10 years old who didn't have access to a mobile phone. With permission from parents and schools, they randomly assigned half of the students to receive phones for one 10-week school term. The students were allowed to keep their phones over the weekend and during one week-long break; during the school week, the researchers took the phones back and transcribed all the text messages that the students had sent or received. Both groups of students were given weekly reading and spelling tests; these tests were analogous to the way participants in a drug trial are monitored so that the study can be stopped immediately if the drug turns out to be harmful. In this case, the students with mobile phones didn't suffer any obvious harm, and the study ran for the full 10 weeks.

Not only did the students with mobile phones suffer no harm, they appeared to be hardly different from the control group at all: Wood et al. found no significant differences between the two groups at the end of the study on any

Table 9.4 *Correlation coefficients between literacy measures and number of text messages sent and received at various points in the study. C. Wood, E. Jackson, L. Hart, B. Plester, and L. Wilde, The effect of text messaging on 9- and 10-year-old children's reading, spelling and phonological processing skills,* Journal of Computer Assisted Learning *2011, Table 3. Reprinted by permission of John Wiley & Sons, Inc.*

	Week 1 sent	Week 1 received	Week 5 sent	Week 5 received	Week 10 sent	Week 10 received
Improvement in reading and spelling	0.242	0.171	0.149	0.096	0.132	0.074
Improvement in phonological awareness	0.057	0.059	−0.076	−0.060	0.324*	0.142
Improvement on fluency measures	0.158	0.225	−0.009	−0.053	0.408**	0.390**
Improvement in rapid naming	−0.219	−0.154	0.157	0.100	−0.243	−0.145

of the literacy tests. Variation within the mobile phone group was relatively uninteresting too; as summarized in Table 9.4, the number of text messages students sent or received at the beginning of the study (Week 1) or in the middle (Week 5) was not related to how much students improved on various literacy tests. There is, however, the suggestion of a relationship at Week 10: students who were sending more text messages at the end of the study improved more on tests of phonological awareness and fluency; the latter included tasks such as listing alliterative or rhyming words. Thus, it appears that texting may have had a small beneficial effect. Wood et al. also found that students who used more textisms tended to improve more on tests of phonological awareness.

This study provides the clearest evidence yet that text messaging doesn't harm a person's literacy, and it may even have a slight benefit. Its primary weakness is the fact that it was very short, less than three months; maybe it takes more exposure before the effects of texting show up. The students in the study also sent relatively few text messages – partly because they had their phones only on the weekends, and partly because their enthusiasm for texting declined over time. (Students sent an average of 45 messages during the first week of the study but only 6 during the last week.) More intensive, long-term use of texting might have had a greater effect on students' literacy skills. Despite these concerns, it's clear that – contrary to the dire predictions in the media – the students in this study who took up text messaging remained just as literate as their peers.

9.3.5 *General conclusions*

Several experimental studies have explored whether texting often, or using more abbreviations, affects a person's literacy. The answer appears to be 'not really': most researchers have found that texting either provides a small benefit or has no effect at all; only occasionally does a study find a negative effect of texting. In this context, the panicked reaction to texting in many quarters starts to look a bit overblown. No study of texting is perfect, but researchers using a variety of methods have found that texting simply doesn't matter very much. If textisms were truly destroying the language and rendering young people unable to articulate simple thoughts, surely we wouldn't be in a situation where study after study finds that text messaging has little or no effect on reading and writing.

This is not, of course, a reason to embrace texting uncritically. People may like or dislike texting for any number of reasons, and the role of technology in society is certainly worth a serious discussion. What we have learned is that the purely *linguistic* argument against texting – that it interferes with a person's ability to use the standard written language – is wrong.

9.4 Summary

- Like all forms of technology, new communication technologies are usually greeted with a mix of enthusiasm and anxiety; electronic modes of communication are no exception.
- The abbreviations popularly associated with text messaging are not unique to that medium; most are common in many digital domains and are much older than texting itself.
- Many texting abbreviations are no different in kind from phenomena that appear in standard written English. Others require readers and writers to think carefully about the relationship between symbols and sounds, and to use their writing system in a creative way.
- Despite popular fears, there is no evidence that texting or using text message abbreviations harms a person's literacy skills.

For further reflection

(1) Collect 20 examples of text messages with abbreviations that you have sent or received. What kinds of abbreviations do you observe in these messages? Overall, what proportion of the words in these messages are abbreviated? What, if any, are places where you could have used an abbreviation but didn't (e.g., words with common abbreviations that

were fully spelled out, use of punctuation even where there was no danger of ambiguity, and so on)?

(2) There are many online 'dictionaries' of text message abbreviations. Find one such dictionary and analyze the abbreviations it lists. How many of these abbreviations, if any, do you use on a regular basis? How many are you familiar with but don't use regularly? How many are completely new to you? Reflect on the impression of text messaging that this dictionary might give to a non-texter. Does it suggest that abbreviation in text messages is more common than it actually is, less common, or about right?

(3) Talk to four people you know who regularly send text messages and ask them about how and why they use abbreviations (if at all). What do they want to say about themselves when they abbreviate a word (or not)? Does their style depend on the person they're communicating with? Reflect on your interviewees' responses: describe the reasons people choose to use or not use abbreviations, and how (if at all) text message style depends on the larger social context. Do your interviewees' responses suggest that they use a single style when texting, or that they are actively controlling how they present themselves to other people?

(4) Learn what you can about text-messaging practices in a language other than English. Do texters in that language use abbreviations or non-standard conventions? How are those conventions similar to, or different from, the kinds of abbreviations that are common in English text messages? What are some of the social attitudes toward text messaging among speakers of that language – is it perceived as a good thing, a bad thing, or both/neither?

(5) Other studies of whether texting affects literacy include Drouin and Davis (2009), Drouin (2011), Kemp (2010), and Coe and Oakhill (2011). Read one of these studies and evaluate it critically. How did the researchers design their experiment, and what did they find? Are you convinced by their results?

Further reading

Crystal (2008) describes text messaging in its historical and modern contexts, and is written for a popular audience. Wood et al. (2009) is a brief and accessible summary of some of the research on texting and literacy. Thurlow (2006) documents attitudes toward text messaging in the popular media.

Another topic of popular concern is technology's potential to help (or hinder) language learning. See Howard Gola et al. (2011) for a review of the role of electronic media in first-language acquisition, and DeWaard (2013) for an evaluation of the Rosetta Stone software.

Other studies of whether and how texting affects literacy include Massengill Shaw et al. (2007), Plester et al. (2008), Kemp (2010), Bushnell et al. (2011), Coe and Oakhill (2011), and De Jonge and Kemp (2012).

Bibliography

Baron, Dennis. *A Better Pencil: Readers, Writers, and the Digital Revolution*. Oxford University Press, Oxford, 2009.

Buncombe, Andrew. The last post: The telegram is dead. Stop. *The Independent*, February 3 2006.

Bushnell, Catherine, Nenagh Kemp, and Frances Heritage Martin. Text-messaging practices and links to general spelling skill: A study of Australian children. *Australian Journal of Educational & Developmental Psychology*, 11:27–38, 2011.

Cabagnot, Ruby Jane L. Text messaging cr8ts a hul nu cltur: Is that gud or bad? *BusinessWorld*, December 28 2000.

Clanchy, M. T. *From Memory to Written Record: England 1066–1307*. Wiley-Blackwell, Oxford, 3rd edition, 2013.

Coe, J. E. L., and J. V. Oakhill. 'txtN is ez f u no h2 rd': The relation between reading ability and text-messaging behaviour. *Journal of Computer Assisted Learning*, 27(1):4–17, 2011.

Collier, Mark, and Bill Manley. *How to Read Egyptian Hieroglyphs*. University of California Press, Berkeley, CA, 1998.

Crystal, David. *Txting: The Gr8 Db8*. Oxford University Press, Oxford, 2008.

De Jonge, Sarah, and Nenagh Kemp. Text-message abbreviations and language skills in high school and university students. *Journal of Research in Reading*, 35(1):49–68, 2012.

Deacon, Michael. Texting is making English a foreign language. *The Telegraph*, August 12 2009. Available at http://www.telegraph.co.uk/comment/personal-view/6017629/Texting-is-making-English-a-foreign-language.html.

DeWaard, Lisa. Is *Rosetta Stone* a viable option for second-language learning? *ADFL Bulletin*, 42(2):61–72, 2013.

Drouin, M. A. College students' text messaging, use of textese and literacy skills. *Journal of Computer Assisted Learning*, 27(1):67–75, 2011.

Drouin, Michelle, and Claire Davis. R u txting? Is the use of text speak hurting your literacy? *Journal of Literacy Research*, 41(1):46–67, 2009.

Drouin, Michelle, and Brent Driver. Texting, textese and literacy abilities: A naturalistic study. *Journal of Research in Reading*, 37(3):250–267, 2014.

Howard Gola, Alice Ann, Lara Mayeux, and Letitia R. Naigles. Electronic media as incidental language teachers. In Dorothy G. Singer and Jerome L. Singer, editors, *Handbook of Children and the Media*, chapter 7, pages 139–156. SAGE Publications, Thousand Oaks, CA, 2011.

Grace, Abbie, Nenagh Kemp, Frances Heritage Martin, and Rauno Parrila. Undergraduates' text messaging language and literacy skills. *Reading & Writing*, 27(5):855–873, 2014.

'Influence' (1848). Influence of the telegraph upon literature. *The United States Democratic Review*, 22(119):409–413, 1848.

Kemp, Nenagh. Texting versus txting: Reading and writing text messages, and links with other linguistic skills. *Writing Systems Research*, 2(1):53–71, 2010.

Kemp, N., and C. Bushnell. Children's text messaging: Abbreviations, input methods and links with literacy. *Journal of Computer Assisted Learning*, 27(1):18–27, 2011.

Liberman, Mark. Telegraphic language. Language Log, December 31 2011. Available at http://languagelog.ldc.upenn.edu/nll/?p=3674.

Ling, Rich, and Naomi S. Baron. Text messaging and IM: Linguistic comparison of American college data. *Journal of Language and Social Psychology*, 26(3):291–298, 2007.

Lyddy, Fiona, Francesca Farina, James Hanney, Lynn Farrell, and Niamh Kelly O'Neill. An analysis of language in university students' text messages. *Journal of Computer-Mediated Communication*, 19(3):546–561, 2014.

Massengill Shaw, Donita, Carolyn Carlson, and Mickey Maxman. An exploratory investigation into the relationship between text messaging and spelling. *The New England Reading Association Journal*, 43(1):57–62, 2007.

Mercer, S. A. B. *Egyptian Hieroglyphic Grammar: With Vocabularies, Exercises, Chrestomathy (A First-Reader), Sign-List & Glossary*. Ares Publishers, Inc., Chicago, IL, 1926.

O'Brien, Robert Lincoln. Machinery and English style. *The Atlantic Monthly*, 94:464–472, July 1904.

Petroski, Henry. *The Pencil: A History of Design and Circumstance*. Alfred A. Knopf, New York, NY, 1989.

Plester, Beverly, Clare Wood, and Victoria Bell. Txt msg n school literacy: Does texting and knowledge of text abbreviations adversely affect children's literacy attainment? *Literacy*, 42(3):137–144, 2008.

Plester, Beverly, Clare Wood, and Puja Joshi. Exploring the relationship between children's knowledge of text message abbreviations and school literacy outcomes. *British Journal of Developmental Psychology*, 27(1):145–161, 2009.

Powell, D., and M. Dixon. Does SMS text messaging help or harm adults' knowledge of standard spelling? *Journal of Computer Assisted Learning*, 27(1):58–66, 2011.

Sutherland, John. Cn u txt? *The Guardian*, November 10 2002. Available at http://www.theguardian.com/technology/2002/nov/11/mobilephones2.

Thurlow, Crispin. From statistical panic to moral panic: The metadiscursive construction and popular exaggeration of new media language in the print media. *Journal of Computer-Mediated Communication*, 11(2):667–701, 2006.

Thurlow, Crispin, and Alex Brown. Generation txt? The sociolinguistics of young people's text-messaging. *Discourse Analysis Online*, 1(1), 2003. Available at http://extra.shu.ac.uk/daol/articles/v1/n1/a3/thurlow2002003.html.

Wood, C., E. Jackson, L. Hart, B. Plester, and L. Wilde. The effect of text messaging on 9- and 10-year-old children's reading, spelling and phonological processing skills. *Journal of Computer Assisted Learning*, 27(1):28–36, 2011a.

Wood, Clare, Beverly Plester, and Samantha Bowyer. Liter8 lrnrs: Is txting valuable or vandalism? *British Academy Review*, 14:52–54, 2009.

Wood, Clare, Sally Meachem, Samantha Bowyer, Emma Jackson, M. Luisa Tarczynski-Bowles, and Beverly Plester. A longitudinal study of children's text messaging and literacy development. *British Journal of Psychology*, 102(3):431–442, 2011b.

10 'The most beautiful language is French'

We use language in many ways: as a practical tool, to communicate ideas; as a social tool, to maintain relationships and mark our identity; as an artistic tool, in poetry, prose, drama, songs, and so on. For many people, using a particular language, or using language in particular ways, goes right to the heart of who they consider themselves to be. Small wonder, then, that so many people have strong opinions about language.

Within a particular language, people argue about whether it's better to use this word or that word, about whether it's okay to use a particular grammatical construction, about how the language should be written, about how to construct a poem or a speech or a contract. Considering languages as wholes, it's common to find claims that a specific language (or dialect of a language) is especially logical, or primitive, or poetic, or spiritual. Ideas like these have been used to argue that certain languages are particularly fit (or unfit) for specific uses, such as science or art.

In this chapter, we will focus on aesthetic judgments of languages: the idea that a language itself (not just an artistic use of that language) can be beautiful or ugly. Along the way, we'll touch on similar descriptions of languages as especially pleasant, clear, or logical – essentially, any kind of broad, hand-wavy judgment about a language or dialect as a whole. We will explore the factors that inform these judgments: To what extent are they a reaction to intrinsic properties of the language itself? To what extent are they related to the language's historical and cultural associations? To what extent are they affected by our beliefs about the people who speak the language?

10.1 Non-linguists' evaluations of dialects

We will begin by investigating what people believe about the dialects of their native language. Traditionally, the field of *dialectology* has involved linguists traveling to different areas and recording the range of variation within a single language. The goal is to document, as accurately as possible, what the dialects of a language are and how they differ from each other. For this reason, dialectologists focus on recording the speech of actual speakers of each dialect, rather

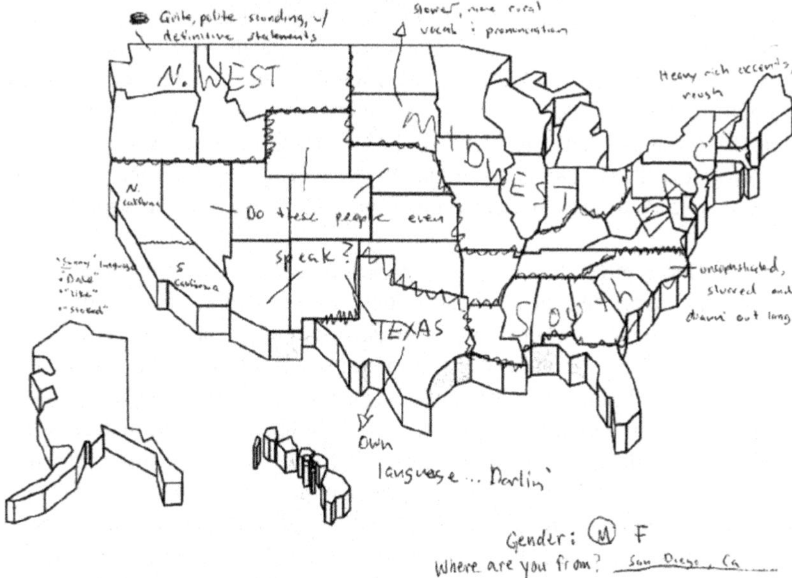

Figure 10.1 U.S. dialects as perceived by a college student from California. Carmen Fought, California students' perceptions of, you know, regions and dialects? *Handbook of Perceptual Dialectology* Vol. 2, Daniel Long and Dennis R. Preston, eds., 2002, Figure 8.4. Reprinted by permission of John Benjamins Publishing Company.

than relying on speakers of other dialects to describe the situation: popular beliefs are often inaccurate.

More recently, though, a number of linguists have argued that studying people's beliefs about other dialects is actually worthwhile – not because it tells us something about those other dialects, but because it helps us understand attitudes about language. The emerging field of *perceptual dialectology* explores these attitudes and attempts to understand where they come from.

10.1.1 Spontaneous evaluation of dialects in a descriptive task

One technique in perceptual dialectology is to give people a blank map and ask them to show where various dialects of their native language are spoken. Figure 10.1 shows a map like this, which was drawn by a college student from California.

Like many respondents, this student identified a number of major dialect regions and gave them geographic labels: *south*, *east*, *midwest*, and so on.

These responses are fairly typical in the United States: almost everyone draws a dialect region for the south(-east), and the midwest is often separated as its own region. This respondent has labeled the entire northeast as a single region; it's also common for subjects to draw more detail in this area (for example, labeling New York City and Boston as having distinctive varieties). Respondents are frequently unsure how to treat the American west; this student has apparently given up and asks *Do these people even speak?*

What's more interesting for our purposes is the fact that even though this is a purely descriptive task – respondents were asked to draw boundaries that separate regions where people speak differently, and to describe how that speech differs if they have any impressions about this – this respondent has spontaneously included evaluative comments on the map. Speakers in the northwest are *quite polite sounding, w/ definitive statements*; the dialect of the south is *unpolished, slurred and drawn out long*; southern Californians use *'sunny' language*. It seems that judgments like these, with charged words like *polite* and *unpolished*, are an integral part of how this respondent thinks about regional variants of English. Nor is this an isolated example; many subjects in these experiments spontaneously describe regional dialects in ways that are evaluative as well as purely descriptive.

The first thing we learn from this task, then, is that linguistic variation isn't socially neutral. Where there are differences in speech, it seems almost inevitable that people will have opinions about how good or bad the different varieties are. Beliefs about which kinds of language are better or worse than others appear to be a fundamental part of how humans 'do' language, no matter how much linguists may argue that all languages are equally valuable.

The other thought-provoking aspect of this task is that it gives us important clues about where these beliefs come from. Many descriptions provided on these maps apparently relate to the way dialects sound: words like *drawl* and *twang* are common in labels of the American South, for example. However, many others seem to refer just as much to the people living in those regions as they do to their language: perceptual dialectology studies document people using terms like *hillbilly*, *cowboy*, *surfer*, *Ivy League*, and so on. Here we have a hint that impressions about a dialect may be based less on personal experience with the sound of that dialect, and more on stereotypes about the people who speak it.

10.1.2 The most pleasant dialect is my own

Another technique in perceptual dialectology is to ask people to rate the speech of various regions according to some criterion. These regions are usually chosen according to convenient political boundaries – for example, US states. One common task is for subjects to rate these areas according to how 'pleasant' that region's dialect is; these ratings give us some idea of people's aesthetic reactions to dialectal variation.

Figure 10.2 shows how the speech of various states was rated by two groups of subjects, one from Nevada and one from Tennessee. On these maps, states in darker colors were rated as more pleasant and states in lighter colors as less pleasant. The Nevada group rated Nevada and Colorado as the states with the most pleasant variety of English; several west-coast states were highly rated too, but other areas of the country were perceived as far less pleasant – notably the south, New Jersey, and New York City. The worst-rated states were Arkansas and Alabama.

The map for the Tennessee group is strikingly different. For these raters, Tennessee was one of the states with the most pleasant English. We don't see the same widespread negative ratings across the south that we saw for the Nevada group, although Arkansas and Alabama are still the states with the lowest ratings. One interpretation of this pattern is that Nevada and Tennessee speakers agree that certain southern accents are bad; the Tennessee speakers just happen to feel that *their* particular variety of southern English is actually quite pleasant.

Similar studies have been carried out around the world – in Japan, Brazil, Germany, and elsewhere – and one of the most consistent findings is that speakers typically rate their own dialects as very pleasant. (Preston 1998 reports that students in Alabama rate the English of Alabama as highly pleasant; clearly, what we have here is a disagreement about the aesthetic qualities of Southern English.) This isn't terribly surprising, and it underscores the fact that judgments about the beauty (or ugliness) of a dialect or language aren't made in a vacuum: they are linked to our beliefs about the people who speak those varieties, and of course our own dialect is likely to hold a special place in our hearts.

Another recurring finding is that raters often say that the standard dialect of their language is especially pleasant. There may be a number of reasons for this: the standard is often familiar (since it's the language of broadcast media), it is spoken by people in positions of power and influence, and it is associated with a powerful ideology that claims that the standard dialect is superior to non-standard varieties. Indeed, when subjects are asked to rate various regions in terms of how *correct* their speech is, they typically give high ratings to regions where they think the standard is spoken; speakers of a non-standard dialect will usually rate their own dialect as not very correct, even if they believe it's still very pleasant.

All these patterns should make us suspicious about that idea that some dialects are objectively more pleasant than others. This doesn't mean that the raters in these studies are lying or fooling themselves – far from it. Our

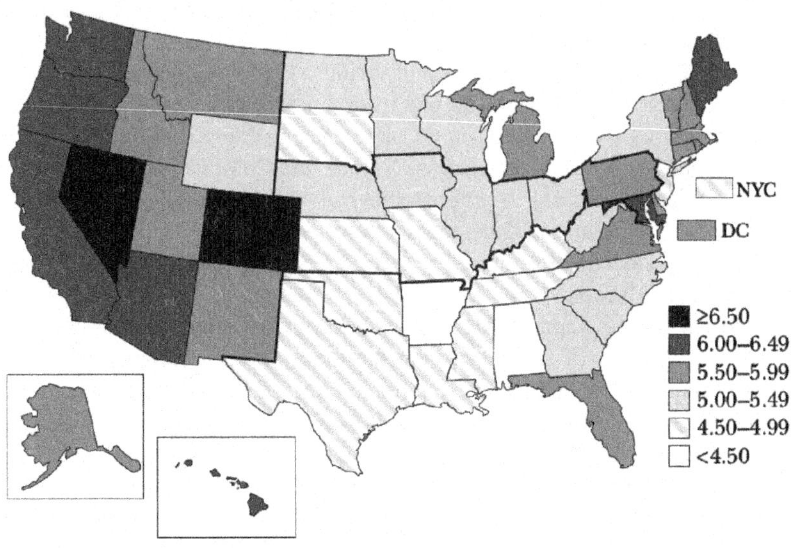

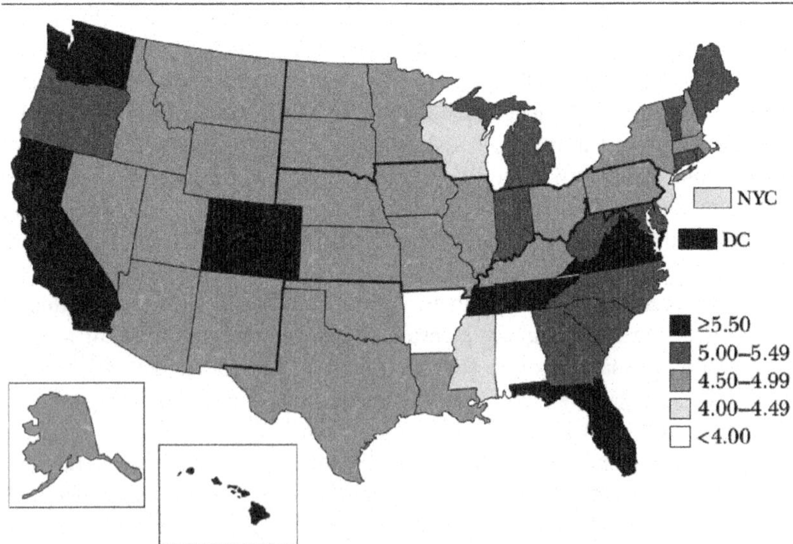

Figure 10.2 Nevada and Tennessee residents' ratings of the pleasantness of English spoken in U.S. states. Valerie Fridland and Kathryn Bartlett, Correctness, pleasantness, and degree of difference ratings across regions – use of Figures 6 and 3, in *American Speech*, Volume 81, No. 4, pp. 358–386. Copyright, 2006, the American Dialect Society. All rights reserved. Republished by permission of the copyright holder, and the present publisher, Duke University Press, www.dukeupress.edu.

reactions to various types of speech, and our judgments that they're pleasant or ugly, are very real; it would be naïve to pretend otherwise. Rather, studies like these help us understand where these reactions come from: apparently, it's impossible to separate our impressions about a kind of speech from our impressions about the people who use it.

10.2 Things that make a language beautiful (or ugly)

It seems, then, that our judgments about whether some variety of speech is beautiful or ugly are inextricably bound up with our ideas about the people who speak it; in fact, many of us are probably already aware of this on some level. But it's also common for people to argue that some languages are *inherently* beautiful or ugly, regardless of the people who speak them. In the next few sections, we'll examine several common claims along these lines. The question we're interested in is whether these 'objective' criteria are applied consistently, or whether they look more like *post hoc* justifications for reactions to a language that are based on something else entirely.

10.2.1 The sounds of language

Guttural consonants

In many parts of the world, French is a strong contender for the title of Most Beloved Language; it stands in stark contrast to German, which is widely despised as ugly and unpleasant. In fact, many people can articulate precisely *why* German is so ugly: sounds like the *ch* of *Bach* give German the unpleasant quality often described with words like *harsh* and *guttural*.

This *ch* sound, which is transcribed as [x] in the International Phonetic Alphabet, is a *voiceless velar fricative*. *Velar* means that the sound is produced by bringing the back part of the tongue near the soft palate, or velum; velar sounds in English include *k*, *g*, and *ng*. The sound is a *fricative* because the tongue doesn't make a complete closure at the velum: there's an opening that allows continuous airflow, but the opening is so narrow that the airflow becomes turbulent; this is what causes the characteristic 'hissing' sound of fricatives. English fricatives include sounds such as *f*, *v*, *s*, and *z*; by contrast, sounds like *k*, *g*, *t*, and *d* are *stops*, meaning that the tongue makes a complete seal that briefly blocks the airflow entirely. Finally, [x] is *voiceless* because the vocal folds don't vibrate while the sound is being produced: compare the voiceless sound *s* and the voiced *z*.

For many people, velar fricatives are inherently ugly sounds. This reaction typically extends to other fricatives produced in the back of the mouth, such as uvulars (where the tongue makes contact with the uvula) and pharyngeals (where the narrow opening for the fricative is made by the throat itself, behind and below the tongue). In fact, in many German dialects, German *r* is a voiced uvular fricative, which makes things even worse. Similar accusations of being harsh and guttural have been leveled at Semitic languages such as Arabic and Hebrew, which have velar, uvular, and pharyngeal fricatives.

Further evidence for the widespread idea that these sounds are unpleasant comes from invented languages (also known as *constructed languages*, or *conlangs*) whose creators specifically wanted them to sound harsh or ugly. In fantasy and science fiction, it's common for writers to have certain groups speak a language that is supposed to sound unpleasant. The idea is to portray the group as primitive, hostile, or both; such languages frequently include velar fricatives. Klingon, the language invented by Marc Okrand for the warlike race of the same name in the *Star Trek* universe, has both voiced and voiceless velar fricatives. It also has a uvular affricate, a sound that begins with a stop-like closure and ends with a prolonged fricative-like period, as in the English affricate *ch*. George R. R. Martin's fantasy series *A Song of Ice and Fire* features the Dothraki, a race of fierce nomads whose language is described as harsh and guttural; David Peterson, who developed the Dothraki language for the associated television series, duly included [x] in its consonant inventory. In J. R. R. Tolkien's *The Lord of the Rings*, the language spoken by the evil being Sauron and his minions includes both voiced and voiceless velar fricatives. This language is so ugly that even the powerful wizard Gandalf is reluctant to speak it; Tolkien describes the effect it has when he finally does:

> The change in the wizard's voice was astounding. Suddenly it became menacing, powerful, harsh as stone. A shadow seemed to pass over the high sun, and the porch for a moment grew dark. All trembled, and the Elves stopped their ears.
>
> Tolkien (1954)

Taken together, all these examples suggest that velar, uvular, and pharyngeal fricatives evoke unpleasant associations. But before we conclude that [x] is an objectively ugly sound, it's worth considering just how consistent this reaction is. Does the presence of [x] inevitably make a language sound ugly?

Absolutely not. The Spanish sound represented by the letter *j* (and by *g* before *e* and *i*), which English speakers are often told to pronounce like an *h*, is actually [x] in many dialects. In addition, Spanish *g* is pronounced as a voiced velar fricative in certain contexts, particularly after vowels. Later stages of Ancient Greek had [x] too, and the sound is still present in modern Greek. But Spanish and Greek don't come in for anything like the abuse suffered by German. In fact, we can even find these sounds in widely admired languages. French, that paragon of beauty, pronounces its *r* sound as a voiced uvular fricative (or as voiceless, depending on the context). Quenya and Sindarin, the beautiful and semi-magical languages spoken by elves in Tolkien's writings, both include [x].

What should we make of all this? Clearly, many people sincerely perceive velar fricatives as ugly sounds, and this idea can be used to great effect in fictional settings. But we aren't so sensitive to these sounds that we invariably find them unpleasant; we're happy to tolerate them in languages that are considered neutral or even beautiful. French and German have very similar pronunciations of *r*, but the former is praised and the latter is criticized: clearly, there's something going on here beyond the actual sounds of the two languages.

Indeed, when we look at the western languages that are commonly described as beautiful or ugly, it's easy to imagine other reasons these languages have the associations they do – reasons that have nothing to do with the way they sound. French, of course, spent centuries as the language of science and art in Europe; today it is still highly prestigious, associated with sophistication and romance. Greek is associated with the first philosophers and the intellectual foundations of western thought; it's also closely connected to the early years of Christianity. By contrast, many westerners still associate Germany primarily with Nazism, and many English speakers' only exposure to the German language is through movies about World War II. In this context, the argument that German is ugly because it has [x] starts to look like *post hoc* reasoning.

Pure vowels

In a book-length treatment of the wonders of the Italian language, Hales (2009) argues that Italian vowels are superior to those of English.

> Even ordinary things... sound better in Italian. The reasons start with its vigorous *vocali*, or vowels, which look like their English counterparts but sound quite different. In my first formal class in Italian, the teacher had us look in a mirror as we mouthed a-e-i-o-u... with the vowels puffing our cheeks, tugging at our lips, and loosening our jaws.
>
> An Italian *a* slides up from the throat into an ecstatic "aaaah." Its *e* (pronounced like a hard English *a*) cheers like the hearty "ay" at the end of *hip-hip-hooray*. The *i* (which sounds like an English *e*) glides with the glee of the double *e* in *bee*. The *o* (an English *o* on steroids) is as perfectly round as the red circle Giotto painted in a single stroke for a pope demanding a sample of his work. The macho *u* (deeper, stronger, and longer than its English counterpart) lunges into the air like a penalty kick from Italy's world-champion soccer team....
>
> Hales (2009, 20–21)

Like most non-linguists writing about language, Hales describes these sounds using impressionistic, non-technical terms that have little to do with the way they're actually pronounced. It's very unlikely, of course, that the students in Hales' Italian class were literally puffing out their cheeks when producing these vowels (try it!). Moreover, *both* English and Italian (like the vast majority of languages around the world) make distinctions among vowels that involve different positions of the lips: *rounded* vowels like *o* require the lips to be drawn together, while *unrounded* vowels like *a* require the lips to be apart.

As it turns out, the five-vowel system that Hales describes isn't unique to Italian; in fact, as documented by Schwartz et al. (1997), it's the single most common vowel system in the world, found in about 30% of all languages. Thus, although this system may be new and pleasing to an English speaker, that's not a good reason to crown Italian with the title of Most Beautiful Language. (To be fair, Hales doesn't explicitly say in her discussion of vowels that Italian is more beautiful than any other language, only that it's superior to English.)[1]

When Hales refers to Italian vowels as 'vigorous' and 'emphatic', she may be referring to the fact that they don't reduce in unstressed syllables. In English, unstressed vowels frequently become schwa ([ə]), a short vowel with approximately the same sound as the vowel in *love* or *hut*. This is especially clear in pairs of words like *atom* and *atomic*. In *atom*, the stress is on the first syllable, and the vowel in the second syllable (written *o*) is pronounced as a schwa. In *atomic*, the stress has moved to the second syllable; now it's the first syllable (still written with *a*) that is pronounced as a schwa.

Italian vowels don't reduce in this way, and English speakers learning Italian (or other languages without this kind of vowel reduction, such as Spanish) have to learn to give every vowel its 'full value', regardless of whether the vowel is stressed or not. Students are sometimes told to be 'precise' and 'clear' when speaking languages like Italian, in contrast to the 'lazy' English way of speaking; it's easy to understand why an English speaker would find such a language aesthetically appealing. However, as with velar fricatives, the fact that a language has schwa doesn't automatically make it an ugly language. Our counterexample, once again, is French, where schwas are abundant and in many cases are dropped from pronunciation entirely (the ultimate in 'laziness'!).

As with consonants, we have little evidence that some vowel sounds are inherently more beautiful than others. Individuals may come to enjoy certain vowels, and it's a wonderful thing for people to be enthusiastic about particular languages, as Hales is about Italian. But these judgments seem to be based more on personal preference (as well as the exoticness of the language

[1] A further issue here is that standard Italian actually has *seven* vowels, not five – another *e*-like vowel and another *o*-like vowel. (These additional vowel differences aren't typically indicated in Italian spelling and are absent in some regional dialects, making them particularly difficult for non-native speakers to learn; many learners aren't told about them at all.) Again, this seven-vowel system is not unusual: of the seven-vowel languages in Schwartz et al.'s sample, about half have the Italian system.

in question and its positive cultural associations) than on systematic phonetic analysis or a cross-linguistic comparison of vowel inventories. What's ordinary and pedestrian in one language becomes beautiful in another.

10.2.2 Grammar: Morphology and syntax

Our last examples of praise for the inherent virtues of certain languages involve what most people associate with the term *grammar*: morphology (building words out of smaller pieces) and syntax (building sentences out of words). It's here, especially, that we find ideas about beauty that are closely linked to impressions of a language as elegant, logical, or precise.

For many English speakers, one of the most daunting parts of studying a language such as Spanish, German, or Finnish is learning how to handle a wide array of noun and verb endings. English has only a bare handful of suffixes of the type known as *inflectional* – roughly, markers of grammatical information such as number (*cat-s*) or tense (*walk-ed*). Many European languages have far more, with the result that a single verb can have dozens or even hundreds of forms. Not only are languages like these particularly exotic for English speakers, but the prestige of Latin and Greek (both highly inflected languages) has led to a long grammatical tradition in the west in which languages with inflectional morphology are highly prized.

Grammatical case, in particular, is sometimes claimed to make a language logical and precise. In a language with *case marking*, nouns take particular forms that indicate their grammatical role in the sentence: subject, object, etc. English marks case only on pronouns; thus, we say *I saw him* but *He saw me*: *I* and *he* are the forms used in subject position, while *him* and *me* appear in object position. In Latin, case is marked on all nouns; thus, it's possible for sentences with very different meanings, such as (1a) and (1b), to be distinguished by case marking alone, whereas the equivalent English sentences require a difference in word order.

(1) a. *Puer puellam amat.*
boy.NOM girl.ACC loves
'The boy loves the girl.'

b. *Puerum puella amat.*
boy.ACC girl.NOM loves
'The girl loves the boy.'

The subject of the verb is marked with *nominative* case (*puer* in example (1a) and *puella* in example (1b)), while the direct object is marked with *accusative* case (*puellam* and *puerum*, respectively). Latin-style case marking, it's sometimes argued, is elegant and precise because it requires the speaker to understand the role of a noun in the larger sentence in order to produce it correctly. However, aside from the long-standing tradition of respect for Latin, it's not clear why indicating the role of a noun via case marking is inherently more precise than using word order for the same purpose. In addition, grammatical case doesn't always map precisely onto a single meaning or function; in Ancient Greek, for example, the dative case could be used for nouns as varied as the indirect object of a verb (*I gave it to him*), the beneficiary of an action or state (*It is better for him*), or the instrument by which an action is performed (*I cut it with a knife*).

Sanskrit has long played a role in India analogous to that of Latin in Europe, as a highly venerated language of scientific and religious tradition. Grammatical analysis of Sanskrit was foundational in Indian intellectual life for centuries; one of the most comprehensive analyses of any language ever produced is the work of the Sanskrit grammarian Pāṇini, who is believed to have lived in the fourth century BC. Pāṇini's work was fantastically detailed, as was that of the grammarians who followed him, and in many ways the Sanskrit grammatical tradition pioneered analytic techniques that weren't seen again in the west until the nineteenth and twentieth centuries. Western scholars who discovered the Indian tradition were impressed by the sophistication of what they found; one scholar famously argued that Sanskrit is 'more perfect than the Greek, more copious than the Latin, and more exquisitely refined than either' (Jones 1824, 28).

One western acknowledgment of the Sanskrit grammatical tradition is found in Briggs (1985), who noted that the technical descriptions employed by Sanskrit grammarians are parallel to certain artificial intelligence programming techniques. Unfortunately, this paper in particular has led to wild reports along the lines of 'NASA is funding research on programming computers with the Sanskrit language' (Briggs was a NASA consultant). The problem here is that there's a difference between the level of attention given to a language and the inherent properties of the language itself. Sanskrit does have a complex morphological system, but there are plenty of equally complex languages that simply happen to lack Sanskrit's tradition of sophisticated analysis. The most thoroughly studied language in modern linguistics is English, which has practically no inflectional morphology to speak of; not surprisingly, then, grammatical analysis of English has focused instead on rules of word order within a sentence. But just because there are sophisticated analyses of English grammar doesn't mean that English itself is more sophisticated than any other language; it's a historical accident that many linguists are English-speaking and therefore, understandably, tend to study their own language.

Once again, we're left with the strong impression that judgments about the beauty, complexity, and elegance of a language's grammar are *social* judgments: the more a language is associated with science, learning, and high culture, the more everyone admires the structure of that language. A famous example is Antoine de Rivarol's 1784 essay *L'Universalité de la Langue Française* (*The Universality of the French Language*), which argues that French syntax contributes to its superiority over other languages:

> What distinguishes our Language from ancient and modern languages is the order and construction of the sentence. This order must always be direct and necessarily clear. French first names the *subject* of speech, then the *verb*, which is the action, and at the end the *object* of the action: behold the Logic that is natural to all men; behold what constitutes common sense....
>
> [T]he syntax of French is incorruptible. This is the source of that admirable clarity, the eternal foundation of our Language: what is not clear is not French; what is not clear is still English, Italian, Greek, or Latin.
>
> Rivarol, quoted in Leavitt (2011, 63)

The word order that Rivarol describes is precisely the same order found in English and many other languages; what's more, there is no evidence that the order subject–verb–object is especially logical. It seems much more likely that Rivarol was influenced by the prestige of his language: if this language is used in scientific discourse across Europe, surely it must be inherently superior to its competitors. It apparently didn't occur to Rivarol that French might have achieved its position just because it was the language of an influential nation. The arbitrariness of which languages are held in high or low prestige is sometimes easier to notice in communities that are removed from us in time or space; Thomason (2001) relates the following anecdote involving some of the indigenous languages of British Columbia:

> The linguist William Poser, when collecting data from a Carrier elder in 1998, was given both a Carrier translation and a Babine translation for each item; his consultant commented that Poser really should know both Carrier and Babine in order to be properly educated.
>
> Thomason (2001, 33)

10.3 Case study: Are some dialects more beautiful than others?

In one sense, the question of whether some languages or dialects are objectively more beautiful than others smacks of contradiction. Aesthetic judgments like these are often thought to sit squarely in the realm of personal opinion: you may find beautiful what I find ugly, and neither of us is necessarily incorrect. There's nothing wrong with being particularly fond of a specific language, but it's a matter of personal taste and the next person is not wrong to feel differently.

On the other hand, though, statements about the aesthetic value of particular languages and dialects often take on a decidedly non-subjective tone, sometimes in ways that have real-world consequences. Standard Italian is heavily influenced by the work of Dante Alighieri, who flouted the conventions of his time by writing in a vernacular language rather than Latin. If Dante chose to write in the most objectively beautiful dialect of Italian (as evidenced by the fine quality of his poetry), then maybe other dialects deserve to disappear. Similarly, minority languages around the world are endangered in part because their speakers have been told for generations that their language is ugly, primitive, and worthless; it's all too common to find people who are ashamed to speak their native language.

10.3.1 Anecdotal evidence from language change and dialect variation

The problem, as we've seen, is that aesthetic judgments like these are inextricably bound up with social realities. In the case of dialects, it's no coincidence that the variety of a language spoken by people in power tends to be the one that's considered beautiful, while the speech of stigmatized groups is often considered ugly. Logically, there are at least two explanations for this state of affairs. The first is that the prestige dialect of a language achieves its position because it's inherently better than other varieties; therefore, educated people with good taste will naturally want to speak it. This idea is known as the *inherent value hypothesis*. The second explanation, called the *imposed norm hypothesis*, is that the prestige dialect is no better or worse than any other dialect; it's considered better simply because it is spoken by people in positions of power and influence.

One piece of evidence in favor of the imposed norm hypothesis comes from the fact that societies in different times and places can have very different ideas about what sounds beautiful. For example, some dialects of English lack *r* in certain positions (roughly, in the last part of a syllable); many words that historically had *r*, and are still spelled that way, are pronounced without *r* in these dialects. In the United States, *r*-dropping is especially associated with parts of the South and with Boston – two regions whose speech is highly stigmatized. Since the Standard English of the United States preserves *r* in these contexts, *r*-dropping is seen as ugly and uneducated. But in Great Britain, *r*-dropping occurs in the highly prestigious variety known as Received Pronunciation.

We see something similar with the sound *h*. Many languages lose *h* over time; this change is so common, in fact, that it shows up regularly on lists of 'sound changes to watch for' provided to beginning students of historical linguistics. Some dialects of English in Great Britain have lost *h*; these dialects happen to have low prestige, such as the Cockney variety of

London. But *h* was also unstable in later varieties of Latin, and it has disappeared entirely in modern Romance languages such as Spanish and (once again) that paragon of linguistic virtue, French. The fact that losing *h* can be standard in one community and highly stigmatized in another suggests that whether or not we perceive a particular sound pattern as beautiful is strongly linked to our opinions about the people who are producing that pattern.[2]

10.3.2 Athenian and Cretan Greek: Giles et al. (1974b)

If it's impossible to separate our opinions about a way of speaking from what we believe about the people who speak that way, then the only way to get 'objective' aesthetic judgments is from people who don't know anything about the language varieties in question. In other words, if Received Pronunciation really is more aesthetically pleasing than a Cockney accent, then someone who knows no English should be able to listen to both varieties and reliably judge that Cockney is less beautiful.

Giles et al. (1974b) took exactly this approach in a study of Greek, comparing the prestigious Athenian dialect with the stigmatized Cretan dialect. The researchers played 30-second samples of various languages for a group of 46 British students, none of whom knew any Greek. Of the six samples that the subjects heard, two were some variety of Greek, either Athenian or Cretan. Both of the Greek samples were recorded by the same speaker, a woman who could speak both varieties.

For each recording, subjects were asked to identify what language was being spoken and rate the voice they heard on qualities such as 'intelligence' or 'toughness'. As summarized in Table 10.1, there is no evidence that the prestige variety is objectively more pleasing: the English-speaking subjects didn't assign significantly different ratings to Athenian and Cretan Greek on any of the six scales that Giles et al. used. (Interestingly, the large t-value for the ratings of the varieties' aesthetic properties shows that this difference came closer than any other to being statistically significant – but it's the *Cretan* dialect that shows a trend toward higher ratings!)

This study is a good beginning in evaluating the inherent value and imposed norm hypotheses, although it's incomplete in a number of respects. One limitation of the study, characteristic of its time, is the fact that all the subjects heard the six language samples in the same order. This is partly because the subjects were all tested together in a single group session, and perhaps partly because creating separate tape recordings with different orders would have

2 Interestingly, Milroy (1983) argues that before the eighteenth century, loss of *h* was widespread in Great Britain and perceived as relatively neutral.

Table 10.1 *Mean ratings of the two Greek dialects.* t-*values test whether the Athenian and Cretan varieties received significantly different ratings; none did. Smaller numbers indicate greater presence of the relevant attribute (prestige, intelligence, etc.). Table 1 of Howard Giles, Richard Bourhis, Peter Trudgill, and Alan Lewis, 'The imposed norm hypothesis: A validation,'* The Quarterly Journal of Speech, *60(4): 1974, 405–410.*

	Evaluative Scales					
Greek Dialects	Prestige	Aesthetic	Intelligent	Tough	Amusing	Sophisticated
Athenian	4.70	5.39	4.22	4.33	6.33	4.89
Cretan	4.61	4.96	4.20	4.46	6.61	4.74
t values (d.f. = 45)	0.28	1.45	0.08	0.19	0.47	0.87

been extremely time-consuming. (Today, of course, it's trivial to administer tests on a computer, which can be programmed to deliver a different random order for each subject, assuming subjects are tested individually.) Randomizing the stimulus order is standard practice because of the danger of order effects: for example, did subjects recognize the language of the German sample, and if so, did they tend to assign higher ratings to Cretan Greek, which came next? ('I'll rate this language higher than the last one – *anything* sounds better than German.')

10.3.3 Wolof: Moreau et al. (2014)

Moreau et al. (2014) conducted a similar study with Wolof, a language of Senegal. The researchers recorded 54 native speakers of Wolof, half of whom were highly educated and half of whom had not completed high school. After eliminating potentially identifying information, they played short samples of these recordings for two groups of students: 116 Senegalese students, all of whom spoke Wolof; and 59 students from various European universities, none of whom knew Wolof. The students were asked to identify whether each speaker had had a short or long education.

Both groups of students were right a little more than 60% of the time; Moreau et al. report that their performance was better than chance ($p < 0.001$ for both groups). Moreover, neither group of students performed significantly better than the other ($p = 0.706$). This second result is especially surprising; we might expect the Senegalese students, who understood the cultural context of the speakers and actually knew the language, to at least do better than the European students. Moreau et al. conclude that their results challenge the imposed norm hypothesis: if high-status ways of speaking are completely arbitrary, then the European students (who lacked the relevant knowledge) shouldn't have been able to do any better than just guessing randomly.

Why did Giles et al. and Moreau et al. get such contradictory results? One possible explanation lies in the fact that these experiments tested subtly different things. Giles et al. had the two varieties of Greek recorded by the *same* speaker; Moreau et al. recorded *different* speakers of high-status and low-status Wolof. The obvious danger of Giles et al.'s approach (known as the *matched-guise* technique) is that the speaker might not be truly bidialectal, and that one or both of the recordings might therefore not be a good representation of the dialect. But its advantage is that it eliminates variation due to individual-level factors such as voice quality. In other words, maybe the students in Moreau et al.'s study weren't responding to the more 'beautiful' speech of educated Wolof speakers; instead, there might be more universal characteristics of vocal quality that tend to vary by socioeconomic status (a possibility that Moreau et al. themselves discuss).

Another relevant factor here is that even though Wolof is spoken somewhat differently by people with high and low levels of education, this difference doesn't exactly rise to the level of distinct 'dialects'. Thus, although Giles et al. were clearly testing listeners' evaluations of different dialects of the same language, Moreau et al. were testing much smaller status-related variations. Again, it's not clear what Moreau et al.'s results tell us about broader judgments of well-defined dialects as 'uneducated' or 'sloppy', independent of the level of education of the person actually speaking that dialect.

10.3.4 General conclusions

There are only a handful of 'pure' tests of the inherent value hypothesis that ask subjects to evaluate dialects of a language they don't speak at all. Most sociolinguistic research tends to focus on social factors that influence perceptions about language, rather than looking for judgments that are clearly *not* based on social factors. This only natural, since sociolinguists by definition are interested in how language is influenced by its social context. Moreover, as linguists have discovered and documented the fascinating complexity that is found in every language studied to date, it's become axiomatic in the field that no language is better or worse than any other. Thus, most linguists simply don't believe that some languages are inherently more beautiful than others, which partly explains the paucity of research in this area.

None of this means that people are wrong to have aesthetic reactions to particular languages or dialects. It's abundantly clear that these kinds of reactions are extremely widespread, perhaps even universal; attempting to get everyone to like all languages equally well is probably a hopeless task. And there's nothing wrong with having a particular interest in a specific language, as Hales does; or with having a special affinity for one's own dialect, as participants in perceptual dialectology research routinely do. The important thing to keep in mind is that beliefs like these are influenced by social factors, not just linguistic ones. There is no purely linguistic justification for condemning a particular dialect to extinction, no matter how much some people may dislike it; or for elevating one language above all others, no matter how ardent its supporters.

10.4 Summary

- Languages, and specific dialects of languages, are frequently judged aesthetically as 'beautiful', 'pleasing', 'ugly', etc.
- Speakers commonly consider their native dialect to be particularly pleasant; the standard dialect of a language is frequently idealized as pleasant, too.
- There seem to be no linguistic features that are universally considered beautiful or ugly. What is thought to be beautiful in one language may be judged ugly in another.
- People's aesthetic judgments about particular languages are inextricably bound up with beliefs about the people who speak those languages. The variety spoken by a prestigious group or a powerful individual tends to be valued more highly by virtue of those associations.
- A few experiments have asked subjects to evaluate various dialects of a language they do not speak. These studies provide little or no evidence that some dialects are objectively better-sounding than others.

For further reflection

(1) Interview five people you know; ask them which dialects of English they find particularly pleasant or unpleasant, and why. Discuss the kinds of reasons your interviewees give to explain their reactions. How often do people refer to the way a dialect sounds, and what kinds of sounds do they mention? How often do people compare the dialect to a standard variety? How often do they explicitly mention associations with the people who speak that dialect?

(2) There are a few additional studies on the inherent value and imposed norm hypotheses; these include Giles et al. (1974a), Brown and Lambert (1976), and Mays (1982). Read one of these studies and evaluate it. What exactly did the researchers do, and what did they conclude? Do you think their results support their conclusions?

Further reading

The classic book on perceptual dialectology is Preston (1989); Preston (1999) and Long and Preston (2002) collect papers in the field. Chapter 2 of Giles and Coupland (1991) summarizes a large body of research on the relationships between social and linguistic attitudes; see also Giles and Watson (2012) for a global overview. Chapters 11 and 17 of Bauer and Trudgill (1998) are brief discussions of popular judgments of languages and dialects.

The World Atlas of Language Structures (http://wals.info/) is an excellent resource for exploring how common particular linguistic features are and how they are distributed across the globe.

Bibliography

Bauer, Laurie, and Peter Trudgill, editors. *Language Myths*. Penguin Books, London, 1998.

Briggs, Rick. Knowledge representation in Sanskrit and artificial intelligence. *AI Magazine*, 6(1):32–39, 1985. Available at http://www.aaai.org/ojs/index.php/aimagazine/article/view/466/402.

Brown, Bruce L., and Wallace E. Lambert. A cross-cultural study of social status markers in speech. *Canadian Journal of Behavioural Science*, 8(1):39–55, 1976.

Fought, Carmen. California students' perceptions of, you know, regions and dialects? In Long and Preston (2002), chapter 8, pages 113–134.

Fridland, Valerie, and Kathryn Bartlett. Correctness, pleasantness, and degree of difference ratings across regions. *American Speech*, 81(4):358–386, 2006.

Giles, Howard, and Nikolas Coupland. *Language: Contexts and Consequences*. Cengage Learning, Boston, MA, 1991.

Giles, Howard, and Bernadette Watson, editors. *The Social Meanings of Language, Dialect and Accent: International Perspectives on Speech Styles*. Number 16 in Language as Social Action. Peter Lang, Bern, 2012.

Giles, Howard, Richard Bourhis, and Ann Davies. Prestige speech styles: The imposed norm and inherent value hypotheses. In William C. McCormack and Stephen A. Wurm, editors, *Language and Society: Anthropological Issues*, pages 589–596. Mouton, The Hague, 1974a.

Giles, Howard, Richard Bourhis, Peter Trudgill, and Alan Lewis. The imposed norm hypothesis: A validation. *The Quarterly Journal of Speech*, 60(4):405–410, 1974b.

Hales, Dianne. *La Bella Lingua: My Love Affair with Italian, the World's Most Enchanting Language*. Broadway Books, New York, NY, 2009.

Jones, William. *Discourses Delivered before the Asiatic Society: And Miscellaneous Papers, on the Religion, Poetry, Literature, Etc. of the Nations of India*, volume I. Charles S. Arnold, London, 1824.

Leavitt, John. *Linguistic Relativities: Language Diversity and Modern Thought*. Cambridge University Press, Cambridge, 2011.

Long, Daniel, and Dennis R. Preston, editors. *Handbook of Perceptual Dialectology*, volume 2. John Benjamins Publishing Company, Amsterdam, 2002.

Mays, David V. Cross cultural social status perception in speech. *Studies in Second Language Acquisition*, 5(1):52–64, 1982.

Milroy, Jim. On the sociolinguistic history of /h/-dropping in English. In Michael Davenport, Erik Hansen, and Hans Frede Nielsen, editors, *Current Topics in Historical Linguistics*, volume 2, pages 37–53. Odense University Press, Odense, 1983.

Moreau, Marie Louise, Ndiassé Thiam, Bernard Harmegnies, and Kathy Huet. Can listeners assess the sociocultural status of speakers who use a language they are unfamiliar with? A case study of Senegalese and European students listening to Wolof speakers. *Language in Society*, 43(3):333–348, 2014.

Preston, Dennis R. *Perceptual Dialectology: Nonlinguists' Views of Areal Linguistics*. Number 7 in Topics in Sociolinguistics. Foris Publications, Dordrecht, 1989.

Preston, Dennis R. They speak really bad English down South and in New York City. In Bauer and Trudgill (1998), pages 139–149.

Preston, Dennis R., editor. *Handbook of Perceptual Dialectology*, volume 1. John Benjamins Publishing Company, Amsterdam, 1999.

Schwartz, Jean-Luc, Louis-Jean Boë, Nathalie Vallée, and Christian Abry. Major trends in vowel system inventories. *Journal of Phonetics*, 25(3):233–253, 1997.

Thomason, Sarah G. *Language Contact: An Introduction*. Georgetown University Press, Washington, DC, 2001.

Tolkien, J. R. R. *The Fellowship of the Ring*. The Lord of the Rings. George Allen & Unwin, London, 1954.

11 'My language limits my thoughts'

There's no denying that speaking and thinking are closely related. We use words to convey ideas to other people, and to organize our own thoughts. We're so accustomed to giving verbal expression to our thoughts that it's easy to believe that we 'think in words'. If language is so central to our thinking, then it seems only logical that the particular *form* of our language – the words that it has, the aspects of the world that it encodes grammatically, and so on – should have a powerful effect on how we think.

The suggestion that language influences thought has a long history, both inside and outside the field of linguistics. The idea is a compelling one; it's intriguing to contemplate the possibility that our minds are shaped in important ways by accidents of our native language. And not only is it a theoretically interesting idea, but if language really does affect thought, then the real-world consequences could be quite serious. Many people are concerned that politicians, advertisers, and others use language in manipulative and misleading ways. It's also been claimed that particular languages are well suited to certain purposes because of the kinds of thought they permit or encourage – or, on a more sinister note, that some languages prevent certain kinds of desirable thought, and therefore confine their speakers to a kind of mental straitjacket. If this is true, then maybe there are languages that deserve to be forgotten.

Unfortunately, the true nature of the relationship between language and thought turns out to be very difficult to study, and the history of thinking about this question is littered with questionable assertions, inaccurate claims, and just plain wild speculation presented as fact. But the good news is that a substantial body of rigorous experimental work on the topic has appeared in the last few decades. In this chapter, we'll look at popular ideas about the relationship between language and thought; then we will examine some relevant experiments, asking what the evidence says about whether, and to what degree, thought is shaped by language.

11.1 The Sapir-Whorf hypothesis

The idea that language influences thought is closely associated with Benjamin Lee Whorf, a linguist who worked in the first half of the twentieth century.

Whorf documented and analyzed several indigenous American languages; at the time, linguists were just starting to grapple with these languages, many of which are different in important ways from more familiar European languages. Their discoveries had profound implications for linguistic theory, in part because they broadened linguists' understanding of what's possible in human language. These differences also invited speculation about the relationship between language and thought: if the grammar of language A seems to divide up the world into concepts that are very different from those of language B, does that mean speakers of language A and language B actually see the world differently?

Whorf thought so. In several of his writings, Whorf discussed words and grammatical constructions in indigenous American languages that have no obvious counterpart in English; he argued that these examples demonstrate different thought patterns. One of his most famous examples involved words for the idea of 'snow': Whorf claimed that Eskimos have many distinct words for 'falling snow, snow on the ground, snow packed hard like ice, slushy snow', and so on, whereas English has only one word for all these things (Whorf 1956, 216). Apparently, what one language takes to be a single concept may be divided up into multiple concepts in another language.

Both Whorf and his mentor, Edward Sapir, argued at times for a close relationship between language and thought; thus, the *Sapir-Whorf hypothesis* is the general idea that the language a person speaks may influence the way that person thinks. We can distinguish between at least two versions of the hypothesis: a *strong* version, whereby your language actually determines and even restricts the way you think; and a *weak* version, whereby your language influences the way you think but doesn't make any idea literally unthinkable. Both Sapir and Whorf argued for stronger and weaker versions of the idea at various times, and it's impossible to know exactly which versions of the hypothesis (if any) they would support if they were still alive today. Even though we credit Sapir and Whorf with the basic suggestion that language and thought are connected, we understand that they wouldn't necessarily endorse every specific proposal that has been put forward under the umbrella of the Sapir-Whorf hypothesis.

Whenever someone claims that some difference between languages A and B causes speakers of those languages to think differently, the first step is to ask whether the languages really are different in the relevant way. One obvious objection to Whorf's Eskimo example, for instance, is that English does *not* have only a single word for the concept 'snow': *snow*, *sleet*, *slush*, *blizzard*, and so on are all words that refer to snow in various states; skiers and other winter athletes have even more precise terms. (Incidentally, Whorf's snow illustration is also at least partly responsible for the modern urban legend that 'Eskimos have hundreds of words for snow'; see Pullum 1991 for an entertaining discussion of the myth.)

But there are other cases where languages really *do* describe the world in different ways. English, for example, has a single basic color term *blue* that covers a range of hues, from the color of the sky to the color of blueberries. Russian, by contrast, has two words: *goluboy* covers lighter blues, and *siniy* darker blues. English speakers can refer to *light blue*, *dark blue*, *sky blue*, *navy blue*, and so on – but these aren't basic terms the way *goluboy* and *siniy* are. Conversely, Russian lacks a single word that covers the entire range of English *blue*. In this case, the linguistic difference is genuine.

But it's not enough to establish that languages A and B really are different; we also have to be certain that speakers of those languages actually *think* differently, and we must do so in a way that avoids simply restating the fact that the two languages are different. It would be very boring, for example, to observe that Russian speakers describe shades of blue with two different words where English speakers use only one – this is just another way of saying that Russian speakers speak Russian and English speakers speak English. What we need is evidence that Russian and English speakers actually *think* about blues differently, independent of the way they talk about them. One criticism of Whorf's writing is that he often failed to do this. Although he sometimes argued for distinct habits of thought based on larger cultural patterns (see, e.g., Whorf 1941), he also sometimes fell into the trap of proclaiming that two groups obviously think about things differently just because they use different words – the snow example is of this type. To be fair, this is true of most discussions of language and thought until the last decades of the twentieth century; studying thought independent of language turns out to be very difficult to do. But we can't accept the Sapir-Whorf hypothesis without good evidence, and we should not abandon the search for good evidence just because it's hard.

Finally, even if we can show that speakers of two languages talk *and* think about something in different ways, that's not enough to prove that their language is affecting how they think. We also have to show that the linguistic differences are *causing* the differences in thought. Take the example of languages that have only a few number words – e.g., words for 'one', 'two', and 'three', and another term meaning 'many' that covers larger quantities. If we find that speakers of a language like this have trouble with mathematical concepts involving larger numbers, is that because their language prevents them from thinking about exact numbers larger than three? Or is it because their society has no need for counting up to larger numbers, which explains *both* speakers' difficulty with the concept (they've never practiced) *and* the lack of number words (speakers simply don't need them)?

The Sapir-Whorf hypothesis, then, turns out to be extremely difficult to test. At the end of this chapter, we will examine some of the creative techniques researchers have come up with to explore the relationship between language and thought. First, though, we will survey some popular Whorfian beliefs and ask how plausible they are.

11.1.1 Reasons to doubt the strong version of the Sapir-Whorf hypothesis

In its strongest form, the Sapir-Whorf hypothesis suggests that I'm literally unable to think about things that can't be expressed in my native language. There are many common-sense reasons to believe that this strong form of the hypothesis simply can't be true. It would be false, for example, to suggest that English speakers can't distinguish among various shades of blue (because they have only a single word *blue*) – English speakers obviously *can* do this, and if they need to refer to a specific type of blue, they will find a way to do so (*light blue*, *pale blue*, *sky blue*, *the color of that guy's shirt*, and so on).

If the strong version of the Sapir-Whorf hypothesis were true, it would be impossible to invent new things or imagine new ideas: if my language doesn't already have a word for the thing, I should be unable to think about it. But of course people come up with new ideas all the time; if they lack a word for the thing, they either create or borrow one. The words *telephone* and *computer* didn't exist in the 1500s, but this didn't stop people from inventing those things and naming them. Similarly, ideas have no problem spreading across linguistic boundaries: it's easy to think of political ideas, religious concepts, and even particular types of food or dress that have been borrowed across language divides. Again, there's no reason to think that people are prevented from thinking about new ideas simply because they happen to lack the relevant word. If my language has no word for the hairstyle known as a *mullet*, and I've never seen one before, it's preposterous to think that I would be unable to understand what I was looking at if you showed me an example, or that I would be unable to describe it to others. If mullets became common enough in my daily life that I needed a single word to refer to them, I would either borrow your word or create a new one.

Indeed, under the strong version of the Sapir-Whorf hypothesis, it's a mystery how we ever learn words at all. Babies are obviously capable of thought long before they learn language: they can recognize familiar faces before they know (or recognize) words like *Mom* and *Dad*; they learn that they can pull on certain kinds of handles to discover interesting things before they learn the word *drawer*; they know how to operate toys and generalize concepts such as 'buttons' or 'lids' before they are even remotely close to being able to describe what they're doing. Under the strong version of the hypothesis, much of what happens in formal education ought to be impossible because it involves a catch-22: to tell you what a new word like *logarithm* or *extradition* means, I have to describe the concept to you, but you won't be able to understand the concept unless you already have a word for it. Similarly, the strongest version of the hypothesis predicts that it should be impossible to learn a second language, or at least impossible to learn those words that don't precisely correspond to words in our first language.[1]

The strong version of the Sapir-Whorf hypothesis assumes that thinking depends on words, but there are plenty of reasons to believe that this isn't necessarily the case. Everyone has had the experience of having a word on the 'tip of your tongue' – you have the concept clearly in mind, and you know that you know a word for it, but you simply can't remember what the word is. Even more tellingly, we can have a concept without having a word to go with it. For example, English has standard names for each of the fingers (*thumb*, *index finger*, and so on), but on the foot, only the *big toe* and the *little toe* have special names. However, the fact that I don't have specific names for my other toes doesn't mean I can't distinguish among them, or that I couldn't describe them to someone else – if pressed, I might refer to my *second toe* or my *index toe* or *the toe next to my big toe*.[2] There are also plenty of people who don't have language but clearly have some form of thought. Babies, as mentioned above, are an obvious example; we could add to the list adults who have conditions that interfere with language, such as severe autism or aphasia. We can also identify aspects of our ordinary thinking that don't seem to involve language at all: imagining music, for example, or picturing a visual image.

All these examples raise serious doubts about the strong version of the Sapir-Whorf hypothesis. We are apparently not slaves to the words we use, even if it turns out that we are more subtly affected by them. Thought and language are, at least to some degree, independent.

11.1.2 Popular beliefs that language influences thought

For all the reasons just discussed, most linguists reject the strong form of the Sapir-Whorf hypothesis. Lucy (1996) takes issue with the fact that linguists typically begin discussions of the hypothesis with an argument against its strong form, much like the one above. He suggests that the strong version is a straw man: since most researchers are actually investigating much weaker forms of the hypothesis, it's unfair to spend so much time discrediting the

1 This is not to say that anyone from any group can understand any concept. There really are societies, for example, whose members have extreme difficulty with basic mathematical operations. It's also common for people who move from one society to another to have trouble understanding the values and practices of the new culture in which they find themselves. The point is that before we attribute these difficulties to *linguistic* differences, we also have to ask whether they could be due to differences in culture or experience.

2 Anatomists, of course, have standard names for the toes as well as for other parts of the body – e.g., the *philtrum*, which is the groove between the nose and upper lip – but these aren't widely known by non-specialists, who nevertheless know that these things exist.

strong form. Lucy may be right about linguists, but outside the ivory tower (or even in academic disciplines other than linguistics), it's surprisingly common to find strong Whorfian ideas about the connection between language and thought.

Someone learning a foreign language, for example, will inevitably discover concepts that the new language encodes differently from his native one. Many people find these differences intriguing, since they point to alternative ways of talking about the world. Combine this with the fact that many people study foreign languages and culture together, and you have a recipe for widespread belief that linguistic differences are linked to differences in thought.

One way languages can differ, of course, is in the particular words they have; it's common knowledge that a given word may have no exact translation from one language into another. Two languages may have words that cover the same range of meaning but divide it differently, as in Russian *goluboy* and *siniy* vs. English *blue*. Alternatively, one language may have a single word for a concept with no exact counterpart in another language; a commonly cited example is German *Schadenfreude*, a word that refers to taking pleasure in someone else's misfortune and has no exact English translation.

What do these differences mean? One conclusion might be that if a language has no word for such-and-such a concept, it must be because speakers of that language don't have the concept itself – indeed, maybe they can't even conceive of the idea. (A collection of claims along these lines in the popular media can be found in Liberman 2009.) Sometimes this is framed as a positive thing: that some language, for example, has no word for 'lying' because its speakers are always honest. But the supposed lack of some concept can also be presented as a moral failing:

> A particularly damaging example of the *No word for X* fallacy is one that one hears here in Northwestern Canada. Many of the Athabascan languages of Canada have a word for "thank you" that is borrowed from French *merci*.... This fact has suggested to the ignorant that these languages previously had no word for "thank you", from which they draw the further conclusion that their speakers had no concept of gratitude. Such a people, of course, must have been sub-human savages. The conclusion is that it's a good thing that white people came to rescue them from their degraded traditional way of life.
>
> Poser (2006)

One problem with this kind of claim is that it's usually false: Athabaskan languages, for example, have plenty of native ways of expressing thanks. But even when the claim is true, we've already seen that lacking a word for something doesn't make a person incapable of thinking about that idea. Speakers will find a way to say what they need to say – they will either come up with a phrase that describes the relevant concept, or they will borrow or invent a new word. In the case of *Schadenfreude*, English speakers have happily borrowed the word from German, with the result that it's now false to say that English has no word for taking pleasure in someone else's misfortune. The upshot is that examples of words without precise equivalents in other languages make nice factoids, but they don't tell us much about deep cultural or cognitive differences.

Languages also differ in the kinds of meaning that are marked grammatically. Whorf (1941, 1956) observed that Hopi doesn't make the same past-present-future distinction found in many European languages, and concluded that speakers of Hopi don't have the same concept of time as Europeans. (The facts of Hopi are still somewhat unclear, but there are certainly other languages, such as Mandarin, that are widely agreed to lack grammatical tense.) In English, many nouns are obligatorily marked for number: *I saw the cat* means I saw exactly one, while *I saw the cats* means I saw two or more. By contrast, some languages have an additional dual marker (i.e., a form meaning 'exactly two'), while others have no grammatical plural at all. Languages such as Turkish (but not English) have grammatical markers, known as *evidentials*, by which the speaker indicates the source of his knowledge about what he is saying: if I personally witnessed Ahmet arrive, I can say *Ahmet gel-di* 'Ahmet came'; but if I only heard about it, I have to say *Ahmet gel-miş*.

Once again, the mere fact that languages can differ in these ways is no reason to jump to strong Whorfian conclusions. The Hopi example has led to the popular belief that Hopi speakers have no sense of time whatsoever, an idea that is contradicted by the fact that the language has plenty of other resources for talking about time. Mandarin speakers, with no grammaticalized plural marker, are nevertheless perfectly capable of telling the difference between one object and more than one. English speakers don't have grammatical evidential markers in their language, but they're perfectly able to describe the source of their information if necessary (compare *John is single again* with *Apparently John is single again*).

Even 'exotic' differences among languages, then, are no reason to embrace the strong version of the Sapir-Whorf hypothesis. But this doesn't necessarily mean that these differences don't matter at all. In recent decades, linguists have started to explore the possibility that grammatical categories can direct speakers' attention in subtle but real ways. The idea is that an English speaker, for example, is constantly forced to pay attention to the difference between single things and multiple things because her language requires her to make this distinction. A Mandarin speaker, on the other hand, is perfectly capable of noticing this difference but isn't forced to do so every time she wants to talk; therefore, maybe Mandarin speakers are less attentive to number differences than English speakers. We will see some examples below of studies that test this kind of weak version of the Sapir-Whorf hypothesis.

One last reason many people find the Sapir-Whorf hypothesis appealing is that it sometimes resonates with their experience of using more than one language. Many bilinguals feel that they think differently when they use different languages, or even that they become different people. On the one hand, reports like these reflect real experiences, and therefore they're something we have to explain if we want to understand language in all its uses. On the other hand, we can't assume too quickly that these experiences are due solely to language differences, as opposed to other factors. An English-Japanese bilingual may feel different in each language, not because the languages themselves are different, but because the act of speaking English brings up one set of associations (with particular people, situations, and cultural practices) while the act of speaking Japanese brings up another. In addition, many bilinguals report other experiences that are actually incompatible with strong versions of the Sapir-Whorf hypothesis. For example, someone may be able to remember the content of a conversation that he has had, but not the language in which it was conducted. Under strong versions of the hypothesis, this should be impossible – if thoughts are determined by words, how can I remember the thoughts I had but not the words I used to express them?

11.2 George Orwell and political language

11.2.1 Newspeak

We see a slightly different flavor of the Sapir-Whorf hypothesis when we consider politics; politicians are widely perceived as using language to manipulate and fool the masses. The basic idea is that unpopular or inconvenient facts are given nice-sounding names to disguise their true nature; this obfuscation fools the public into supporting policies, people, and institutions they would otherwise reject.

Popular discussion of these issues has been enormously influenced by the writings of George Orwell. In one well-known essay, 'Politics and the English language', Orwell identifies several specific examples of pleasant expressions being used in his own day to cover up unpleasant realities:

> Defenceless villages are bombarded from the air, the inhabitants driven out into the countryside, the cattle machine-gunned, the huts set on fire with incendiary bullets: this is called *pacification*. Millions of peasants are robbed of their farms and sent trudging along the roads with no more than they can carry: this is called *transfer of population* or *rectification of frontiers*. People are imprisoned for years without trial, or shot in the back of the neck or sent to die of scurvy in Arctic lumber camps: this is called *elimination of unreliable elements*.
>
> Orwell (1968, 136)

Orwell's argument in this essay is that politicians use vague language to hide what they're actually doing. Everyone, he insists, should use language in a way that is clear, precise, and concrete.

An even more sinister view of political uses of language appears in Orwell's work of dystopian fiction, *1984*. This novel depicts a totalitarian government that has unprecedented control over every aspect of citizens' lives; leaders demand absolute obedience in action and even in thought. The appendix to the novel describes the government's long-term plan for enforcing compliance: a language called *Newspeak*.

> The purpose of Newspeak was not only to provide a medium of expression for the world-view and mental habits proper to the devotees of Ingsoc, but to make all other modes of thought impossible. It was intended that when Newspeak had been adopted once and for all and Oldspeak forgotten, a heretical thought – that is, a thought diverging from the principles of Ingsoc – should be literally unthinkable, at least so far as thought is dependent on words.
>
> Orwell (1949)

This goal was to be accomplished by eliminating words such as *justice* or *democracy* that were incompatible with the ruling party's ideology. Without access to words like these, citizens would be unable to think about the relevant ideas, and thus would be unable to desire or demand them. Note that Newspeak could succeed only under a very strong version of the Sapir-Whorf hypothesis: its crucial assumption is that not having a word for something means not being able to think about that thing.

Orwell's writings have been widely hailed as prophetic, and words such as *Newspeak* and *Orwellian* have entered the general vocabulary. A quick search of major newspapers, blogs, or other venues for public writing turns up plenty of complaints about this or that politician's use of language, often explicitly invoking Orwell or accusing the target of Newspeak. The fear is that if the public passively accepts politicians' misleading descriptions, they'll end up acquiescing to policies that are obviously wrong; the situation could be avoided if only politicians and the media were forced to use clear, neutral language.

11.2.2 Real-world examples: Can misleading language disguise the truth?

How frightened should we be? Are we really in danger of becoming slaves to manipulative political language? There are several reasons to think the situation isn't quite so dire. The first is the fact that Newspeak depends on such a strong version of the Sapir-Whorf hypothesis – but, as we have already seen, it's highly unlikely that thought really does depend totally on language.

Another reason to suspect that even manipulative language can't fool everyone is the very fact that we're able to talk about it. Surely Orwell didn't think it was impossible to see the real meaning of terms like *pacification*; after all, Orwell himself managed to do it. The very act of pointing out a term that you find offensively misleading, such as *collateral damage* or *revenue enhancement*, demonstrates that at least one person (namely, you) wasn't fooled.

Indeed, when we look at real-world examples, we see that even nice-sounding phrases can easily acquire negative associations. Consider some examples from the United States:

- Some institutions give favorable treatment or consideration to members of minority groups; policies like these are known as *affirmative action*. The positive word *affirmative* hasn't prevented some people from concluding that such policies are unjust; the result has been a vigorous, decades-long debate over whether affirmative action is a good or bad thing. For people who disagree with these policies, *affirmative action* is a distinctly negative term.
- Shortly after the terrorist attacks of September 11, 2001, Congress passed a law that expanded the authority of law enforcement agencies. This law is known as the *Patriot Act* – again, a vaguely positive term obviously meant to encourage support for the law. Critics, though, have argued that the law is intrusive and violates civil liberties. *Patriot Act* is a highly negative term among people who disagree with the law.
- On a lighter note, the halftime show of the 2004 Superbowl became notorious for a performance by singers Justin Timberlake and Janet Jackson: Timberlake uncovered part of Jackson's costume, exposing one of her breasts on live television. The ensuing controversy was intense, with commentators debating whether the exposure was intentional, whether anyone deserved to be penalized, and whether the incident was newsworthy at all. There was one thing, though, that everyone could agree on: when Timberlake referred to the incident as a *wardrobe malfunction*, the term met with instant and universal ridicule. The euphemistic language didn't cause the public to view the incident more mildly; rather, the public's knowledge of what had really happened made the euphemistic language risible.

Authoritarian governments in the real world, unlike the one in *1984*, have had little success in using Newspeak-like language to prevent their citizens from recognizing what is plainly before their eyes. Kershaw (1983, 194–199) observes that when ordinary Germans saw that Nazi propaganda conflicted with the reality on the ground, their reaction was to disbelieve nearly everything the government said – in fact, radio broadcasts from Great Britain became more trusted than the German government's own pronouncements. Cameron (1995, 152–155) cites an unpublished paper by Julian Konstantinov describing how the collapse of Communism in Bulgaria revealed Bulgarians' real attitudes toward the words they had been forced to use: citizens immediately abandoned terms such as *People's Army* or *People's Republic*, for example, because they observed that these institutions served not the people but the party. In other words, the meaning of *People's* had changed so that it corresponded to reality; the meaning intended by those in power (that these institutions reflected the will of the people) collapsed under the weight of fact.

Contemporary examples of similar phenomena can be found in modern China. Public speech is tightly controlled, particularly on the Internet, and one of the official justifications for restrictions on free speech is the need to promote a 'harmonious society'. Some citizens have responded by adopting the official language but giving it a subversive meaning: a blog post or online comment can be *harmonized*, which simply means that it's been censored. Again, people's perception of reality doesn't change just because they have to use euphemistic words; rather, the meanings of the words change so that they match reality.[3]

Finally, Cameron (1995, 72–75) notes that Orwell's goal of clear and unbiased language may be impossible anyway. The problem is that we use language *both* to describe 'the plain facts of the matter' *and* to show what we think about those facts. Consider, for example, an opponent of Newspeak who argues that every action that involves ending a human life should be described as *murder*. On the face of it, this sounds like a sensible proposal. But things become much more complicated when we consider practices that are controversial precisely because people disagree over whether they fall into the moral category of murder. It's easy to find opinion pieces, for example, that explicitly invoke Newspeak in their criticism of abortion (Broomstreet 2006), euthanasia (Hentoff 1987), or capital punishment (Aronson 2007). No one disagrees about the relevant facts (namely, that all of these actions result in death); rather, it's our *evaluation* of those facts that is at issue.

Note that all these examples involve a population that knows the truth of the matter, and is therefore able to notice the difference between the facts and what's said about them. When people do *not* know the facts, then of course the

[3] Another popular technique is to replace potentially sensitive words with homophones or near-homophones. 'River crabs' have become a symbol of censorship because, in Mandarin, *river crab* sounds like *harmony*. River crabs are said to threaten the beautiful but endangered *grass-mud horse* – a fictional creature whose name sounds like an obscene phrase, and which symbolizes resistance to censorship. The *China Digital Times* (http://www.chinadigitaltimes.net/) maintains a list of phrases like these in its 'Grass-mud horse lexicon'.

situation is different, and language can easily be used to disguise and mislead. When a politician falsely declares that she's never taken a bribe, her constituents may well believe her if they have no reason to think otherwise. But we can understand this phenomenon without ascribing any magical powers to language; it's an ordinary part of our everyday experience, called *lying*.

The real world, then, gives us little reason to believe that large-scale linguistic manipulations like Newspeak will become reality anytime soon. This is not to say, though, that the words we use don't matter at all. As noted above, we use language for taking positions as well as describing facts, and the world has no shortage of issues that are well worth discussing. In addition, we use language as a framing device, and there's evidence that different ways of framing a situation really matter (see section 11.3.5). But language isn't the only tool we use to influence people; this is why executives wear suits, negative political ads feature ominous music, and consumer products are covered with pictures of smiling faces. We can appreciate the framing potential of language without concluding that language is unique, or that we're slaves to the words we hear.

11.3 Case study: Does our language affect the way we think?

The strong version of the Sapir-Whorf hypothesis seems highly improbable – our thoughts aren't completely determined by the language we use. But the weak version, the idea that language has a subtle influence on the way we think, could very well be true. As discussed above, the weak version of the hypothesis is difficult to test because we have to find a way to assess thought independent of language. In this section, we will look at several experiments designed to do just that. As we do so, we'll ask whether they provide us with good evidence for a link between language and thought, and if so, what the nature of that link is.

11.3.1 Color terms: Winawer et al. (2007)

For several decades during the early and middle twentieth century, variants on the Sapir-Whorf hypothesis were very popular. The domain of color terms, in particular, seemed to confirm that languages (and therefore, presumably, thought) could differ in large and unexpected ways. Linguists and anthropologists observed that languages divide up the color spectrum differently: some languages, for example, have separate basic color terms for 'light blue' and 'dark blue'; others, such as Japanese, have a single basic term that describes both 'blue' and 'green'. Many languages have no word at all for colors that English speakers would consider basic, such as pink or grey. Some languages have only a tiny number of basic color terms, as few as two or three. This range of variation suggested to many people that whether or not a person considers two colors to be 'the same' will depend on whether they are called by the same name in that person's language.

Received opinion about the implications of these differences began to change in the 1960s and 1970s; many researchers came to accept the idea that the variation they saw actually reflected fundamental similarities in human cognition across cultures. Several factors contributed to this shift. One was the growing influence of Noam Chomsky, who argued that humans are born with much of their knowledge of language 'pre-programmed', and that differences in grammatical structure across language are actually just variations on a universal core. Chomsky's proposals aren't actually incompatible with the Sapir-Whorf hypothesis – it could be that even those differences end up affecting thought in profound ways – but in practice, linguists who are sympathetic to Chomsky's ideas tend to be skeptical of Whorfianism, and vice versa.

Another factor that contributed to the shift towards a universalist view of color was Berlin and Kay's (1969) influential survey of color terms in 98 languages. Berlin and Kay argued that there are actually strict constraints on the color terms in a given language: if a language has *n* basic color terms, there are only a few possibilities for what those terms will be. They proposed a hierarchy of color terms based on when they appear in a language's vocabulary: a language with only two color terms will have words for 'dark' and 'light'; a language with three terms will additionally have a word for 'red'; and so on. The observation that color terminology doesn't vary without limit suggested to many linguists that the color spectrum can't be divided up in arbitrary ways; there must be innate constraints on how color is perceived that can't be overridden by language.

Finally, Heider (1972) and Heider and Olivier (1972) conducted a series of experiments with the Dani people of New Guinea, a group with only two basic color terms: *mola* ('light') and *mili* ('dark'). Dani and English speakers actually performed very similarly on some tasks, such as remembering colors or learning new names for colors, despite the differences in their native color vocabulary. Heider argued that there are certain colors – 'focal colors', such as a prototypical red – that are inherently salient, and people are much better at identifying and remembering focal colors than non-focal colors. By this argument, a language doesn't make its speakers better at seeing some colors than others; rather, some colors are inherently more noticeable, and languages tend to have basic color terms that cluster around those focal points. Not every language has a word for every focal color, but speakers will be sensitive to focal colors regardless of whether they happen to have words for them.

Studies like these, combined with the changing Zeitgeist, convinced many linguists in the second half of the twentieth century that the effect of a person's native color terms on her perception of color is weak or non-existent. But in recent decades, a number of researchers have begun to argue that color perception really *is* influenced by a person's native vocabulary, albeit in subtle ways. Roberson et al. (2000), for example, replicated several of Heider's experiments with a different group and found that native language did affect color perception. Other researchers have explored how people perceive hues that lie at the boundary between one color term and another – for example, how English speakers perceive colors that are very close to the boundary between *blue* and *green*.

In one such study, Winawer et al. (2007) investigated the phenomenon known as *categorical perception*, in which a person is more sensitive to differences across categories than between categories. English speakers, for example, are known to perceive the difference between *blue* and *green* categorically: they do well at distinguishing between two colors if one is 'blue' and the other is 'green', but they're much worse at distinguishing between equally distinct colors if both are 'blue' or both are 'green'.

If a language's color terms cause speakers to perceive a category boundary wherever they have a linguistic boundary, then we might expect Russian speakers to perceive the difference between light and dark blue (*goluboy* and *siniy*) categorically where English speakers do not. Winawer et al. studied 26 native speakers of Russian and 24 native speakers of English. During the experiment, each subject would see three blue squares on a computer screen, one at the top and two at the bottom; the subject's job was to identify which of the two bottom squares exactly matched the shade of the top square.

Russian and English speakers did in fact behave differently. Russian speakers responded faster when the two bottom squares straddled the boundary between *goluboy* and *siniy*; in other words, they performed better when they were distinguishing between colors that belonged to two different categories. They responded more slowly when the two bottom squares were both *goluboy* or both *siniy*. English speakers, by contrast, responded equally quickly regardless of whether the two squares were both *light blue* or *dark blue*, or whether one was *light blue* and the other *dark blue*. Thus, Russian speakers showed evidence of a category boundary in the middle of the blue spectrum, but English speakers didn't.

So far, these results look promising. Moreover, Winawer et al. found these differences in a non-linguistic task – that is, subjects were apparently just matching colors, not describing them verbally. But it turns out that things aren't quite so simple. Although subjects weren't *required* to name the colors during the color-matching task, they might have done so anyway. Maybe, for example, the Russian subjects were covertly saying *goluboy* and *siniy* to themselves when they saw the colored squares, and if they found that one of the bottom two squares was *goluboy* while the other was *siniy*, that linguistic label gave them an extra boost in matching them to the top square. In other words, maybe language differences helped the Russian speakers only because they were actively using language to perform the task, not because their perception had been permanently altered by their language. It could even be that Russian speakers were naming the colors subconsciously, not fully aware of what they were doing. This issue turns out to be a serious and recurring problem for studies of language and thought: even if researchers don't explicitly ask subjects to use their language to accomplish some task, subjects may invoke language anyway. The result is that even differences that appear to be purely non-linguistic may turn out to be linguistic after all. Papafragou et al. (2002, 216) sum up the dilemma by concluding that 'many apparent effects of language on thought are more appropriately interpreted as effects of language on language.'

Winawer et al. addressed this possibility by conducting two more versions of the same experiment, which they made harder by asking subjects to perform an extra task at the same time that they were matching the colored squares. In one of these interference conditions, subjects were given an eight-digit number and asked to recite it to themselves silently; after several color-matching trials, they had to recall the number. The idea was that if subjects were performing a demanding verbal task (reciting a number), they couldn't use language to help them in the color-matching task, and the category advantage for Russian speakers would disappear. In the other interference condition, subjects saw a grid of black and white squares; they had to hold a picture of the grid in mind for several color-matching trials and then recall it. The idea was that because this task is demanding but doesn't involve language, subjects would be free to use language for the simultaneous color-matching task, and the category advantage for Russian speakers would remain.

Figure 11.1 shows the results for all three types of interference (none, spatial, and verbal). The predictions are confirmed perfectly: Russian speakers maintained their advantage for cross-category comparisons when they were performing the spatial interference task, but the advantage disappeared in the verbal interference task. English speakers made no distinction between cross-category and within-category comparisons, regardless of the type of interference (or lack thereof).

So, do the differences between Russian and English affect thought, or not? The answer appears to be both yes and no. On the one hand, Russian speakers were slightly better at distinguishing between *goluboy* and *siniy*, although the effect sped up Russian speakers' inter-category responses by only about a tenth of a second. On the other hand, this effect seems to depend crucially on subjects' ability to use language (perhaps unconsciously) to perform the task. In other words, having both *goluboy* and *siniy* doesn't permanently alter Russian speakers' color perception; it merely gives them a slight advantage in some situations to have rapid access to simple color terms that distinguish the two

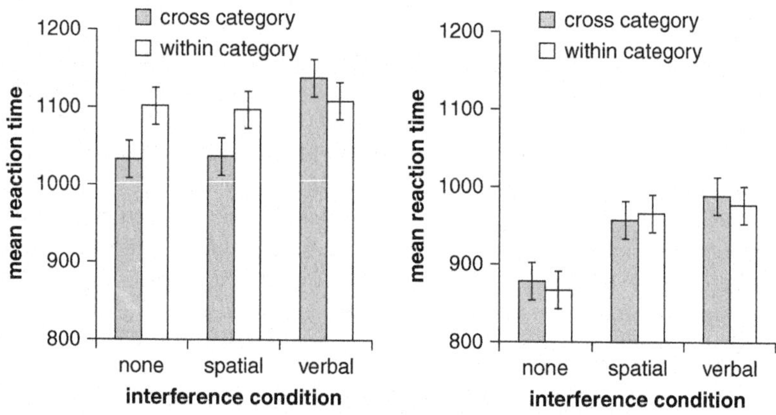

Figure 11.1 Response times (in milliseconds) for across- and within-category comparisons for Russian speakers (left) and English speakers (right) by interference condition. Jonathan Winawer, Nathan Witthoft, Michael C. Frank, Lisa Wu, Alex R. Wade, and Lera Boroditsky, Russian blues reveal effects of language on color discrimination, *Proceedings of the National Academy of Sciences* 104(19):7780–7785, Figure 2. Copyright (2007) National Academy of Sciences, U.S.A.

types of blue. What we have here is evidence for a weak Whorfian effect of language.

11.3.2 Grammatical gender: Konishi (1993)

In languages with grammatical gender, each noun belongs to a specific sub-class – its gender – that affects its grammatical behavior. Often, other words in the sentence are required to carry information about the gender of a particular noun. The adjective modifying a noun, for example, might be required to match the gender of the noun; in some languages, the verb indicates the gender of its subject or object. Thus, a person who speaks a language with grammatical gender has to keep track of which sub-class each noun belongs to.

The basis of these groupings can be more or less arbitrary. In some indigenous American languages, the gender of a noun is based on criteria such as the shape of the thing it refers to (round and compact versus long and thin, for example) or whether or not it's human. In many European languages, by contrast, the gender of a noun has little or no connection to its meaning; the gender is either completely arbitrary or linked to some morphological property of the noun (e.g., Spanish words ending in *-ción* are typically feminine). The interesting thing about gender in European languages is that noun classes are linked to biological sex: the forms used with one class of nouns ('masculines') are also used for male humans; the forms used with the other class of nouns ('feminines') are also used for female humans. The result is that speakers of such languages regularly talk about inanimate objects with the same grammatical forms that they also use for distinguishing humans according to biological sex.

No one would argue, of course, that speakers of languages with sex-based gender systems literally believe that inanimate objects are male or female. The Spanish word for 'table' (*mesa*) is feminine, but Spanish speakers are perfectly aware that tables don't have ovaries. Mark Twain famously noted that the German word for 'girl', *Mädchen*, is grammatically neuter – neither masculine nor feminine. But no one thinks German speakers don't know the difference between boys and girls.

It's possible, though, that gender influences speakers in more subtle ways. Maybe Spanish speakers, for example, vaguely associate tables with femaleness because of their grammatical gender; Konishi (1993) tested this idea. He asked 40 native speakers each of Spanish and German to rate 32 words along several dimensions such as 'weak'–'strong'. These dimensions were grouped into larger categories related to ideas that are known to be associated with biological sex; for example, the 'potency' category (which included dimensions such as 'weak'–'strong' and 'small'–'big') is associated with sex, with males perceived as more potent ('strong', 'big', etc.) than females.

Crucially, many of the words in Konishi's study have different genders in Spanish and German. Some, such as *puente* and *Brücke* (both meaning 'bridge'), involve a masculine Spanish word and a feminine German word; others, such as *manzana* and *Apfel* ('apple'), involve a feminine Spanish word and a masculine German one. If grammatical gender affects how speakers think, we might expect speakers of each language to rate masculine words as more potent and feminine words as less so, regardless of their meanings.

Figure 11.2 shows that this is exactly what happened: within each language, masculine nouns were rated as more potent than feminine nouns, even though the masculine nouns in one language corresponded to the feminine nouns in the other and vice versa. Konishi reports that the effect was statistically significant at $p < .01$. These differences suggest that speakers' ideas about these words were indeed influenced by the words' grammatical gender: objects described by masculine nouns tended to be thought of as slightly bigger, stronger, etc. than objects described by feminine nouns. Notice, though, that the effect is tiny – just a tenth of a point on a seven-point scale. Clearly, grammatical gender is not causing speakers of these languages to see some objects as entirely masculine and others as entirely feminine; the difference may be real, but it's also extremely subtle.

We might also ask how much these results are mediated by language. Konishi's subjects were instructed to rate 'concepts', not 'words', but the fact remains that they saw the actual words during the experiment. Maybe the

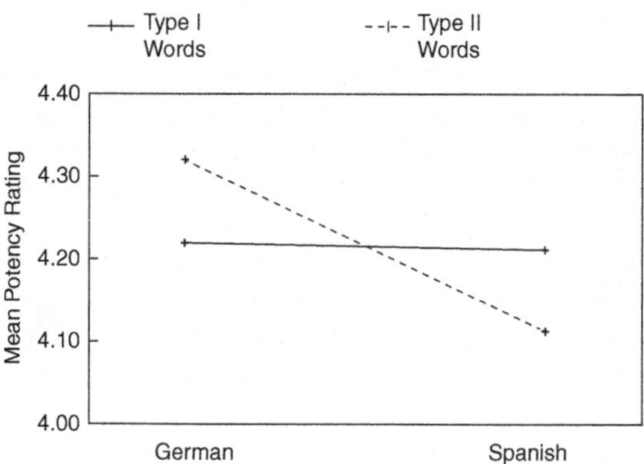

Figure 11.2 Mean potency rating of German and Spanish Type I and Type II words. *Note:* Type I words: feminine gender in German and masculine gender in Spanish (e.g., *sun, fork, pan, brush*); Type II words: masculine gender in German and feminine gender in Spanish (e.g., *moon, spoon, pot, broom*). Toshi Konishi, The semantics of grammatical gender: A cross-cultural study, *Journal of Psycholinguistic Research* 22(5):519–534, 1993. With kind permission from Springer Science and Business Media.

experience of seeing the word *manzana*, complete with the morphological cue to its gender (the final *-a*), brings up feminine associations that don't arise in the experience of seeing an actual apple. In other words, maybe subjects associate gender with the word, but not the thing.

Overall, the results of Konishi (1993) suggest a weak version of the Sapir-Whorf hypothesis: grammatical gender may indeed give inanimate objects subtle associations with biological sex that they otherwise wouldn't have. But the effects are small, and gender is only one of the many factors that affect how these objects are perceived. Grammatical gender does *not* overwhelm everything else people know about apples and bridges.

11.3.3 Motion events: Papafragou et al. (2002)

Movement can be encoded linguistically in different ways. Compare, for example, the sentences in (1) and (2) (Papafragou et al. 2002, 195):

(1)	The man	walked	across	the street.
	FIGURE	MOTION+MANNER	PATH	GROUND

(2)	O andras	dieshise	to dromo	(me ta podia/perpatontas).
	the man	crossed	the street	(on foot/walking)
	FIGURE	MOTION+PATH	GROUND	(MANNER)

Both of these sentences convey the same information: that the man was in motion, that his movement began on one side of the street and ended on the other side, and that he accomplished this movement by walking. The sentences are different in how they use specific grammatical structures to encode various parts of the motion event. In the English sentence in (1), the main verb (*walked*) encodes both the fact that the man was moving and the MANNER in which he moved (namely, walking). The PATH that he took is encoded in the following prepositional phrase (*across the street*). The Greek sentence in (2) is different. Here, the main verb (*dieshise*) encodes the man's PATH (namely, that he was moving across something – in this case, the street). The MANNER of the motion is expressed in a separate phrase (*me ta podia* or *perpatontas*).

Talmy (1985) first observed that languages differ systematically in how they encode motion events. In some languages, like English, motion verbs typically encode the MANNER of the movement but not the PATH: *walk, crawl, float, roll, bounce*, and so on. (English does have verbs that encode PATH rather than MANNER, but they're less common: *cross, ascend*, etc.) Other languages, like Greek, have the opposite tendency: motion verbs typically encode the PATH of the movement, and MANNER (if expressed at all) requires a separate phrase. Note that these differences affect the type of information that has to be specified in a sentence that describes motion. If the verb encodes the MANNER of motion, it's possible to produce a sentence that doesn't mention the PATH at all: *The man walked*. Conversely, if the verb encodes information about the PATH, it's possible to produce a sentence that doesn't mention the MANNER of motion: *The man crossed the street* (but he could have been walking, running, crawling, flying, etc.).

What we have, then, are not differences in what English or Greek *can* express, but rather differences in what they *usually* express. A number of studies (e.g., Slobin 1991) have confirmed that speakers of English are far more likely to use MANNER verbs when describing motion events, while speakers of Spanish (a 'path' language like Greek) are far more likely to use PATH verbs. Could it be that English speakers actually pay more attention to the MANNER of motion events, while Spanish or Greek speakers pay more attention to PATH?

Papafragou et al. (2002) studied speakers of English and Greek from a wide range of ages (four years old to fifty) to test whether the two groups actually think about events differently. They showed each subject a series of drawings that depicted people or animals in motion and asked subjects to describe what they saw; not surprisingly, Greek speakers were more likely than English speakers to use PATH verbs (e.g., *The frog is entering the room [jumping]*), while English speakers were more likely to use MANNER verbs (e.g., *The frog is jumping [into the room]*). Two days later, the researchers showed more pictures to the same subjects and asked them to remember whether these were

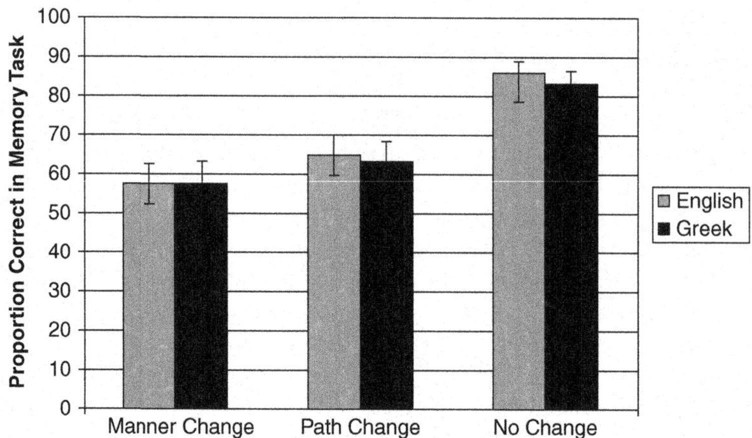

Figure 11.3 Performance on the memory task of Experiment 1 by native language and picture type. Reprinted from *Cognition*, 84, Anna Papafragou, Christine Massey, and Lila Gleitman, Shake, rattle, 'n' roll: The representation of motion in language and cognition, 189–219, copyright 2002, Figure 3, with permission from Elsevier.

the same pictures they'd seen before. Some of the pictures really were the same; others were similar to the earlier pictures but different in some crucial way. Some of the modified pictures changed the PATH of the original motion (e.g., a frog jumping out of a room instead of into it), while others changed the MANNER (e.g., a boy stumbling over a log instead of jumping over it). If Greek speakers pay more attention to PATH and English speakers to MANNER, then we might expect Greek speakers to do better at noticing pictures whose PATH had changed, while English speakers would do better at noticing pictures whose MANNER had changed.

As shown in Figure 11.3, subjects remembered pictures about equally well regardless of their native language. All subjects were better at correctly identifying pictures with no change (i.e., pictures they really had seen before) than rejecting pictures that had been changed, but there were no statistically significant differences between English and Greek speakers for either MANNER or PATH changes. These results, then, provide no evidence that English and Greek speakers think differently about motion events.

11.3.4 The direction of time: Boroditsky (2001)

Many languages use some of the same words to talk about space and time. In English, time is often imagined as an invisible horizontal line: the future is *ahead* of us and the past is *behind* us; we move *forward* to new things and think *back* on what's happened before. Cross-linguistically, it's very common for words that originally had spatial meanings to acquire temporal meanings as well.

Mandarin has expressions that use the same front-back line to talk about time that English speakers do. But Mandarin speakers can also talk about time using a different imaginary axis – a vertical one. In this conception, the past is 'above' and the future is 'below'; examples are given in (3) and (4).

(3) Vertical metaphors: 'earlier' (Boroditsky 2001, Figure 2)

a. māo shàng shù
'cats climb trees'

b. shàng ge yuè
'last (or previous) month'

(4) Vertical metaphors: 'later' (Boroditsky 2001, Figure 2)

a. tā xià le shān méi yǒu
'has she descended the mountain or not?'

b. xià ge yuè
'next (or following) month'

Obviously, time isn't literally a horizontal or vertical line, but it's possible that spatial metaphors like these lead us to think about it that way. Boroditsky (2001) asked whether the specific metaphors a language uses could influence how speakers imagine time: since Mandarin has both horizontal and vertical metaphors, are Mandarin speakers more likely to think about time as a vertical line than English speakers, whose metaphors are almost exclusively horizontal?

To explore this question, Boroditsky used a psychological phenomenon known as *priming*. The basic idea is that people are often faster at some task if they've just seen or done something related; for example, if a subject's job is to recognize words, she will be faster at recognizing the word *doctor* if she's just seen a related word such as *nurse*. Boroditsky studied 26 native speakers of English and 20 native speakers of Mandarin; she asked them to answer true-false questions about the relative order of events (e.g., *March comes before April*). Two types of time words were used in these questions, either *before/after* (which some English speakers can use with a spatial meaning) or *earlier/later* (which are purely temporal). Interspersed with these time-related questions were spatial questions, in which subjects saw two objects and had to judge their relative location (some examples are given in Figure 11.4). Some of the spatial questions involved the horizontal axis, while others involved the vertical axis. Boroditsky predicted that English speakers would be primed to answer time-related questions after they had just

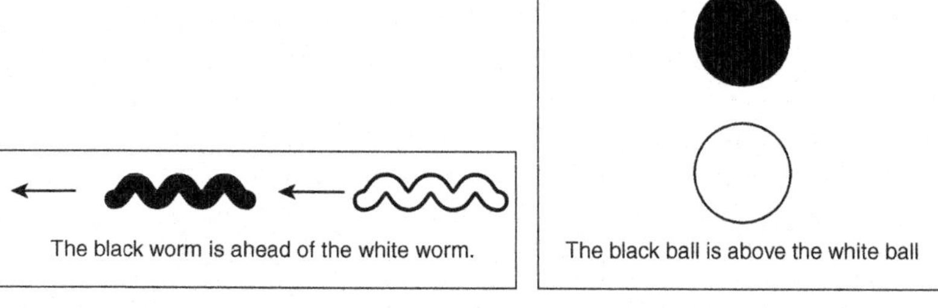

Figure 11.4 Examples of spatial questions used as primes. Reprinted from *Cognitive Psychology*, 43, Lera Boroditsky, Does language shape thought? Mandarin and English speakers' conceptions of time, 1–22, copyright 2001, Figure 3, with permission from Elsevier.

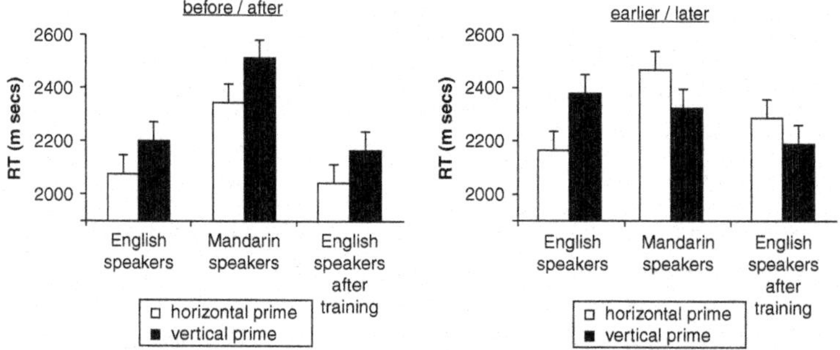

Figure 11.5 Reaction times to temporal questions by native language, type of spatial prime, and temporal language (*before/after* vs. *earlier/later*). Reprinted from *Cognitive Psychology*, 43, Lera Boroditsky, Does language shape thought? Mandarin and English speakers' conceptions of time, 1–22, copyright 2001, Figure 4, with permission from Elsevier.

answered horizontal spatial questions; in other words, thinking about horizontal space would help English speakers think about time because they imagine time that way. Mandarin speakers, on the other hand, might be primed by the vertical spatial questions, because their language makes a vertical metaphor available.

Figure 11.5 summarizes the results. For the time questions that used *before/after*, both English and Mandarin speakers answered faster if they had just seen a horizontal prime than if they had just seen a vertical prime; in other words, reasoning about horizontal space helped speakers of both languages reason about time. For the time questions that used *earlier/later*, the two groups were different: English speakers benefited from the horizontal primes, as before, but Mandarin speakers benefited from the vertical primes. In other words, when they were answering questions about time that didn't use any spatial language at all, English speakers appeared to associate time with horizontal space, while Mandarin speakers associated time with vertical space.

Boroditsky conducted two other experiments to assess how much this effect really depends on language. In one experiment, she asked English speakers to complete an identical task – but before they did so, she trained them in what she called 'a new way to talk about time'. Subjects learned to use vertical spatial metaphors to describe the relative order of events, e.g., *Monday is above Tuesday*. As shown in Figure 11.5, English-speaking subjects who received this training performed like the Mandarin-speaking subjects of the original experiment: they answered *earlier/later* questions faster after vertical primes than after horizontal primes. Boroditsky concluded that even brief training in a different way of using language can cause people to think differently about time. In another experiment, Boroditsky asked 25 Mandarin-English bilinguals to complete part of the original experiment (with only the *earlier/later* questions included); she found that the priming effect of vertical spatial questions was bigger for subjects who had begun learning English later in life, and concluded that early exposure to English made the Mandarin speakers less likely to think about time as a vertical space.

Taken together, all of these experiments suggest that these metaphors do encourage speakers to think about time in particular ways; what we have, then, is support for a weak version of the Sapir-Whorf hypothesis. Interestingly, some of these same results also provide evidence *against* the strong version of the hypothesis: even though English speakers are apparently biased to think about time horizontally, they could be brought to think about time vertically after just a brief training period. In other words, a lifetime of using horizontal metaphors for time could be counteracted by just a little practice; English speakers were clearly not trapped by their habitual way of speaking.

We should also keep in mind that language isn't the only tool we have for representing time spatially. For English speakers, the idea of time as a horizontal line is reinforced in many other ways: the direction of writing, the traditional left-to-right layout of timelines, the arrangement of days within a week on a calendar, the horizontal control bars we use to navigate audio and video files, and so on. (We also have vertical representations of time, such as the arrangement of weeks on a calendar, but these are less common.) Confronted with all these ways of representing time, we might ask which way the causation goes: do horizontal metaphors cause English speakers to represent time horizontally in all these other domains too, or is language just one more consequence of a general cultural agreement that time is horizontal? Similarly, we might ask whether alternative forms of training could encourage English speakers to think about time vertically. For example, suppose English speakers were trained to arrange the days of the week in a vertical layout – would this have had the same effect as the linguistic training?

Finally, it's important to note that although Boroditsky's study is well known and has been highly influential, it's also controversial. In particular, a number of other researchers (Chen 2007; January and Kako 2007; Tse and Altarriba 2008) have tried and failed to replicate the results, which raises the question of whether these apparent differences between English and Mandarin speakers are even real. Either there is no difference, and Boroditsky obtained a significant result by chance; or other labs used slightly different procedures that made the difference disappear – and if the latter is true, then the effect of language is apparently very fragile and unlikely to matter in real-world situations.

11.3.5 Framing events: Loftus and Palmer (1974)

Loftus and Palmer (1974) conducted a famous study on how language can be used to frame events in a way that affects how observers interpret those events. In one experiment, they showed several videos of traffic accidents to 45 students and then asked them about what they had seen. The crucial question was *About how fast were the cars going when they ___ each other?* Each subject saw a version of this question with one of five verbs: *hit*, *smashed*, *collided*, *bumped*, and *contacted*. As summarized in Table 11.1, Loftus and Palmer found that subjects' speed estimates depended in part on what verb they had seen in the question – their speed estimates were higher for more 'forceful' verbs, a significant difference at $p < .005$. Apparently, the way you ask someone about an event can affect the way that person remembers it.

In a second experiment, Loftus and Palmer asked 150 students to watch a single video of a traffic accident and answer questions about it. Some subjects were asked the same question as before, this time with one of two verbs (*hit* or *smashed*); other subjects weren't asked about the speed of the cars at all. One week later, the same subjects answered different questions about the accident; here, the crucial question was *Did you see any broken glass?* As shown in Table 11.2, Loftus and Palmer found that subjects were significantly ($p < .025$) more likely to answer *yes* if they had seen the verb *smashed* a week earlier than if they had seen the verb *hit* or hadn't been asked about speed at all – despite the fact that there was actually no broken glass in the video.

Did these different ways of phrasing the question actually affect how subjects remembered the accidents they had seen with their own eyes? Apparently so. Although we have seen that language doesn't put speakers in a straitjacket, it does seem possible for specific linguistic choices to 'nudge' people in one direction or another. In a similar study, Fausey and Boroditsky (2010) asked students about Janet Jackson and Justin Timberlake's 'wardrobe malfunction'

Table 11.1 *Mean speed estimates in response to questions with different verbs. Reprinted from* Journal of Verbal Learning and Verbal Behavior, *13, Elizabeth F. Loftus and John C. Palmer, Reconstruction of automobile destruction: An example of the interaction between language and memory, 585–589, copyright 1974, Table 1, with permission from Elsevier.*

Verb	Mean speed estimate
Smashed	40.8
Collided	39.3
Bumped	38.1
Hit	34.0
Contacted	31.8

Table 11.2 *Subjects who responded* yes *and* no *to the question* Did you see any broken glass? *by verb condition. Reprinted from* Journal of Verbal Learning and Verbal Behavior, *13, Elizabeth F. Loftus and John C. Palmer, Reconstruction of automobile destruction: An example of the interaction between language and memory, 585–589, copyright 1974, Table 2, with permission from Elsevier.*

	Verb condition		
Response	Smashed	Hit	Control
Yes	16	7	6
No	34	43	44

(see section 11.2.2); they found that subjects recommended larger monetary penalties when they read that Timberlake *tore the bodice* than when they read that *the bodice tore*, even when they had just watched a video of the incident.

However, as discussed above, we can understand these effects without concluding that language has some magical power over us. For obvious reasons, no politician will propose *An Act for Giving Tax Breaks to Corporations That Give Me Money*, even if that's what the bill does; similarly, cigarette manufacturers don't voluntarily cover their products with pictures of yellow teeth or tar-covered lungs. We are influenced by many things, and language is no exception.

11.3.6 General conclusions

Although some of the studies we have seen don't support any version of the Sapir-Whorf hypothesis, others suggest that a weak version may in fact be true: the way we perceive color, for example, may be subtlely influenced by the language we speak. It's often hard to tell whether we're really seeing an influence of language on thought, as opposed to an influence of larger cultural patterns on both thought and language, but in at least some cases (e.g., grammatical gender in Spanish and German) it seems plausible that language is playing a causal role.

However, the evidence above also suggests that our understanding of the Sapir-Whorf hypothesis should be nuanced in at least two important ways. One is that most of the effects we've seen are very small – differences of less than a second in reaction times, or differences of a tenth of a point on a seven-point scale. These aren't the kinds of differences that would be obvious in everyday life; we can't point to a Spanish speaker, for example, and say, 'The only reason you think these apples are beautiful is because *manzana* is feminine in your language.'

The other important nuance is that, at least in some cases, the effect of language seems to be restricted to situations where the person is actually using language in some way, either consciously or not. English and Russian speakers, for example, behave the same when they're prevented from using language in a color-matching task. Language, it seems, hasn't altered speakers' color perception permanently; rather, it matters only for the kind of thought that is crucially connected to language – what Slobin (1991) calls 'thinking for speaking'.

The good news, then, is twofold. Language does have some very interesting effects on how people think, and working out exactly what those effects are will occupy researchers for decades to come. But the effects are subtle, and all the evidence suggests that we are *not* slaves to our language in the way Orwell feared. Newspeak isn't going to become a reality anytime soon.

11.4 Summary

- The *Sapir-Whorf hypothesis* is the idea that a person's language influences the way he or she thinks. The hypothesis comes in strong and weak versions.
- Many popular beliefs about language, especially in the realm of politics, assume a strong version of the Sapir-Whorf hypothesis: that language can make some thoughts unthinkable. However, there are many reasons to believe that the strong version of the hypothesis is not true.
- Several studies have found evidence for the weak version of the Sapir-Whorf hypothesis: language has a non-deterministic influence on some kinds of

thought. Some of these studies suggest that the effect is present only when people are actively using language to accomplish some task.

- It is often difficult in a given situation to determine whether language is really affecting how speakers think, or whether they way people think affects the language they use.
- There is good evidence that language can be used to 'frame' events and ideas, subtlely influencing how people think about them; however, language is not the only tool that can be used in this way.

For further reflection

(1) Choose a controversial political topic, and do an internet search for people explicitly comparing certain ways of talking about that topic to Newspeak. Analyze the discussions you find. Do commentators seem genuinely concerned that specific words or phrases will fool the public into accepting bad policies? Do you agree? Why or why not? To what extent do you think these terms can be used to frame public discussion in a way that influences people's opinions? To what extent do you think people choose their words in order to show where they stand on the issue? To what extent could these words or phrases be characterized as ordinary lying?

(2) Another example of linguistic diversity is the difference between languages that use *egocentric* directions ('left', 'right', 'behind', etc.) and those that exclusively use *cardinal* directions ('north', 'south', etc.). Read the extended discussion of this difference in Deutscher (2010a) or chapter 7 of Deutscher (2010b) and consider what it might imply about the Sapir-Whorf hypothesis. Do you find it plausible that speaking a language like Guugu Yimithirr might encourage a person to think differently about space? Do you think it's possible that the language might reflect cultural convention? Think about your own experience with egocentric and cardinal directions: what kinds of situations make it easier or harder for you to keep track of directions such as 'left' or 'north'?

(3) Two more studies of the relationship between language and thought include Mazuka and Friedman (2000) (shape vs. material in English and Japanese) and Gennari et al. (2002) (motion in English and Spanish). Read and evaluate one of these papers. How did the authors go about testing thought independent of language, and to what extent do you think they succeeded? Are you convinced by the authors' conclusions? In what ways, if any, might the two groups of speakers be different other than in their language?

Further reading

Two of Whorf's essays most often cited in connection with the Sapir-Whorf hypothesis are Whorf (1941) and Whorf (1956). Recent discussions of the psycholinguistic literature, written for a general audience, include Boroditsky (2010), Deutscher (2010b), and McWhorter (2014). The latter two books position themselves on opposite sides of the issue (Deutscher argues in favor of the hypothesis; McWhorter argues against it), but they actually come to the same conclusion: a weak version of the hypothesis is true, but the strong version is not. For an even more skeptical view, see Chapter 3 of Pinker (1994).

Orwell's famous essay on politics and language is Orwell (1968). Cameron (1995) is a thoughtful review of language use in the political sphere, particularly with regard to political correctness.

Bloom (1981) is a well-known early study of the Sapir-Whorf hypothesis, but with many methodological flaws; see Au (1984) for criticism. Boroditsky et al. (2003) reviews some of the literature, with a special focus on grammatical gender; however, several of the experiments described here seem to have never been peer-reviewed or published. Lucy and Gaskins (2001) and Imai and Gentner (1997) are experiments testing whether language affects how much a person pays attention to the shape of an object vs. the material it is made of. Fausey and Boroditsky (2011) is a study of whether language affects how well a person remembers the agents involved in an event.

Bibliography

Aronson, Stanley M. Commentary: Refining the art of doublespeak. *The Providence Journal*, pages C–05, March 26 2007.

Au, Terry Kit-Fong. Counterfactuals: In reply to Alfred Bloom. *Cognition*, 17(3):289–302, 1984.

Berlin, Brent, and Paul Kay. *Basic Color Terms: Their Universality and Evolution*. University of California Press, Berkeley, CA, 1969.

Bloom, Alfred. *The Linguistic Shaping of Thought: A Study in the Impact of Language on Thinking in China and the West*. Lawrence Erlbaum Associates, Hillsdale, NJ, 1981.

Boroditsky, Lera. Does language shape thought?: Mandarin and English speakers' conceptions of time. *Cognitive Psychology*, 43(1):1–22, 2001.

Boroditsky, Lera. Lost in translation. *The Wall Street Journal*, July 23 2010. Available at http://www.wsj.com/articles/SB10001424052748703467304575383131592767868.

Boroditsky, Lera, Lauren A. Schmidt, and Webb Phillips. Sex, syntax, and semantics. In Dedre Gentner and Susan Goldin-Meadow, editors, *Language in Mind: Advances in the Study of Language and Thought*, chapter 4, pages 61–79. The MIT Press, Cambridge, MA, 2003.

Broomstreet, Henry. Letter to the editor: Abortion doublespeak. *San Bernardino Sun*, March 13 2006.

Cameron, Deborah. *Verbal Hygiene*. Routledge, London, 1995.

Chen, Jenn-Yeu. Do Chinese and English speakers think about time differently? Failure of replicating Boroditsky (2001). *Cognition*, 104(2):427–436, 2007.

Deutscher, Guy. *Through the Language Glass: Why the World Looks Different in Other Languages*. Metropolitan Books, New York, NY, 2010a.

Deutscher, Guy. Does your language shape how you think? *The New York Times*, August 29 2010b. Available at http://www.nytimes.com/2010/08/29/magazine/29language-t.html?fta=y.

Fausey, Caitlin M., and Lera Boroditsky. Subtle linguistic cues influence perceived blame and financial liability. *Psychonomic Bulletin & Review*, 17(5):644–650, 2010.

Fausey, Caitlin M., and Lera Boroditsky. Who dunnit? Cross-linguistic differences in eye-witness memory. *Psychonomic Bulletin & Review*, 18(1):150–157, 2011.

Gennari, Silvia P., Steven A. Sloman, Barbara C. Malt, and W. Tecumseh Fitch. Motion events in language and cognition. *Cognition*, 83(1):49–79, 2002.

Heider, Eleanor Rosch. Universals in color naming and memory. *Journal of Experimental Psychology*, 93(1):10–20, 1972.

Heider, Eleanor Rosch, and Donald C. Olivier. The structure of the color space in naming and memory for two languages. *Cognitive Psychology*, 3(2):337–354, 1972.

Hentoff, Nat. Euthanasia: Another warning from the Surgeon General. *The Washington Post*, page A21, April 11 1987.

Imai, Mutsumi, and Dedre Gentner. A cross-linguistic study of early word meaning: Universal ontology and linguistic influence. *Cognition*, 62(2):169–200, 1997.

January, David, and Edward Kako. Re-evaluating evidence for linguistic relativity: Reply to Boroditsky (2001). *Cognition*, 104(2):417–426, 2007.

Kershaw, Ian. How effective was Nazi propaganda? In David Welch, editor, *Nazi Propaganda: The Power and the Limitations*, chapter 10, pages 180–205. Croom Helm, London, 1983.

Konishi, Toshi. The semantics of grammatical gender: A cross-cultural study. *Journal of Psycholinguistic Research*, 22(5):519–534, 1993.

Liberman, Mark. 'No word for X' archive. Language Log, January 28 2009. Available at http://languagelog.ldc.upenn.edu/nll/?p=1081.

Loftus, Elizabeth F., and John C. Palmer. Reconstruction of automobile destruction: An example of the interaction between language and memory. *Journal of Verbal Learning and Verbal Behavior*, 13(5):585–589, 1974.

Lucy, John A. The scope of linguistic relativity: An analysis and review of empirical research. In John J. Gumperz and Stephen C. Levinson, editors, *Rethinking Linguistic Relativity*, number 17 in Studies in the Social and Cultural Foundations of Language, chapter 2, pages 37–69. Cambridge University Press, Cambridge, 1996.

Lucy, John A., and Suzanne Gaskins. Grammatical categories and the development of classification preferences: A comparative approach. In Melissa Bowerman and Stephen C. Levinson, editors, *Language Acquisition and Conceptual Development*, number 3 in Language, Culture and Cognition, chapter 9, pages 257–283. Cambridge University Press, Cambridge, 2001.

Mazuka, Reiko, and Ronald S. Friedman. Linguistic relativity in Japanese and English: Is language the primary determinant in object classification? *Journal of East Asian Linguistics*, 9(4):353–377, 2000.

McWhorter, John H. *The Language Hoax: Why the World Looks the Same in Any Language*. Oxford University Press, Oxford, 2014.

Orwell, George. *1984*. Harcourt Brace Jovanovich, New York, NY, 1949.

Orwell, George. Politics and the English language. In Sonia Orwell and Ian Angus, editors, *The Collected Essays, Journalism and Letters of George Orwell*, volume 4: In Front of Your Nose, 1945–1950, pages 127–140. Penguin Books, London, 1968.

Papafragou, Anna, Christine Massey, and Lila Gleitman. Shake, rattle, 'n' roll: The representation of motion in language and cognition. *Cognition*, 84(2):189–219, 2002.

Pinker, Steven. *The Language Instinct: How the Mind Creates Language*. William Morrow and Company, New York, NY, 1994.

Poser, Bill. No word for thank you. Language Log, May 6 2006. Available at http://itre.cis.upenn.edu/~myl/languagelog/archives/003120.html.

Pullum, Geoffrey K. *The Great Eskimo Vocabulary Hoax and Other Irreverent Essays on the Study of Language*, chapter 19: The Great Eskimo Vocabulary Hoax, pages 159–171. The University of Chicago Press, Chicago, IL, 1991.

Qiang, Xiao. The grass-mud horse lexicon. Available at http://chinadigitaltimes.net/space/The_Grass-Mud_Horse_Lexicon.

Roberson, Debi, Ian Davies, and Jules Davidoff. Color categories are not universal: Replications and new evidence from a stone-age culture. *Journal of Experimental Psychology: General*, 129(3):369–398, 2000.

Slobin, Dan I. Learning to think for speaking: Native language, cognition, and rhetorical style. *Pragmatics*, 1(1):7–25, 1991.

Talmy, Leonard. Lexicalization patterns: Semantic structure in lexical forms. In Timothy Shopen, editor, *Language Typology and Syntactic Description*, volume 3: Grammatical Categories and the Lexicon, chapter 2, pages 57–149. Cambridge University Press, Cambridge, 1st edition, 1985.

Tse, Chi-Shing, and Jeanette Altarriba. Evidence against linguistic relativity in Chinese and English: A case study of spatial and temporal metaphors. *Journal of Cognition and Culture*, 8(3/4):335–357, 2008.

Whorf, B. L. The relation of habitual thought and behavior to language. In Leslie Spier, A. Irving Hallowell, and Stanley S. Newman, editors, *Language, Culture, and Personality: Essays in Memory of Edward Sapir*, pages 75–93. Sapir Memorial Publication Fund, Menahsa, WI, 1941.

Whorf, Benjamin Lee. Science and linguistics. In John B. Carroll, editor, *Language, Thought, and Reality: Selected Writings of Benjamin Lee Whorf*, pages 207–219. The MIT Press, Cambridge, MA, 1956.

Winawer, Jonathan, Nathan Witthoft, Michael C. Frank, Lisa Wu, Alex R. Wade, and Lera Boroditsky. Russian blues reveal effects of language on color discrimination. *Proceedings of the National Academy of Sciences*, 104(19):7780–7785, 2007. Available at http://www.pnas.org/content/104/19/7780.full.

Appendix
Statistics brief reference

The purpose of this chapter is to provide you with enough information to begin to read, understand, and evaluate published research in the social sciences. It is *not* a comprehensive introduction to statistics; for more information, see the 'Further reading' suggested below.

The first part of the chapter reviews some common methods for summarizing data, both numerically and graphically. The second part gives an overview of significance testing: why it's important, how it's usually reported, and how to interpret it. With the background provided in these two sections, you should be able to read a typical scholarly paper reporting the results of social science research and understand the gist of what's going on, even if you cannot follow all the details.

The last part of this chapter describes some of the major issues in conducting social science research. This section will expose you to some of the most important questions you can ask about how an experiment was designed and carried out; learning to ask those questions is the first step towards being able to evaluate the results of a particular study.

The examples in this chapter are taken from a study of the effects of intoxication on speech. In that experiment, eight subjects recorded a list of several dozen words, once while sober and once while moderately drunk; see Kaplan (2010) for a more detailed description of the methods involved. I've chosen these examples for convenience: the experiment generated a large amount of data that lends itself to many different types of analysis. The results presented here are meant to illustrate statistical points; they aren't novel (or even representative) findings about the general effect of alcohol on speech, nor are they necessarily the best way to analyze the data. For an overview of the literature on intoxicated speech, see Chin and Pisoni (1997).

A.1 Descriptive statistics

The purpose of *descriptive statistics* is to summarize datasets in a concise way. This section reviews some common descriptive techniques, both numeric and graphical.

Table A.1 *Average pitch (fundamental frequency), duration, and loudness (intensity) of consonant-vowel-consonant words in sober and intoxicated speech.*

	Sober		Intoxicated	
Measure	*M*	(*SD*)	*M*	(*SD*)
Pitch (Hz)	154.0	(51.7)	156.4	(52.3)
Duration (ms)	442	(120)	467	(127)
Loudness (dB)	78.2	(5.8)	75.1	(5.3)

A.1.1 Some common statistics for summarizing data

Perhaps the most common statistic for summarizing a large set of numbers is the familiar *mean* (or *average*), which is a single number intended to reflect a typical value for the set. *Mean* is often abbreviated with the capital letter *M*.

The mean of a set of numbers often represents a 'typical' or 'usual' value, but of course this doesn't have to be the case. Imagine, for example, a pediatrician's waiting room that contains 10 parents in their late 20s, each with a 2-year-old child. The average age in this room would be about 15, even though there are no teenagers in the room at all. It's better to think of the mean as something like a 'center' value for the entire set, but even this can be misleading. A single extreme value can skew the mean; this is why income averages, for example, are often misleadingly high (because a few individuals have extremely high incomes relative to the rest of the population). At the University of North Carolina at Chapel Hill, campus legend holds that geography majors have the highest average salary after graduation – not because geography is a lucrative field, but because basketball star Michael Jordan was a geography major.

When describing a set of numbers, researchers often report both the mean and the *standard deviation* (*SD*). The standard deviation reflects the amount of 'spread' in the data: a small SD means that the numbers in the set are clustered tightly around the mean, while a larger SD means that the numbers are more spread out. As a rule of thumb, more than half of the numbers in the set will fall within one standard deviation of the mean, and the vast majority will fall within two standard deviations – but all this depends on the specific properties of the set, and there are no guarantees.

Table A.1 reports some descriptive statistics for sober and intoxicated speech; the results here are restricted to subjects' pronunciations of words with the shape consonant-vowel-consonant. The measures reported in this table are the pitch of the subject's voice (measured at the midpoint of the vowel), the duration of the word, and the maximum intensity (loudness) the subject achieved during the word.

If we looked only at the means, it might seem that these properties are affected by alcohol: intoxicated speech was apparently higher-pitched, slower, and quieter. But when we look at the standard deviations, we see that the amount of variation *within* each type of speech dwarfs the differences *between* the two types of speech. In the case of duration, for example, the words that the subjects produced while drunk averaged 25 ms longer than the words that they produced while sober – but the standard deviations are over 100 ms. In other words, it's emphatically *not* the case that all of the words in intoxicated speech lasted longer than all of the words in sober speech. At best, the intoxicated words *as a group* tended to be slightly longer – and the difference between the two groups is so small, relative to the amount of variation within the groups, that we might even question whether this difference is real at all.

Means and standard deviations are sometimes abbreviated $\bar{x}$ and σ, respectively. An extremely common practice is to give the standard deviation in parentheses immediately after the mean; when results are reported in this way, the caption of the table will usually (but not always) include a note to this effect. Some researchers also report the size of the dataset as N (short for *number*); in social science research, this is usually the number of people who participated in the experiment. The tables in this book that report both means and standard deviations are Tables 2.1, 3.1, 3.2, 7.1, 7.2, 7.3, 8.1, 9.1, and 9.2.

The mean and standard deviation tell us something about a single variable. The last statistic we will examine in this section, r, provides information about the relationship between two variables – specifically, how closely they are *correlated*. When we can predict one variable perfectly from the other, the two are perfectly correlated; for example, if we know the volume of water in a bucket, we can calculate the weight of that water precisely. In this situation, $r = 1$ or -1. Perfect correlations can be found in the physical sciences (after accounting for measurement error), but they're almost non-existent in the social sciences, where there are many factors that affect almost anything a social scientist is likely to measure. When a correlation is less than perfect, the absolute value of r decreases; the closer r is to zero, the weaker the relationship between the two variables is.

Figure A.1 illustrates what correlations of different strengths look like. Part A.1a shows the relationship between the intensity (loudness) of the first and second vowels in disyllabic words like *rapid*. Unsurprisingly, there's a very strong correlation between the two ($r = .894$): the louder the first vowel, the louder the second vowel. Part A.1b shows the relationship between the duration of the nasal consonant (*m*) and the stop consonant (*p*) in words like *trumpet*; here, the correlation is less strong ($r = -.565$). The negative value of r reflects the fact that as the stop gets longer, the nasal tends to get shorter – more

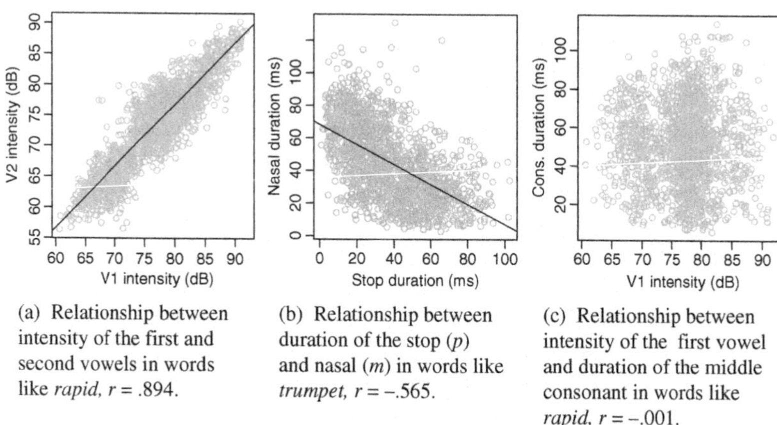

(a) Relationship between intensity of the first and second vowels in words like *rapid*, $r = .894$.

(b) Relationship between duration of the stop (*p*) and nasal (*m*) in words like *trumpet*, $r = -.565$.

(c) Relationship between intensity of the first vowel and duration of the middle consonant in words like *rapid*, $r = -.001$.

Figure A.1 Examples of strong (a), moderate (b), and no (c) correlation.

generally, a negative *r* means that as one variable goes up, the other goes down. Finally, part A.1c shows the relationship between the intensity of the first vowel and the duration of the middle consonant in words like *rapid*. There is absolutely no correlation between these two variables; thus, *r* is practically zero (−.001).

A.1.2 Graphical techniques

When analyzing a dataset, it's good practice to graph the data: visual representations may reveal patterns that can't be seen with just a mean and standard deviation. This section reviews several common types of graphs used in social science papers.

Bar graphs, of course, are a staple of publications in this area; the height of each bar shows the mean for some subset of the data, allowing for a quick visual comparison among groups of interest. The graph in Figure A.2a, for example, shows the average duration of the middle consonant in words like *rapid* in sober and intoxicated speech. Middle [t]s are clearly much shorter on average than [p]s and [k]s; in addition, it appears that consonants were slightly longer in intoxicated speech than in sober speech. The *error bars* in this graph show one standard deviation around each mean; they're useful for conveying how much variation there is in the data.[1] In this case, we can see that the difference between sober and intoxicated speech is very small compared to the variation within each type of speech; on the other hand, the difference between

[1] Error bars may be used to indicated other quantities as well, such as the standard error or a confidence interval. Unfortunately, researchers often don't specify what the error bars on a given graph represent.

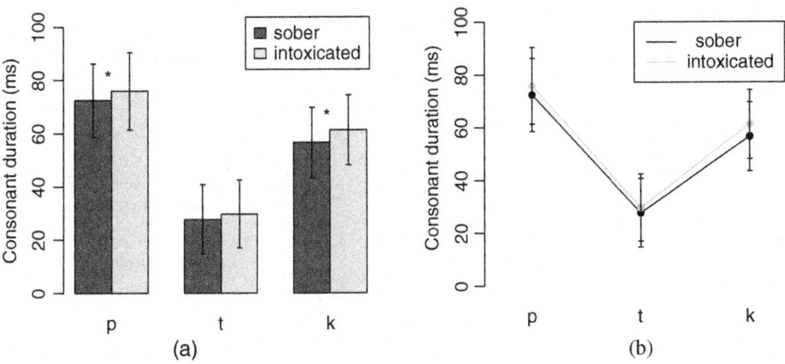

Figure A.2 Duration of the middle consonant in words like *rapid* in sober and intoxicated speech, presented as a bar graph and a line graph. Asterisks in the bar graph mark consonants with significant differences between sober and intoxicated speech at $\alpha = 0.05$.

[p]/[k] and [t] is quite large. In this book, you can find bar graphs with error bars in Figures 2.1, 11.1, 11.3, and 11.5. Bar graphs without error bars can be found in Figures 8.2 and 8.3.

An alternative to bar graphs is the *line graph*, which shows group means with dots instead of bars and connects related groups with lines. The line graph in A.2b conveys at a glance just how similar consonant duration is in sober and intoxicated speech: the lines for the two conditions lie almost on top of each other. Line graphs in this book can be found in Figures 6.3, 6.5, 8.1, and 11.2.

Although they're less commonly used, *histograms* are helpful for showing the characteristics of a dataset in more detail. For example, suppose I tell you that subjects 06 and 07 together had an average pitch of 159 Hz (approximately the E♭ below middle C) and a standard deviation of 64 Hz. You might imagine that these subjects mostly produced words with a pitch around the mean of 159, but that they were occasionally as high as 265 Hz (two standard deviations above the mean) or as low as 53 Hz (two standard deviations below).

The histogram on the left side of Figure A.3 shows that this is actually very misleading. A histogram shows the variable of interest (in this case, pitch) along the horizontal axis. This axis is divided into a series of discrete 'bins'; for each bin, a vertical bar shows how many times a number within that range occurs in the dataset – in this case, the number of words spoken by either subject with that pitch. We see here that *neither* subject produced very many words with a pitch close to 159 Hz; instead, there appears to be one large set of words around 100 Hz, and another set between 200 and 250 Hz. It turns out that there's a very good reason for this: subject 06 had a high-pitched voice, and subject 07 had a low-pitched voice. The two histograms on the right side of Figure A.3 show the data for these two subjects separately. This kind of

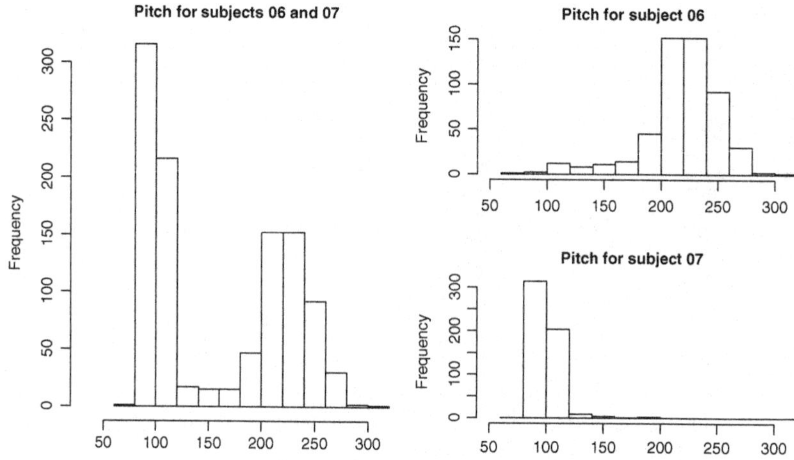

Figure A.3 Histograms of the pitch of words spoken by subjects 06 and 07.

situation is an example of why it's good practice to graph your data: if we had focused exclusively on the mean and standard deviation of the original dataset, we would have missed the fact that another factor (namely, the identity of the subject) was having a huge effect on pitch.

Finally, *scatterplots* are useful for showing the relationship between two continuous variables; each variable is represented by one of the axes. The scatterplots in Figure A.1, for example, make it easy to see at a glance that the relationship in the first plot is much stronger than the relationship in the second plot, and that the third plot exhibits no correlation whatsoever. Scatterplots in this book are in Figures 6.2, 6.4, and 7.1.

A.2 Inferential statistics

All of the statistical techniques discussed in the previous section let us summarize large datasets in a way that's easy to digest, either numerically or graphically. In other words, the descriptive statistics we've seen so far are a way of describing aspects of the world that we have actually observed during an experiment.

We sometimes want to go beyond this and use what we've already observed to make predictions about things that we have *not* observed directly. In fact, this is often the whole point of an experiment: we observe some small part of the world, and hope to use what we learn there to make broader generalizations about how the world works. Making predictions is the purpose of *inferential statistics*, to which we now turn.

A.2.1 *Statistical significance: The* p*-value*

Descriptive techniques make it easier for humans to see patterns in the data. Once we've discovered a pattern, a natural next step is to ask, 'Is this pattern real, or is it just a coincidence?' Unfortunately, it turns out that humans are pretty bad at answering this kind of question intuitively. We're very good at finding patterns, but we are often tempted to conclude that most of the patterns we see are meaningful, even when they're not. In addition, once we think we've discovered a pattern, we tend to look for more evidence that the pattern is real and ignore any evidence to the contrary.

To address this problem, statisticians have developed rigorous mathematical techniques for estimating how likely it is that a given pattern is a coincidence or not. At the heart of this enterprise is the concept of *statistical significance*. The basic idea is that we can perform a statistical test on the data to determine the probability that the pattern we found is due to pure chance. If the chances are simply too low that the pattern is a coincidence, we conclude that the pattern is 'real' – that it reflects some difference or relationship in the real world. The technical way to describe this situation is to say that the pattern is *statistically significant*.

To make this idea more concrete, imagine that you and I are playing a game that involves tossing a coin. When the coin comes up heads, you give me a dollar; when it comes up tails, I give you a dollar. If the coin is fair, then over the course of many tosses we expect to come out about even: heads and tails should come up approximately the same number of times.

Suppose, then, that we toss the coin ten times and get six heads (and four tails). This isn't a perfectly even outcome, and I am 'winning' the game (since I have taken more money from you than you took from me). But you probably won't accuse me of cheating, since six heads out of ten is very close to an even result and we know that there's no guarantee that the number of heads and tails will always be perfectly matched. But if we continue to play the game and keep getting more heads than tails, you may eventually become suspicious. By the time we've tossed the coin 500 times and gotten 300 heads, you're probably ready to ask for a new coin. Your reasoning would go something like this: 'If this were a fair coin, we would expect to get about the same number of heads and tails. But 300 heads out of 500 tosses is not even, and it's very unlikely that a fair coin would do this. Therefore, instead of believing that this is just a huge coincidence, I conclude that the most likely explanation is that this coin is *not* fair, and that it's weighted to give more heads than tails.'

The technical term for your default assumption that the coin is fair is the *null hypothesis* – essentially, a state of affairs where nothing interesting is going on. A test of statistical significance is an attempt to answer the question, 'If

Table A.2 p-*values for various outcomes of a coin-tossing experiment, testing the null hypothesis that heads and tails are equally likely.*

Tosses	Heads	p
10	6	.754
20	12	.503
50	30	.203
100	60	.0569
200	120	.00569
500	300	.00000894

the null hypothesis were true, how likely is it that my data would look the way it does?' We make 'how likely?' precise with a quantity known as p. The p-value of a statistical test is an estimate of how probable it is that we could have gotten the results we actually did if the null hypothesis were true. If our data is reasonably likely under the null hypothesis, then we conclude that there's no reason to believe anything else. But if p is too small – if it would take a big coincidence to get results like ours under the null hypothesis – then we *reject* the null hypothesis and conclude that the pattern we saw is a real one: it is *statistically significant*.

Table A.2 illustrates this line of reasoning for the coin-toss game. Each row of the table shows, for a given number of heads out of a given number of tosses, the probability of getting at least that number of heads if the coin were fair. If we get 6 heads out of 10 tosses, the p-value is .754; in other words, if we repeated our game of 10 tosses many times with a fair coin, then we would get a heads-tails difference at least this uneven about 75% of the time. This tells us that 6 heads out of 10 is not an unusual outcome for a fair coin, so you have no reason to conclude that I'm cheating.

For a larger number of tosses, the difference eventually starts to look a little more surprising. 12 heads out of 20 tosses is a result we would expect about 50% of the time; 30 heads out of 50 tosses, only about 20% of the time. Still, even a one-in-five result isn't *too* unlikely; I could still make a plausible argument that we got all those extra heads by chance. That argument becomes less persuasive as the game goes on; by the time we get to 300 heads out of 500 tosses, the odds against that outcome are enormous, and the only reasonable conclusion is that the coin is *not* fair. Thus, you will probably reject the null hypothesis and conclude that the coin is weighted to give me an advantage.

Statistical significance, then, is not all-or-nothing; a given set of results may be more or less likely, and reasonable people can disagree about how small

p has to be before we reject the null hypothesis. In practice, researchers in the social sciences typically choose a cut-off, known as an α level, before they conduct their experiment. If p falls below α, we conclude that the results are statistically significant; otherwise, there is no reason to reject the null hypothesis. The most common choice for α in the social sciences is 0.05, although researchers sometimes set a more rigorous standard (e.g., $\alpha = 0.01$). By this criterion, 60 heads out of 100 tosses wouldn't be enough to conclude that the coin is weighted (because p is just over 0.05), but 120 heads out of 200 tosses gives us a statistically significant p-value.

Statisticians have developed many different ways to calculate p, depending on the type of data involved. In reporting a set of results, it's good practice for authors to include at least three pieces of information: the specific test that they used, the value of the *test statistic* that they obtained when they conducted the test, and p. For example, a test of whether medial consonants get longer in intoxicated speech (see Figure A.2) might be reported as follows:

> Intoxicated subjects produced significantly longer [p] ($t(346) = -2.27$, $p = 0.024$, two-tailed) and [k] ($t(353) = -3.35$, $p = 0.00088$) between vowels in word-medial position. However, the difference in duration between sober and intoxicated [t] was not statistically significant ($t(171) = -0.998$, $p = 0.32$).

Here, the null hypothesis (not explicitly stated) is that these consonants have the same duration in sober and intoxicated speech. The test statistic is t, which tells the reader that this statistical result is based on a test known as Student's t-test; this passage also notes that the two-tailed version of the test was used. Finally, the p-values for both [p] and [k] are less than 0.05, while the p-value for [t] is greater; therefore, the author concludes that alcohol has a significant effect on [p] and [k], but that there is no evidence for an effect on [t]. In other words, the difference between drunk and sober [t] is so small that it may well be due to chance; the differences for [p] and [k] are large enough that it's simply not plausible that they're coincidental.

Another method for reporting statistical significance, especially when there are several comparisons involved and the author wants to show at a glance which differences are significant and which are not, is to mark statistically significant effects with asterisks. Figure A.2a illustrates this approach in a bar graph; asterisks are also used in other types of graphs and in tables.

Researchers are often interested in studying several factors at once in a given dataset; in addition, they may want to explore how those factors interact. Suppose, for example, that we want to investigate the *first formant* (an acoustic measure of vowel quality) of subject 06's sober and intoxicated vowels. An analysis of the vowels [a] (as in *dock*) and [i] (as in *beef*) might be reported as follows:

> There was a significant main effect of Vowel ($F(1, 89) = 7755.97$, $p < 0.0001$), such that the first formant was smaller for [i] than for [a]. There was no main effect of Condition ($F(1, 89) = 0.48$, $p = 0.49$); however, there was a significant interaction between Vowel and Condition ($F(1, 89) = 57.76$, $p < 0.0001$): the first formant of [i] was higher in the intoxicated condition, while the first formant of [a] was higher in the sober condition.

Here, the test statistic is F. In this type of analysis, a *main effect* is the effect of a single factor by itself. The main effect of Vowel (i.e., whether the vowel is [i] or [a]) is significant; this isn't surprising, since the first formant is one of the properties that we use to distinguish between [i] and [a] in the first place. The main effect of Condition (whether the subject was sober or intoxicated) is *not* significant; in other words, being drunk neither increased nor decreased subject 06's first formants overall. However, this analysis also revealed a statistically significant *interaction* between these two factors; this means that the effect of one factor depends on the value of the other factor. In this case, it turns out that Condition does matter, but that its effect depends on the vowel: intoxication increased subject 06's first formant for [i] but decreased it for [a].

A.2.2 Beyond the p*-value*

If the moral of section A.2.1 is 'Look for p', the moral of this section is 'Not just p!' It's tempting to use the p-value of a statistical test as a binary decision-making tool: if $p < 0.05$, the result is real; otherwise, it's not. Statistical tests are a tool; like any tool, they must be used appropriately. This section reviews just a few of the important issues that can and should influence how we interpret the results of a given test.

Experimental power

One property common to just about all statistical tests is that results become more reliable as the sample size increases. We've already seen an example of this with the coin-tossing game: 60% heads out of 10 tosses does not constitute convincing evidence that the coin is loaded, but 60% heads out of 500 tosses does.

The corollary of this is that if an experiment is too small, it may fail to collect enough data to find a difference that's really there. For example, if a coin is weighted so that it will come up heads 60% of the time, then 10 tosses are simply not enough to detect this weighting reliably – it will be indistinguishable from a fair coin. Therefore, if we find that a difference is *not* significant, we can never conclude that there is no difference between the relevant groups; all we can say is that the experiment failed to find evidence for a difference.

To take a real-world example, recall from Table A.1 that consonant-vowel-consonant words lasted a bit longer when pronounced by subjects who were intoxicated. It turns out that this difference is statistically significant; subjects reliably spoke a little more slowly when they were drunk. We might also want to ask whether a person's speech rate is related to *how* drunk he or she is: does speech get slower and slower as a person's blood alcohol content (BAC) increases? Suppose we explore this question by looking at the relationship between each subject's average word duration and his or her BAC as measured at the end of the experiment (BACs ranged between .09 and .18). It turns out that this analysis gives us no evidence that drunker people speak even more slowly; r for the correlation between these two variables is a weak -0.115, and the correlation isn't significant. But computing averages in this way leaves us with only eight data points to include in our correlation (one for each subject); maybe this just isn't enough. Thus, although this analysis provides no evidence that speech slows down with increasing BAC, it doesn't prove that there is no such effect.

This is one weakness of significance testing: a test can tell us that two groups are most likely different from each other, or that two variables are related; but it can't tell us that two groups are the same, or that two variables *aren't* related. In other words, if we fail to find a significant result, it's always possible that our study was just too small. Of course, if a very large study fails to find a significant effect – or if many smaller studies consistently fail to find an effect – then we will eventually conclude that there is simply nothing to be found. For individual experiments, the most important thing to keep in mind when interpreting a p-value is that the more data the researchers collected, the more reliable the results are.

Confounding factors: correlation and causation

Another well-known issue in inferential statistics is the difference between correlation and causation. A significant p-value may tell us that two variables are related to each other, but it doesn't tell us whether a change in one variable directly causes a change in the other, or whether both are affected by some third factor.

This problem is especially obvious when we look at real-world behavior, so we'll leave the alcohol experiment aside for a moment and examine the results of a study conducted by Plester et al. (2008). These researchers found (among other things) that 11- and 12-year-old students who sent text messages more frequently tended to have lower verbal intelligence scores. One obvious interpretation of this result is that sending lots of text messages lowers a person's intelligence. Another possibility, though, is that people with lower intelligence are more likely to send text messages. A third possibility is that some other factor affects both intelligence scores and texting frequency. For example, students who aren't invested in the values of school and the institutions it represents may try less hard on standardized tests and therefore have lower intelligence scores (regardless of their actual abilities). These same students might be more likely to engage in extracurricular activities, such as texting, that are frowned on by teachers and other authority figures. By itself, the p-value doesn't distinguish among these possibilities.

If we're interested in the direct relationship between two variables such as texting frequency and intelligence – and, in fact, this is exactly what Plester et al. set out to study – then 'outside' influences such as student motivation are known as *confounding factors*. That is, the direct relationship between intelligence and text messaging (if there is one) may be confounded by the existence of other factors that influence both. Confounding factors are an especially difficult problem in the social sciences, where it's impossible to control for all irrelevant differences among the real, complex, and messy human subjects we study. The best experiments do everything possible to avoid obvious confounds, but there is essentially no such thing as a perfect study.

The upshot of all this is that *discovering* a statistically significant result can be more straightforward than *interpreting* it. A significant relationship between X and Y doesn't automatically tell us that X affects Y directly. To come up with the most reasonable interpretation of a given result, we need to consider the entire context – how the study was conducted, in addition to the things we think are more or less likely based on what else we already know about how the world works.

Statistical significance versus practical significance

Another temptation in interpreting p-values is to assume that if a result is statistically significant, then it must involve a large or important effect. But statistical significance and practical significance are emphatically *not* the same thing. For the correlation between two variables, for example, there's a difference between p and r: p tells us whether the correlation is 'real' (that is, whether it is probably due to chance or not); r tells us, if the correlation is real, how strong it is (that is, how accurately we can predict one variable from the other).

Figure A.2 illustrates the same point. Recall that [p]s and [k]s were pronounced a little bit slower in intoxicated speech, and that this difference turned out to be statistically significant. This does *not* mean that we can figure out whether or not someone is drunk based on how long that person's [p]s and [k]s are: there is a dramatic amount of overlap between sober and intoxicated speech. At best, intoxication seems to 'nudge' subjects to speak a little more slowly. Voice analysis can't replace blood alcohol tests.

The difference between statistical and practical significance is especially important to keep in mind when we're comparing groups of people. Chapter 8, for example, discusses many experiments that suggest some kind of difference between the way men speak and the way women speak. But even if we find a significant difference between men and women, this doesn't mean that all men speak one way and all women speak another way. In fact, the linguistic differences between men and women are almost always much smaller than, for example, the average gender difference in height. We all know better than to say that men in general are tall or women in general are short; it would be even less accurate to claim that women in general use tag questions and men in general do not (section 8.4).

A.3 Experimental design

As we have seen, statistical tests are extremely important in determining whether there is a relationship between two variables. But they are neither the beginning nor the end of the process. Section A.2.2 describes how thoughtful and informed reflection is vital for properly interpreting a p-value after the test has been performed. This section focuses on the other side of the process: the kinds of considerations that go into designing a good experiment, one that will yield a meaningful p-value in the first place.

A.3.1 Subject selection

In a field that studies human beings, the process of choosing particular human beings to study is obviously very important. The first consideration, of course, is to make sure that the people you study are representative of the people you want to learn about. If you want to learn how native speakers of French perceive English vowels, then at some point you're going to have to study some actual native speakers of French.

This point can be much less obvious than it seems. Researchers who work at universities typically study college undergraduates, because they have easy access to this group. This is sometimes okay, but it means that we have to think carefully before we conclude that 'people in general do X' on the basis of the behavior of 40 sophomores in a laboratory.

An even more difficult problem is the issue of confounding variables. Usually, the variable we want to study is related to a number of other variables we do *not* want to study. For example, if we want to study whether texting causes a child to do better or worse in school, we will have to deal with the fact that children (and their parents) make choices about texting that are related to many other factors, including attitudes toward school, technology-related values, financial wherewithal, and so on. Similarly, it's very difficult to study how being biologically male or female affects behavior; a person's biological sex has a profound impact on that person's life experiences, with the result that biological sex and social gender are almost impossible to untangle. Any time we find a statistically significant difference between two groups of people, we should think carefully about exactly what difference between the groups caused them to behave differently – is it the variable we were originally interested in, or could some other difference between the groups be responsible?

A.3.2 *Task design*

Another difficult problem is the question of what kind of behavior to measure. A very common technique is to bring subjects into the laboratory and give them a task that, we hope, will cause them to do things that are similar to what they do out in the real world. Sometimes, though, this is easier said than done. A formal language test, for example, may or may not measure what a person actually knows about a language. Asking subjects to have a conversation with a stranger may not be the best source of information on how people normally talk to their friends. Being drunk in a laboratory is different from being drunk at a party.

An unnatural task isn't necessarily bad, particularly if it affects everyone the same way. The real trouble arises when different groups of people respond to the same task in different ways. For example, suppose a group of schoolchildren is asked to write down short messages that contain 'textese' abbreviations. Students who value the approval of teachers and authority figures might make a special effort to use lots of abbreviations, even if they wouldn't ordinarily do so in their daily lives, because they think the researcher wants them to do this. By contrast, students whose identity is not invested in the institution of school might make no special effort to use abbreviations on a test like this, even if they typically use abbreviations when texting with their friends.

A.3.3 *Data analysis*

In a perfect world, we could be completely objective whenever we evaluated the results of an experiment. But in reality, data analysis often requires a certain amount of judgment and selectivity, and it's all too easy for researchers to allow their conscious or unconscious biases to creep in at this stage.

In some experiments, the first step of data analysis involves coding subjects' behavior in some way – deciding when someone has interrupted someone else, interpreting a child's unclear speech, and so on. People might reasonably disagree as to whether a given utterance was really an interruption, or exactly what the toddler said. If the researcher knows what outcome he wants to get, he may unintentionally make these decisions on the basis of what he expects to happen. He might be more likely to code an utterance as an interruption, for example, if it was spoken by the kind of person he thinks is more likely to interrupt in the first place.

There are a number of procedures that researchers use to try to avoid this problem, either individually or in combination. One is to list the criteria for how to code the data as explicitly as possible, leaving less room for bias to affect the decisions. Another is to make sure that the person who codes the data doesn't know what the hypothesis is, or even what the experiment is about, so that the coder is (we hope) free of bias entirely. A third option is to have several different people code the same data; the better their judgments agree, the more reliable the coding is.

A similar problem arises if the researcher wants to throw out some of the data. Sometimes it's obvious that this needs to happen – for example, if a subject was obviously not paying attention during a test because she answered 'yes' to every question. Unfortunately, once we allow ourselves to exclude part of the data, it becomes very tempting to throw out anything that doesn't fit our hypothesis. As with the coding issue, one solution is to establish very strict criteria for which data stays and which goes (e.g., deciding that only subjects who got at least 70% of the questions on a test right will be analyzed).

A final issue has to do with running statistical tests in an appropriate way. One aspect of this process is that the researcher has to be sure to choose the right statistical test for her data; this is a complex problem in the social sciences and is outside the scope of this chapter.

A problem that's easier to see is the temptation to conduct too many statistical tests. Remember that a statistically significant test doesn't *guarantee* that the effect is real; it only means that the results of the experiment are very unlikely to have happened if the effect is *not* real. But unlikely isn't the same as impossible; a few statistical tests are going to turn up significant just by chance. If a researcher wants to compare the intelligence of two groups and gives both groups 47 different intelligence tests, but only one of those intelligence tests shows a significant difference, we may start to get suspicious that the one significant result was a fluke.

There are statistical techniques for avoiding this problem; many of them boil down to using a stricter criterion – a smaller α – for multiple significance tests. More generally, we should look out for studies where it appears that the researchers may have been 'fishing' in their data for a significant result. A single significant result when only one test was conducted is much more impressive than one significant result out of 100 tests.

A.3.4 Publication bias and replication

The last issue we will consider is how experimental results are reported to the broader community. Not every experiment gets published, and the publication process has its own biases. Most importantly, it's usually much more exciting to report a result that is significant than one that is not significant. Scientific journals may be reluctant to publish non-significant results, and authors may be reluctant to try. The effect of all this is that we never hear about many non-significant results because they're never published. If 100 studies investigate men and women and only 5 find a significant difference between the two on some measure, then we might conclude that men and women aren't so different on this measure after all. But if the 5 significant findings are the only ones that are published, our conclusions will be very different because we simply don't know about the other 95.

In addition, all this assumes that there are multiple studies on the same question in the first place. No single experiment is enough to prove something once and for all; to be truly convinced of a result, we want to see it replicated by different researchers using different methods.

Neither of these things helps us very much in evaluating an individual study. But keeping the entire process in mind helps remind us that every experiment takes place in a larger context; coming to a general conclusion about a broad and complicated question means judging and synthesizing evidence from a wide range of sources. We can appreciate the scientific process best when we understand that it is principled and rigorous without being a magic bullet.

A.4 Summary

- Descriptive statistics are a tool for summarizing datasets and giving us an overview of possible patterns in the data.
- Descriptive statistics that are commonly reported in the social sciences include means, standard deviations, and r.
- Graphical tools can help us see patterns in data that are not obvious from descriptive statistics alone. Social scientists frequently use bar graphs, line graphs, and scatterplots to present their data.
- Statistical inference involves extrapolating from a limited dataset to draw conclusions about the broader world. Statistical significance is a formal process for estimating whether a given pattern that we see in the data is likely to be due to chance or not.
- Statistical significance does not prove the direction of causation. It is not the same as practical significance.
- The results of a statistical analysis are only meaningful if the data comes from a well-designed study in the first place. Researchers must be careful at all levels of designing and conducting an experiment.

Further reading

Huck (2008) is an excellent and detailed guide to evaluating the results of social science research; the book is a textbook written at the undergraduate level and covers an extensive array of topics in statistics and experimental design. Johnson (2008) and Baayen (2008) are introductions to statistics intended specifically for linguists; the latter is more technical and assumes some elementary statistics background. Both books also introduce R, a free software package for doing statistical analysis.

Bibliography

Baayen, R. H. *Analyzing Linguistic Data: A Practical Introduction to Statistics Using R*. Cambridge University Press, Cambridge, 2008.

Chin, Steven B., and David B. Pisoni. *Alcohol and Speech*. Academic Press, New York, NY, 1997.

Huck, Schuyler W. *Reading Statistics and Research*. Pearson Education, Boston, MA, 5th edition, 2008.

Johnson, Keith. *Quantitative Methods in Linguistics*. Wiley-Blackwell, Oxford, 2008.

Kaplan, Abby. *Phonology Shaped by Phonetics: The Case of Intervocalic Lenition*. PhD thesis, University of California, Santa Cruz, Santa Cruz, CA, 2010.

Plester, Beverly, Clare Wood, and Victoria Bell. Txt msg n school literacy: Does texting and knowledge of text abbreviations adversely affect children's literacy attainment? *Literacy*, 42(3):137–144, 2008.

Language index

People index

General index

CPSIA information can be obtained
at www.ICGtesting.com
Printed in the USA
LVOW13s0156020218
564987LV00016B/163/P